NASA SP-2000-4517

The History of the XV-15 Tilt Rotor Research Aircraft:

From Concept to Flight

Martin D. Maisel
Demo J. Giulianetti
and
Daniel C. Dugan

Monographs in Aerospace History #17

The NASA History Series

National Aeronautics and Space Administration
Office of Policy and Plans
NASA History Division
Washington, D.C.
2000

For sale by the U.S. Government Printing Office
Superintendent of Documents, Mail Stop: SSOP, Washington, DC 20402-9328
ISBN 0-16-050276-4

Contents

Prologue

This monograph is a testament to the efforts of many people overcoming multiple technical challenges encountered while developing the XV-15 tilt rotor research aircraft.

The Ames involvement with the tilt rotor aircraft began in 1957 with investigations of the performance and dynamic behavior of the Bell XV-3 tilt rotor aircraft. At that time, Ames Research Center was known as the Ames Aeronautical Laboratory of the National Advisory Committee for Aeronautics (NACA).

As we approach the new millennium, and after more than 40 years of effort and the successful completion of our initial goals, it is appropriate to reflect on the technical accomplishments and consider the future applications of this unique aircraft class, the tilt rotor.

The talented engineers, technicians, managers, and leaders at Ames have worked hard with their counterparts in the U.S. rotorcraft industry to overcome technology barriers and to make the military and civil tilt rotor aircraft safer, environmentally acceptable, and more efficient.

The tilt rotor aircraft combines the advantages of vertical takeoff and landing capabilities, inherent to the helicopter, with the forward speed and range of a fixed wing turboprop airplane. Our studies have shown that this new vehicle type can provide the aviation transportation industry with the flexibility for high-speed, long-range flight, coupled with runway-independent operations, thus having a significant potential to relieve airport congestion. We see the tilt rotor aircraft as an element of the solution to this growing air transport problem.

I am proud of our past accomplishments and ongoing efforts in the development of tilt rotor technology. Much remains to be done to continue to develop and further enable quiet, ultra-safe, cost-efficient flight for this class of vehicles. I am convinced that Ames Research Center will continue to provide the leadership necessary to be in the forefront of new developments leading to the introduction of tilt rotor aircraft into the aviation transportation system of the 21st century.

Enjoy the aviation historical journey that unfolds on the following pages.

Harry McDonald
Director,
NASA Ames Research Center

Dedication

The story of the successful development of the tilt rotor aircraft is not just about technology, but also about the efforts of many capable people who dedicated themselves to what they believed would be an important advancement in aviation. The tasks proved to be technically challenging and involved both high financial and safety risks. This history, therefore, is dedicated to all of the people who held on to the dream and made it possible, and especially to those who, unfortunately, have passed on and are not able to witness the remarkable product of their work. A partial list of these people includes: Bob Lichten and Lovette Coulter of Bell Helicopter Textron Inc.; Pip Gilmore of the Boeing Helicopter Company; Laurel (Shorty) Schroers and Gary Churchill of the U.S. Army; and Jim Weiberg, Dr. Leonard Roberts, and Jerry Bree of the NASA Ames Research Center. Their efforts have advanced aeronautical technology significantly and made their mark on aviation history.

Acknowledgments

The authors wish to acknowledge Frank J. Aguilera, manager of the Ames Advanced Tilt Rotor Technology Office, who requested the writing of this history and who sponsored the work. This account of the history of the development of tilt rotor technology is the product of valuable contributions from many people, each of whom played a key role in the long chain of events that led to the successful accomplishment of the tilt rotor research aircraft program goals. Firsthand recollections and comments were provided by Bell Helicopter personnel, both active and retired, including Dick Stansbury, Jerry Pickard, Jose Caero, Claude Liebensberger, Jack DeTore, John Williams, Sam Ferguson, and Hank Smyth. We are especially indebted for assistance provided by Ron Reber of Bell Helicopter Textron Inc., who provided the link to other Bell personnel and who generously made available Bell's large resource of XV-3 and XV-15 still photographs. Former and current Government employees who provided important information included Paul Yaggy and Dave Sharpe of the Army laboratory at Ames; Woody Cook, Dave Few, Mike Bondi, Don Reynolds, and John Wilson of NASA Ames; John Ward of NASA Headquarters; and Hal Andrews of NAVAIR. The authors also thank John Schneider (retired), Ken Bartie and Hal Rosenstein of the Boeing Helicopter Company for photographs and information, and Jay Hendrickson for background about the Platt-LePage Aircraft Company. In addition, the authors wish to thank tilt rotor pioneer Mario Guerrieri for his input regarding the Transcendental Aircraft Corporation. Finally, the authors wish to acknowledge Roger W. Ashbaugh of the Documentation and Technology Branch and Lynn L. Albaugh, Capitol Resource Management, both at Ames, for their assistance in preparing this publication.

The authors have made every effort to ensure that the historical accounts in this document are reported accurately and that the people associated with these events are correctly identified. However, due to limitations of the available documentation, the names of some individuals may have been inadvertently omitted. Also, the reader should be aware that some information is not presented chronologically because events that are important in telling this story often occurred separately but during the same time period.

There are also a number of people at NASA Headquarters who helped in various ways. In the NASA History Office, M. Louise Alstork edited, proofread, and prepared the index while Stephen J. Garber and Nadine J. Andreassen also assisted with editing and production. Roger D. Launius, the NASA Senior Historian, provided much useful overall guidance. The Printing and Design Office developed the layout and handled the printing. Geoff Hartman and Joel Vendette handled the editing and design, respectively, while Jeffery Thompson and Stanley Artis saw this work through the publication process. Thanks are due them all.

Foreword

The development of tilt rotor aircraft technology involved some of the same factors that led to other important aeronautical accomplishments of this century. The vision of a few individuals in search of a practical and efficient new aircraft design, commitment to their goals, and their willingness to continue to pursue their objective while encountering major technical problems and programmatic challenges were critical ingredients in this tale. However, the unique aspect of the tilt rotor story was the combined Government and industry focused effort that was sustained for over four decades to explore, comprehend, develop, and refine this technology. The remarkable product of the investment of public and private funds, and the efforts of the people dedicated to the concept, is an aircraft type that will have an impact on civil and military aviation that will rival the introduction of the practical helicopter more than 60 years ago.

As this book is being written, the first production V-22 Osprey tilt rotor aircraft is being prepared for delivery to the U.S. Marine Corps and the Bell-Augusta BA609 six- to nine-passenger civil tilt rotor aircraft is well into the development phase. When these new vehicles enter service, I am confident that other visionaries will find new uses for this capability, both in the civil transport and military arenas. The tilt rotor aircraft has come of age.

I have had the good fortune to have been closely associated with a significant element of this activity, the XV-15 tilt rotor research aircraft project, for several decades. It is fitting that this adventure in aeronautical technology development be recorded. I know firsthand that the success of the tilt rotor can be credited to the capable industry and Government individuals whose story is told in the following pages.

Hans Mark
Director of Defense Research and Engineering
Office of the Secretary of Defense
Director, NASA Ames Research Center, 1969-1977

Foreword

The XV-15 tilt rotor research aircraft program resulted in part from earlier investigations by the U.S. military seeking new and more efficient concepts for air support of field operations. The XV-3 tilt rotor emerged from the Army/Air Force convertiplane program of the 50s as a strong contender. However, it faced significant stability problems that discouraged many supporters and threatened to swamp the program. The program was continued by those in industry and Government who believed in the concept and its potential, and were willing to risk their investment. They were rewarded by the discovery of new techniques and the incorporation of new materials technology that made it possible to propose the XV-15 tilt rotor research aircraft project. It was my privilege to successfully advocate Army participation in the program with both funding and personnel. The unique aspects and synergistic values of the Army AARL/AMRDL-NASA interagency participation made this possible. It demonstrated the value of sharing resources in direct partnership toward common goals. Although not yet integrated into Army field strategies, the tilt rotor aircraft holds significant potential for consideration in future missions. The soon-to-be deployed Marine V-22 Osprey demonstrates the rewards of the investment of defense dollars in the tilt rotor research aircraft project. There likely will be more.

It was my good fortune to be directly associated with and participate in the development and testing of the tilt rotor for almost three decades; first in NACA/NASA working with the XV-3 and then as Director of AARL/AMRDL with the XV-15 tilt rotor research aircraft project. I am grateful for the effort of the authors to document and preserve this story of remarkable achievement. The persistence and dedication of those who made it happen against many challenges and discouragement demonstrates high standards that deserve to be acknowledged. It is a fitting tribute to their vision and expertise.

Paul Yaggy

Director,
Army Aeronautical Research Laboratory (AARL)/Army Air Mobility Research and Development Laboratory (AMRDL), 1965-1974

Director,
Research, Development and Engineering
U.S. Army Aviation Systems Command, 1972-1974

List of Figures

List of Acronyms

AARL	Army Aeronautical Research Laboratory
AATD	Army Aeronautical Test Directorate
ADTA	Aviation Development Test Activity
AEFA	Army Engineering and Flight Activity
AFAPL	Air Force Aero Propulsion Laboratory
AFSRB	Airworthiness and Flight Safety Review Board
AGARD	Advisory Group for Aerospace Research and Development, North Atlantic Treaty Organization
AHS	American Helicopter Society
AIAA	American Institute of Aeronautics and Astronautics
AMRDL	Army Air Mobility Research and Development Laboratory
APA	Airport Planners Association
ARC	Ames Research Center
ASME	American Society of Mechanical Engineers
ASRO	Advanced Systems Research Office
ASW	Anti-Submarine Warfare
ATB	Advanced Technology Blade
ATM	Air Traffic Management
ATTT	Advanced Tiltrotor Transport Technology
BHTI	Bell Helicopter Textron Inc.
CAP	Composite Aircraft Program
CNO	Chief of Naval Operations
COD	Carrier Onboard Delivery
CPIF	Cost Plus Incentive Fee
CTR	Civil Tilt Rotor
CTRDAC	Civil Tiltrotor Development Advisory Committee
DCAA	Defense Contract Audit Agency
DFRC	Dryden Flight Research Center
DOD	Department of Defense
DOT	Department of Transportation
ECGB	Engine Coupling Gearbox
EMD	Engineering Manufacturing Development
EMI	Electromagnetic Interference
EUROFAR	European Future Advanced Rotorcraft
FAA	Federal Aviation Administration
FAI	Federation Aeronautique Internationale
FFS	Force Feel System
FSAA	Flight Simulator for Advanced Aircraft
FSD	Full Scale Development
GPS	Global Positioning System
HAI	Helicopter Association International
HUM	Health and Usage Monitoring
IAS	Institute of Aeronautical Sciences
IGE	In-ground-effect
IOC	Initial Operating Capability
IR&D	Independent Research and Development

JAA	Joint Aviation Authorities
JARG	Joint Aeronautical Research Group
JTAG	Joint Technology Assessment Group
JTR	Joint Transport Rotorcraft
JVX	Joint Vertical Experimental
LaRC	Langley Research Center
LHX	Light Helicopter Experimental
LPH	Amphibious Assault Ship (helicopters)
MAC	Military Airlift Command
MCAS	Marine Corps Air Station
NACA	National Advisory Committee for Aeronautics
NALF	Naval Auxiliary Landing Field
NAS	National Aerodynamic Simulation
NASA	National Aeronautics and Space Administration
NATC	Naval Air Test Center
NATO	North Atlantic Treaty Organization
NAVAIR	Naval Air Systems Command
NAVMAT	Naval Materiel Command
NOE	Nap-of-the-earth
NRTC	National Rotorcraft Technology Center
NTSB	National Transportation Safety Board
OARF	Outdoor Aerodynamic Research Facility
OART	Office of Aeronautical Research and Technology
OEI	One engine inoperative
OGE	Out-of-ground effect
ONERA	Office National d'Etudes et de Recherches Aerospatiales
PCM	Pulse Code Modulation
QSRA	Quiet Short-Haul Research Aircraft
R&QA	Reliability and Quality Assurance
RFP	Request for Proposal
RMDU	Remote Multiplex/Digitizer Unit
RPV	Remotely Piloted Vehicle
RSRA	Rotor Systems Research Aircraft
SAE	Society of Automotive Engineers
SAR	Search and Rescue
SAWE	Society of Allied Weight Engineers
SBA-MS	Sea Based Air-Master Study
SCAS	Stability and Control Augmentation System
SCS	Sea Control Ship
SEB	Source Evaluation Board
SETP	Society of Experimental Test Pilots
SHCT	Short-Haul Civil Tiltrotor
SNI	Simultaneous non-Interfering
STO	Short Takeoff
STOL	Short Takeoff and Landing
TDT	Transonic Dynamics Tunnel

TRENDS	Tilt Rotor Engineering Database
TRRA	Tilt Rotor Research Aircraft
UAV	Unmanned Aerial Vehicle
UT	University of Texas
VDTR	Variable Diameter Tilt Rotor
V/STOL	Vertical or Short Takeoff and Landing
VDTR	Variable Diameter Tilt Rotor
VMS	Vertical Motion Simulator
VTOL	Vertical Takeoff and Landing
WBSE	Work Breakdown Structure Elements
WPAFB	Wright-Patterson Air Force Base

Introduction

For as long as can be remembered, humans have always wanted to fly... to be able to soar into the sky and alight wherever their fancy takes them. One such individual was Leonardo da Vinci (1452-1519), who was the first person to approach heavier-than-air-flight in a somewhat scientific manner. Da Vinci is credited with the design of the first helicopter, basically a helical air screw (figure 1), which was conceived to lift off the ground vertically—no ground roll required, no runway needed. However, nearly four centuries later, when technology advancements allowed sustained, powered manned flight, the practical solution demonstrated by the Wright brothers used a fixed-surface to provide the lift. This required the aircraft to accelerate along the ground until a sufficient speed was reached so that the necessary force could be generated for the vehicle to become airborne. The da Vinci dream of vertical liftoff was finally achieved with the development of the successful helicopter more than 30 years after the first fixed-wing flight.[1] While, in the second half of this century, this remarkable machine has become an essential vehicle for numerous civil and military applications, because of its vertical lift capabilities, it remains extremely limited in the speed and range that it can attain. By the middle of this century, these limitations to the helicopter's effectiveness and the demonstrated capabilities of the fixed-wing airplane had fostered a new dream... the development of an aircraft with the vertical takeoff and hover capability of the helicopter, and with the speed and range of the fixed-wing aircraft. This is the story of the quest for a new type of aircraft that would make that dream a reality.

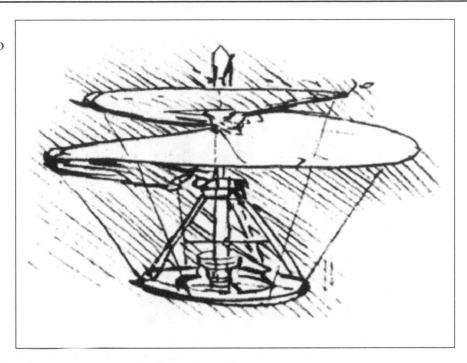

Figure 1.
Leonardo da Vinci 15th century helical air screw flying machine.

The search for an aircraft type with Vertical Takeoff and Landing (VTOL) capabilities triggered the imagination of designers and inventors to produce numerous configurations using a wide variety of lifting and propulsion devices. A summary of these configurations is shown in the V/STOL (Vertical or Short Takeoff and Landing) concepts illustration[2] prepared by the McDonnell Aircraft Company in the 1960s (figure 2). For the various aircraft types considered, one of the key distinguishing features is associated with the device used for providing the vertical

---

[1] While several helicopters became airborne during the first three decades of the 20th century, the Focke-Wulf Fw-61 is generally credited with being the first helicopter to demonstrate performance and precision control, essential characteristics of a successful helicopter. The first flight occurred in Germany in 1937 and public flight demonstrations were made in 1938.
[2] Seth B. Anderson, "Historic Overview of V/STOL Aircraft Technology," NASA TM 81280, March 1981.

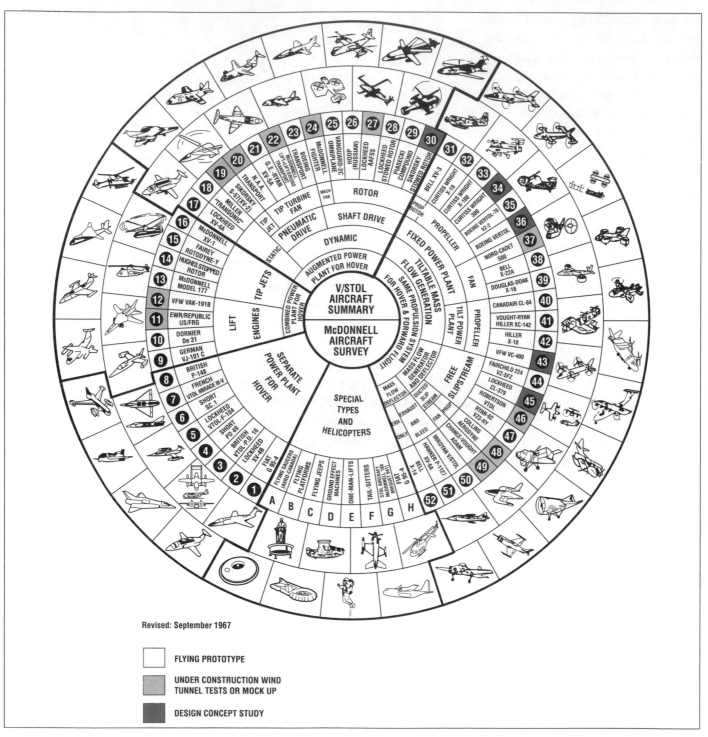

Figure 2.
Illustration of vertical and short takeoff and landing (V/STOL) aircraft developed by the McDonnell Aircraft Company in the mid-1960s.

lift. If the thrust for vertical takeoff is produced over a small area, such as the exhaust nozzle area of a "direct-lift" jet engine, the lifting device is referred to as a "high disc loading" type (where disc loading is defined as the thrust divided by the area over which it is produced). On the other end of the spectrum, if a large area is used to generate the vertical lift, as in the case of a helicopter with its large diameter rotors, the system is called a "low disc loading" device. This singular parameter (disc loading) is a direct indicator of the achievable level of efficiency in the production of the required hover thrust, as shown in figure 3. Low disc loading lifting systems are capable of delivering significantly more thrust per horsepower than higher disc loading devices. Therefore, for applications where extended-duration hover or near-hover conditions are required, or where lower installed power or lower fuel consumption in hover is important, low disc loading aircraft concepts appear to be the right choice.

The vertical lift efficiency of a VTOL aircraft, however, is not the only area of interest in the selection of a configuration. In addition to the need for vertical liftoff, these aircraft need to be designed to perform a cruise mission, usually with certain speed and range requirements. Performance in the cruise flight regime, therefore, needs to be assessed for each VTOL configuration. The challenge of finding an aircraft type that meets both the hover- and cruise-mode performance criteria, while also meeting other operational, economic, and environmental requirements was the major task encountered by the developers of VTOL technology.

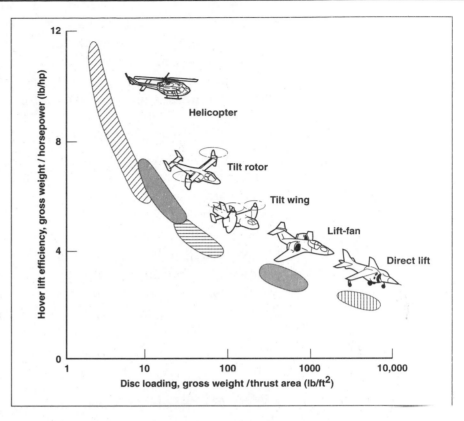

Figure 3.
Hover vertical lift efficiency as a function of disc loading.

Early Efforts

For one group of military planners in the late 1940s and early 1950s, the mission requirements included significant hover duration, low speed maneuvering and agility, and a speed and range greater than current helicopter capabilities. This, and additional mission factors such as the need for moderate downwash velocities below the hovering aircraft to enable safe rescue operations, led the planners to specify low disc loading for the new VTOL vehicle. These considerations resulted in the August 1950 initiation of the joint U.S. Army and U.S. Air Force Convertiplane Program. This program was formulated to provide demonstrations of different approaches to meeting the convertiplane requirements. The aircraft selected from the design competition were the XV-1 compound helicopter, figure 4 (proposed by the McDonnell Aircraft Co.), the XV-2 stoppable rotor aircraft, figure 5 (proposed by Sikorsky Aircraft), and the XV-3 tilt rotor aircraft, figure 6 (submitted by the Bell Helicopter Company). A discussion of the aircraft concepts addressed in the Convertiplane Program is provided by R. W. Prouty's February 1984 *Rotor and Wing International* article "From XV-1 to JVX—A Chronicle of the Coveted Convertiplane."

Two designs, the XV-1 and the XV-3, survived the initial evaluation phase and were developed as test aircraft for limited flight evaluations. While the XV-1

Figure 4.
McDonnell XV-1 compound helicopter. (Boeing Photograph AD98-0209-13)

Figure 5.
Sikorsky XV-2 Convertible Aircraft.

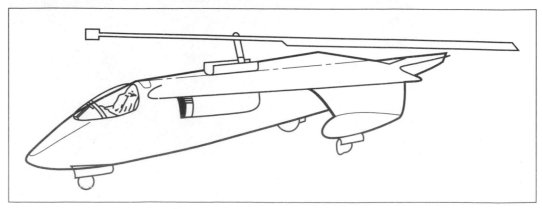

achieved a speed of 200 mph in 1955 (as the XV-3 was encountering technical problems, to be discussed later), it became apparent that the compound helicopter, in high speed flight, would still experience the type of severe oscillatory load conditions that limits the speed capability of the conventional helicopter. These vibrations are due to the edgewise movement of the rotor through the air during cruise flight. Helicopter rotors operating in the cruise mode are burdened with the tasks of producing the required thrust and lift while delivering the forces and moments to maintain a balanced, or trimmed, flight state. Because of the essentially edgewise motion of the rotor, the blades experience an aerodynamic acceleration and deceleration as they "advance" into and "retreat" from the airstream. Although the compound helicopter uses a conventional fixed-wing to produce the required lift while in the cruise flight mode, thereby unloading the rotor from the burden of producing lift and trim moments, it still encounters the variations in rotor blade drag due to the advancing and retreating airloads during each rotation. In addition, the edgewise rotor limits maneuver capability at high speeds because of the extreme load oscillations that occur on the rotor. Also, the exposed rotor hub and control hardware contribute significantly to drag in the high speed cruise mode, further limiting maximum airspeed. The compound helicopter also suffered the weight penalty of carrying the additional cruise mode propulsion system hardware. Collectively, these issues inhibit the performance potential of the compound helicopter. The compound helicopter was not the answer to the search for a viable low disc loading VTOL high performance aircraft.

Figure 6.
Bell helicopter XV-3
tilt rotor aircraft.
(Bell Photograph 209854)

According to advocates during the 1950s, the tilt rotor configuration was projected to have the potential to overcome many of the limitations or deficiencies of the helicopter and compound helicopter. The XV-3 provided an opportunity to demonstrate the effectiveness of the tilt rotor aircraft and learn about unknown problems of this aircraft type. However, before the story of the XV-3 program is told, the evolution and early history of the tilt rotor aircraft will be briefly reviewed.

During the 1920s and 1930s, the numerous innovative flying machines devised included several concepts that were expected to provide vertical takeoff capabilities. One of these was developed in the U.S. by Henry Berliner[3] in the early

---

[3] Jay P. Spenser, *Whirlybirds, A History of U.S. Helicopter Pioneers,* University of Washington Press, 1998.

1920s (figure 7). This design resembled a fixed-wing biplane of the period, except that it had a large diameter fixed-pitch propeller mounted on a vertical shaft near the tip of each wing. For forward flight, the shafts would be tilted forward. Reports indicate that the Berliner helicopter achieved forward speeds of about 40 mph. While the propellers were not designed to convert fully to the conventional airplane mode, the Berliner side-by-side helicopter was an early example of the rotor arrangement used on current tilt rotor aircraft.

Figure 7.
Henry Berliner tilt-propeller helicopter. (National Air and Space Museum–NASM–Photo)

Another design conceived to provide vertical lift and forward flight is the "Flying Machine" for which George Lehberger was issued a patent in September 1930 (figure 8). His approach contained the basic concept of the tilt rotor aircraft, that is, the use of a relatively low disc loading thruster (propeller) that can tilt its axis from the vertical (for vertical lift) to the horizontal (for propulsive thrust). While the authors are not aware of any attempt by inventor George Lehberger to develop this vehicle, it would be expected to encounter performance, loads, structural dynamics, and control deficiencies if built as indicated in the patent illustration. The vectored thrust low disc loading VTOL aircraft required many technology advancements before it would be a practical aircraft type.

In the late 1930s, a British patent was issued for the Baynes Heliplane (figure 9) which resembled the configuration of the current tilt rotor aircraft. Inadequate financial backing prevented development work, leaving the exploration of tilt rotor technology to other engineers in the four decades that followed.

In Germany, the Focke-Achgelis FA-269 trail-rotor convertiplane project was initiated in 1942. This aircraft, illustrated in figure 10, followed the moderately successful lateral twin-rotor helicopter, the Focke-Wulf Fw-61 flown in 1937. The FA-269 used pusher propellers that tilted below the wing for takeoff. This project was discontinued after a full-scale mockup was destroyed during a bombing in WWII. Years later, variants of the trail-rotor tilt rotor configuration would surface again in design studies at Bell and McDonnell Douglas.

The accomplishments of the German Focke-Wulf activities did not go unnoticed by the americans. Two enterprising engineers, Dr. Wynn Laurence LePage and Haviland Hull Platt of the Platt-LePage Aircraft Company of Eddystone, Pennsylvania, became intrigued with the success of the German helicopter and decided to pursue the development of a viable helicopter in the U.S. with the same general arrangement of the Fw-61. The product of this work was the 1941 Platt-LePage XR-1A lateral

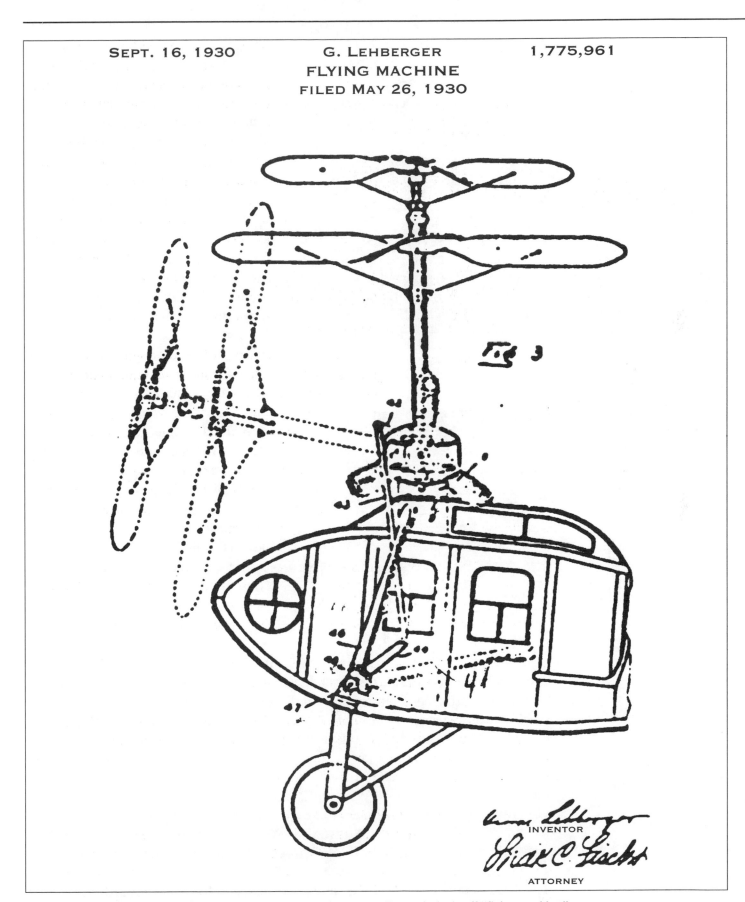

INVENTOR

ATTORNEY

Figure 8. U.S. patent illustration of George Lehberger's 1930 tilting propeller vertical takeoff "flying machine."

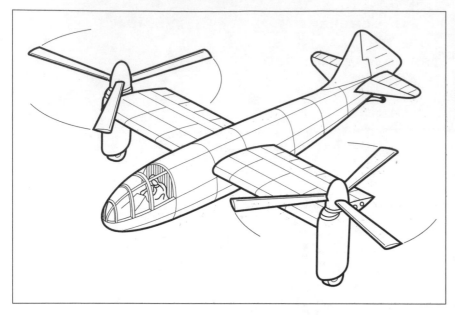

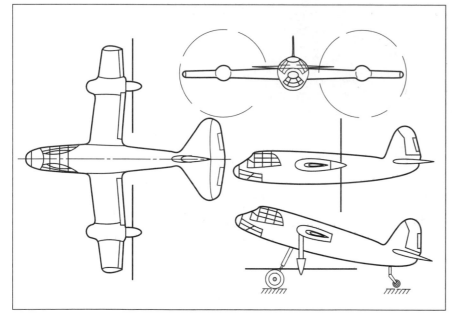

Top:

Figure 9.
The Baynes Helicopter.

Bottom:

Figure 10.
Three-view drawing of the Focke-Achgelis FA-269 convertiplane.

twin-rotor helicopter (figure 11). This aircraft inspired the design of a large (53,000-lb.) tilt rotor aircraft (figure 12), which resembled the XR-1A configuration, but incorporated mechanisms that permitted the rotors to be tilted for-ward flight. While Platt-LePage never developed their tilt rotor design, Haviland Platt applied for a patent for the concept on July 7, 1950, and was granted U. S. patent 2,702,168 on February 15, 1955 (figure 13).

The next significant appearance of the tilt rotor occurred in early 1947 when the Transcendental Aircraft Corporation of New Castle, Delaware, initiated work that led to the development of the Model 1-G tilt rotor aircraft (figure 14). The founding principals of Transcendental were Mario A. Guerrieri and Robert (Bob) L. Lichten, who had been coworkers at the Kellett Aircraft Company. Bob Lichten had earlier worked for pioneer helicopter designers LePage and Platt and had become intrigued with the tilt rotor concept. His experience at Platt-LePage provided him a mission that he pursued for the rest of his life.

While at Kellett, Guerrieri and Lichten investigated the performance of a heli-copter rotor acting as a propeller and, encouraged by the results, decided to demonstrate tilt rotor technology by independently building and flying a small, single-place experimental aircraft. Appendix A contains a brief description and the general characteristics of this aircraft, the Transcendental Model 1-G.

Lichten left Transcendental in 1948, and, in September 1952, Guerrieri sold his interests in the company to William E. Cobey, a Kellett Aircraft Corporation vibrations expert who continued the development of the Model 1-G. With some funding provided by a 1952 Army/Air Force contract for flight data reports and analyses, hover testing of the 1750 lb. Model 1-G began on June 15, 1954.

The Transcendental Model 1-G, however, met an unfortunate end. After success-fully completing more than 100 flights in a period of just over one year, includ-

Figure 11.
Platt LePage XR-1A lateral twin-rotor helicopter. (Photograph courtesy of Jay Hendrickson)

Figure 12.
Platt LePage tilt rotor transport aircraft design (Boeing print-Ames AD98 0209-22)

ing partial conversions to within 10 degrees of the airplane mode, an inadvertent reduction of the rotor collective pitch while flying with the rotors tilted forward led to a crash into the Chesapeake Bay on July 20, 1955. Although the aircraft was destroyed, the crash occurred near land in shallow water, which allowed the pilot, who sustained minor injuries, to wade ashore.[4]

---

[4] This description of the Transcendental Model 1-G accident was based on an account by Mario Guerrieri (Letters to the Editor, *Vertiflite*, Vol. 34, Number 5, Sept./Oct. 1988) in which he relates information provided to him by William Cobey. This information disputes the account noted by Mark and Lynn in "Aircraft Without Airports—Changing the Way Men Fly" (*Vertiflite*, May/June 1988) that states that the accident was fatal to the pilot.

United States Patent Office

2,702,168
Patented Feb. 15, 1955

2,702,168

CONVERTIBLE AIRCRAFT

Haviland H. Platt, New York, N. Y.

Application July 7, 1950, Serial No. 172,507

15 Claims. (Cl. 244–7)

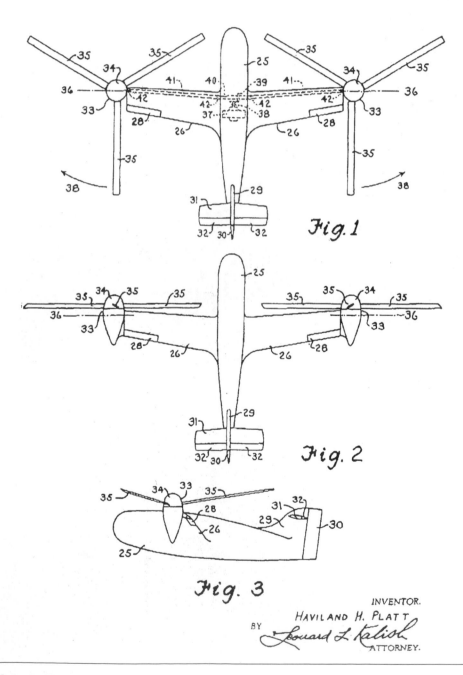

Fig. 1

Fig. 2

Fig. 3

INVENTOR.
HAVILAND H. PLATT
BY
Leonard L. Kalish
ATTORNEY.

Figure 13. Illustration from the Haviland Platt patent of the tilt rotor concept.

A second, improved, Transcendental tilt rotor aircraft, the 2,249 lb., two-place Model 2 (figure 15), was subsequently developed by Cobey but funding limitations resulting from the withdrawal of Air Force support prevented the expansion of the flight envelope, and the program was terminated in 1957. Transcendental became associated with the short-lived Helicopter Division of the Republic Aviation Corporation, Farmingdale, Long Island, but the failure to gain Government interest ended the venture. The Transcendental Model 2 is described in Appendix A. While never attaining flight in the airplane mode (but having flown within 10 degrees of airplane mode), the Model 1-G is generally recognized as the first vehicle to successfully explore the conversion mode of flight of the tilt rotor aircraft.

Other tilt rotor aircraft designs appeared during the 1950s but most never left the drawing board. One aircraft, the York convertiplane (figure 16) was developed by C. H. York in 1956. However, no record of its operational experience was found.

Figure 14. Transcendental Model 1-G experimental tilt rotor aircraft. (Photograph courtesy of John Schneider)

Figure 15. Transcendental Model. (John Schneider-Ames Photograph AD98-0209-19)

Figure 16. York convertiplane. (John Schneider-Ames Photograph AD98-0209-16)

XV-3 Program

Figure 17.
Bob Lichten, extreme left, et al. in front of the XV-3. (Bell Photograph 214838)

Long before Transcendental initiated flight tests of the Model 1-G, Bob Lichten had joined Bell Aircraft where he was given the opportunity to further the advancement of the tilt rotor with the research and development resources of a major rotorcraft company. At Bell, Lichten began the task of developing a new technology base associated with the tilt rotor aircraft. In 1951, in response to the Convertible Aircraft Program Request For Proposal (RFP) for the design of a "convertiplane," the Bell proposal offered Lichten's tilt rotor, the Bell Model 200. With the subsequent award of a contract for two full-scale "tilting-thrust-vector converti-planes" in October 1953, and the infu-sion of Army and Air Force funds, the exploration of this new technology was accelerated. The Bell Model 200, designat-ed the XV-3[5] by the Army and Air Force, produced some interesting technical chal-lenges for Lichten and his team during the next thirteen years. Figure 17 shows Bob Lichten, the principal advocate of the tilt rotor concept, standing in front of his creation, the XV-3.

Figure 18.
XV-3 at Bell, August 11, 1955. (Bell Photograph 210021)

Instability

Following an extensive series of ground tests by Bell, the initial hover trial of the XV-3 was flown on August 11, 1955 (figure 18). After noting satisfac-tory characteristics during the begin-ning of the flight, Bell test pilot Floyd Carlson experienced a high vibration in hover. During a subsequent flight on August 18, 1955, a reappearance of the rotor dynamic instability problem resulted in a hard landing that caused minor airframe damage. A thorough ground investigation was conducted to

---

[5] Interesting summaries of the early years of Bell's development of tilt rotor technology are pro-vided in *Aerophile,* Volume 2, Number 1, June 1979; "The Rebirth of the Tiltrotor - The 1992 Alexander A. Nikolsky Lecture" by Robert Lynn (*Journal of the American Helicopter Society,* Vol. 38, No. 1, Jan. 1993); and "Aircraft Without Airports - Changing the Way Men Fly" by Hans Mark and Robert Lynn (*Vertiflite,* May/June 1988).

understand and resolve the cause of the dynamic instability. Flight testing resumed on March 29, 1956, but on July 25 the instability occurred again, causing Bell to conduct another series of ground tiedown tests which lasted until late September of that year.

It is important to note that the ability of the rotorcraft dynamicists of that period to analyze complex systems (such as the rotor/pylon/wing of the tilt rotor) was quite primitive compared to the computational capabilities of the 1990s. The attempts to correct the instability that occurred on the XV-3 had to be done by combining the available analytical methods with experimental data. Therefore, ground tiedown tests were needed to expand the database documenting the fundamental characteristics of the tilt rotor as well as to evaluate configuration changes.

Figure 19.
Crash of the XV-3 on October 25, 1956.
(Bell Photograph 217259)

Following the second ground test effort, flight testing continued with the goal of expanding the speed and conversion envelope of the XV-3. On October 25, 1956, as Bell test pilot Dick Stansbury moved the rotor shaft 17 degrees forward from the vertical, a severe rotor instability occurred that resulted in extremely high cockpit vibrations and caused the pilot to black out. The subsequent loss of control caused the number 1 XV-3 (aircraft tail number 4147) to crash, seriously injuring the pilot (figure 19).

The XV-3 program faced a crisis. The inability to solve the instability using traditional analyses, experimentation, and trial-and-error empirical methods made even some of the tilt rotor's most avid supporters question the readiness of this technology. But the believers held on. A satisfactory solution to the rotor/pylon/wing dynamic instability problem had to be found. Advocates of the tilt rotor at Bell and the Government decided to continue the work and authorized the initiation of a major design change as well as plans for testing the XV-3 in the NACA Ames Aeronautical Laboratory[6] 40- by 80-foot wind tunnel. The original three-bladed, 25-ft diameter articulated rotor was replaced with a two-bladed stiff-inplane rotor. By July 18, 1957, with isolated two-bladed rotor static tests and rotors-installed XV-3 tiedown tests completed (figure 20), investigations of the performance and dynamic behavior of the modified XV-3 began.

---

[6] The NACA (National Advisory Committee for Aeronautics) was the predecessor to the NASA (National Aeronautics and Space Administration). The NACA became the NASA in October 1958 and the Ames Aeronautical Laboratory was renamed the Ames Research Center (ARC). ARC is located at Moffett Federal Airfield, formerly Moffett Naval Air Station, about 40 miles south of San Francisco, California.

In the following 18 months, the XV-3 (tail number 4148) with its new rotor system underwent two wind tunnel entries in the 40- by 80-foot wind tunnel (September-October 1957 and October 1958) and an additional series of ground tiedown and flight tests. During this period further changes were made to improve stability, including the reduction of the rotor diameter to 23 feet, the addition of external struts to stiffen the wing, and a significant increase in the stiffness of the rotor controls. The configuration that emerged accomplished the elusive goal of completing a dynamically stable full conversion to the airplane mode. This occurred at Bell on December 18, 1958, with test pilot Bill Quinlan at the controls. Subsequent flights explored the effect of wing stiffness (by modifying the strut attachments) and expanded the flight envelope within the fairly narrow range of the XV-3's performance capabilities.

Figure 20.
Tiedown tests of the XV-3 with protective shields at Bell in July, 1957.
(Bell Photograph 220955)

Government Flight Tests

The XV-3 was transported to Edwards Air Force Base where, from May through July 1959, Air Force Major Robert Ferry conducted a Government flight evaluation. The tests included handling qualities assessments, Short Takeoff and Landing (STOL) operations, and autorotation demonstrations. The Air Force test report,[7] authored by Project Engineer Lt. Wallace H. (Wally) Deckert, USAF, and Major Ferry, noted numerous deficiencies in the performance and flying qualities of the aircraft. However, in spite of the deficiencies, the report concluded that "the fixed-wing prop-rotor (i.e. the tilt rotor) principle is feasible and should be given serious consideration in future Vertical or Short Takeoff and Landing (V/STOL) aircraft design competition." "The XV-3 demonstrated that the fixed-wing prop-rotor con-

Figure 21.
XV-3 in hover at Ames Research Center.
(Bell Photograph 228649)

---

[7] W. H. Deckert, R. G. Ferry, "Limited Flight Evaluation of the XV-3 Aircraft," TR-60-4 ARDC XV-3, May 1960.

cept is operationally practical with safety and complexity comparable to helicopters."

After the conclusion of the flight program at Edwards AFB, the XV-3 was transported to NASA ARC onboard an Air Force C-130, where flight testing continued until July 1962 (figure 21). The first full tilt rotor conversion at Ames was performed by test pilot Fred Drinkwater on August 12, 1959 (figure 22). This flight program was followed by an additional entry in the Ames 40- by 80-foot wind tunnel (in June-July 1962, figure 23) to investigate the effects of changes to the pitch-flap coupling on rotor flapping and high-speed airplane mode stability.

Pitch-flap coupling refers to a feature provided by the hub design wherein the blade pitch angle is changed in a manner that alters the amount of out-of-plane flapping motion that occurs. A standard stabilizing pitch-flap coupling, referred to as d_3, reduces the flapping displacement by reducing the pitch angle as flapping increases. After another modification (this time to increase the pylon/wing stiffness) the XV-3 was able to reach a speed of 155 knots before indications of low damping, i.e. aeroelastic instability, were seen. While this was a definite improvement over the earlier stability limits of the XV-3, it would still be inadequate for the intended military mission application of the tilt rotor aircraft and was substantially below the predicted performance capability of this aircraft type.

Top:
Figure 22.
XV-3 in airplane mode of flight near Ames Research Center.
(Bell Photograph 028304)

Bottom:
Figure 23.
XV-3 in the Ames Research Center 40- by 80- ft. wind tunnel.
(AMES Photograph A37017)

Stability Validation

In 1965, after a period of model-scale testing and analytical studies, Bell funded a ground test to continue its investigation of XV-3 tilt rotor dynamics. To further pursue this work in a full-scale wind tunnel test, Robert (Bob) Lynn, Bell's Chief of Research and Development (who later was Bell's Senior Vice President,

Research and Engineering), obtained support from C. W. (Bill) Harper, Chief of the Aeronautics Division in the Office of Advanced Research and Technology (OART) at NASA Headquarters, for another entry in the Ames 40- by 80-foot wind tunnel. This test involved configuration variations that were predicted to alter the rotor/pylon/wing aeroelastic stability. The test results were compared with the pre-test predictions to determine if the evolving analytical methodology adequately represented the aircraft's structural dynamics. Without a speed capability well in excess of the helicopter's maximum speed, the tilt rotor aircraft did not fulfill the performance requirements of the VTOL mission. Lacking a valid structural stability prediction method, the design of a new tilt rotor aircraft was considered to have a high level of uncertainty and therefore an unacceptable high-risk undertaking.

The planned test could have exposed the XV-3 aircraft, as well as the 40- by 80-foot wind tunnel, to possible damage due to the potential for an explosively rapid failure caused by instability. Could Ames accept this unusual risk? Showing great confidence in the technical approach, the decision to accept the test was made by Mark Kelly, NASA's Chief of the Large Scale Aerodynamics Branch, and Woodrow L. (Woody) Cook, Chief of the Advanced Aircraft Programs Office.

The Bell test team was led by Kipling (Kip) Edenborough, who served as test director, and included Claude Leibensberger, Flight Test Engineer for the XV-3 project. The test, which ran from October to November 1968, proceeded remarkably well for all of the planned test conditions. The level of damping (i.e. stability) was assessed by disturbing the pylon and measuring the resulting vibrations. Decaying vibration amplitudes indicated a stable structure, constant amplitude vibrations indicated neutral stability, and growing amplitudes revealed a dangerous unstable condition. Test results showed that configurations predicted to be stable were in fact stable, and those predicted to be unstable showed signs of decreasing stability as the stability limit speed was approached. With the aircraft in its most stable condition, a run at maximum wind tunnel speed, recognized as a high risk condition, completed the test activity. When the wind tunnel was taken to its maximum airspeed capability (of nearly 200 knots), the vibratory loads data once again verified the predicted stability.

Disaster Strikes

Suddenly both pylons separated from the wing and were blown down the tunnel. The XV-3 was extensively damaged in what appeared to be the result of the inability to design an aeroelastically stable tilt rotor aircraft. However, after months of careful examination of the damaged structure and analyses of the incident, the test data revealed this was not the case. The failure was traced to a fatigue crack and rivets working loose in the left wingtip spar. The progressing crack and loose rivets reduced the stiffness of the pylon attachment to the level where a resonance occurred, producing the high oscillatory loads that led to the subsequent massive structural failure. The right rotor, exposed to extremely high overloads as the aircraft was being shaken during the initial failure, failed under a whirl divergence condition. In the final analysis, the wind tunnel investigation successfully accomplished its goals, but this wind tunnel entry would be the final research activity conducted with the XV-3 experimental aircraft.[8]

XV-3 Legacy

At first look, an assessment of the results of 13 years of flight, ground, and wind tunnel investigations with the XV-3 did not present a favorable prospect for the future of the tilt rotor aircraft. The severely underpowered XV-3 had limited hover capability and cruise performance. The maximum level flight speed of 115 knots (155 knots in a dive) was not adequate to prove that the tilt rotor had a useful airplane mode capability. However, it was fortunate that the airplane-mode speed was so restricted since the aircraft would likely have been destroyed in flight, due to the rotor/pylon/wing aeroelastic instability. The XV-3 also suffered from handling qualities problems, including lateral and roll instabilities when hovering in ground effect (IGE), and a directional divergent oscillation and poor control responses in the longitudinal and directional axes at low airspeeds. In addition, a complex gear shifting process, required to reduce rotor RPM after converting to the airplane mode (to improve rotor efficiency), produced an unacceptably high pilot workload.

On the positive side, the significant achievement of the XV-3 project was clearly the demonstration of the ability of the tilt rotor aircraft to perform in-flight conversion from the helicopter configuration to the fixed-wing (airplane) configuration and back to the helicopter mode in a safe, stable, controllable manner. This was accomplished with sufficient airspeed margins and maneuverability and adequate tolerance to gusts and turbulence throughout the process. A total of 110 full conversions were performed during the 125 flight hours logged by the 10 XV-3 test pilots (three Bell, three Army, two Air Force and two NASA). The proven conversion capability, coupled with the predicted but unproven performance potential in the hover and cruise flight regimes, provided the basis for continued interest in the tilt rotor concept in the military and within the NASA Langley and Ames Research Centers that were focusing on the search for new VTOL vehicle technologies. A description of the XV-3 is provided in Appendix A.

---

[8] After years of storage at Moffett Field, California, Tucson, Arizona, and the Wright-Patterson AFB near Dayton, Ohio, the remains of the XV-3, tail number 4148, were found at the U.S. Army Air Museum at Fort Rucker, Alabama, in 1984. This unexpected discovery occurred when the Bell XV-15 flight test team visited the museum while conducting a demonstration tour with the XV-15 tilt rotor research aircraft. The XV-3 had been stored outside and was in need of extensive repair (including the damage from the wind tunnel accident). Claude Leibensberger, an XV-3 engineer who at the time was retired from Bell, led the restoration accomplished with Army support. The refurbishment was completed by December 1986 but the aircraft was not put on display due to limited museum space. By late 1995, the XV-3 was again seen disassembled in an indoor storage area where it remains as of the time of this writing.

Encouraged by the outcome of the flight and wind tunnel tests of the XV-3, Bell management continued to show interest in pursuing the development of tilt rotor technology. In 1966, to ensure they could legally proceed with the work, Bell paid Haviland Platt for the rights to the convertible (tilt rotor) aircraft described in his patent.

NASA-Army Cooperation

During the late 1960s, the U.S. Army established the Army Aeronautical Research Laboratory (AARL) at the NASA Ames Research Center. In 1969, a "Master Agreement" between the National Aeronautics and Space Administration and the U.S. Army Materiel Command was authorized which provided for the joint (Army/NASA) participation in the development of advanced aircraft technology. The cooperative effort conducted under this agreement would be performed by NASA and Army personnel assigned to the Joint Aeronautical Research Group (JARG). The NASA Ames Aeronautics and Flight Mechanics Directorate and the Army Aeronautical Research Laboratory, later designated the Army Air Mobility Research and Development Laboratory (AMRDL), began a cooperative activity to address an array of tilt rotor aircraft aeromechanics issues and deficiencies that had surfaced during the flight and wind tunnel tests of the XV-3. The initial staff members of this joint tilt rotor focused effort were James (Jim) Weiberg[9] (NASA) and Martin D. (Marty) Maisel[10] and Gary B. Churchill[11] of the AMRDL. During the early phases of this cooperative effort, the Air Force joined the Army and NASA in funding some of the research activities. The focused tilt rotor technology investigations included in-house Government research, contracted work, and combined Government/industry efforts. In addition, tilt rotor related work was conducted within the rotorcraft industry under both company funded and Independent Research and Development (IR&D) efforts. The following review will focus on the NASA Ames/Army funded activities.

---

[9] At the beginning of the tilt rotor activity, Weiberg had accrued nearly 30 years as an aerodynamics, wind tunnel, and flight-test engineer at the Ames Research Center.

[10] Maisel had worked on the design and test of tilt wing propellers and tilt rotor proprotors at Boeing Vertol before joining the AMRDL in 1970.

[11] Churchill came to the AMRDL in 1971 from Boeing Vertol with an extensive background in V/STOL flight control system development. Prior to working at Vertol, he participated in the development of the LTV XC-142 tilt wing aircraft.

Building the Technology Base

Aeroelastic Stability

One of the principal areas of interest was the structural instability that plagued the XV-3 when operating in the airplane flight mode. Although this condition was found to occur on aircraft with wing-mounted propellers, such as the Lockheed Electra, a complete understanding of the phenomenon and a validated analysis capable of assessing the tilt rotor configuration did not exist in the late 1960s. Therefore, the rotor/pylon/wing aeroelastic instability[12] subsequently became the focus of analytical and experimental work initially at the NASA Langley Research Center[13] and then at NASA Ames.

A basic understanding of the physical phenomenon that causes the airplane mode aeroelastic instability problem was developed by Earl Hall[14] of the Bell Helicopter Company in 1966. By 1968, this insight was applied by Troy Gaffey, a Bell dynamicists (and later, Bell's vice president for engineering) who developed an effective solution to provide the required high-speed airplane-mode rotor/pylon/wing stability for the tiltrotor aircraft.[15] His solution involved the use of a hinged, or "gimbaled," rotor hub design with a pitch change mechanism that increased blade flapping when out-of-plane motion occurred. This pitch-flap coupling, called $-\delta_3$, combined with a high wing stiffness and a reduced rotor-hub to wing torsional axis distance, was predicted to provide stability up to and beyond the desired airspeeds. Small-scale wind tunnel test data cited in Gaffey's paper demonstrated that satisfactory high-speed aeroelastic stability was achievable.

---

[12] In this airplane-mode flight condition, when the rotor encounters small inflow variations, large differences in the distribution of loads are generated at a sufficient distance from the rotor hub to cause the pylon (or nacelle) structure and wing structure to bend or twist. These dynamic deformations can build up to the point where the structure's elastic, or spring, characteristics moves its shape back toward the original, undeformed configuration. The inertial forces, however, continue the "unwinding" past the original shape and a repetitive cycle of aeroelastic oscillation is initiated. Under certain conditions, once initiated, the deformations continue to grow ultimately leading to a catastrophic structural failure.

[13] When the Army initiated the Composite Aircraft Program (CAP) in 1965, with the objective of developing the technology for an aircraft that combines the characteristics of an airplane and a helicopter, the Bell Helicopter Company proposed a tilt rotor design (the Bell Model 266) based on their experience with the XV-3. Following the termination of the CAP in 1967, a 0.133-scale semispan dynamic and aeroelastic wind tunnel model, representing the Model 266, was given to the Langley Research Center (LaRC) by the Army. The availability of this model and NASA Langley's interest in exploring the aeroelastic characteristics of the tilt rotor aircraft led to a joint NASA/Bell experimental investigation in the Langley Transonic Dynamics Tunnel (TDT). A series of other tests in this facility, establishing an important aeroelastics/dynamics/loads data base, continued into the early 1970s (using other Bell models and a Grumman Aircraft model). See "A Historic Overview of Tiltrotor Aeroelastic Research at Langley Research Center" by Raymond G. Kvaternik (NASA Technical Memorandum 107578, April 1992).

[14] Earl Hall Jr., "Prop-Rotor Stability at High Advance Ratios." *Journal of the American Helicopter Society,* vol. 11, no. 2, April 1966.

[15] Troy M. Gaffey, *The Effect of Positive Pitch-Flap Coupling (Negative d3) on Rotor Blade Motion Stability and Flapping.* Paper No. 227, Presented at the 24th Annual Forum of the AHS, Washington, D.C., May 8–10, 1968.

Meanwhile, the Boeing Vertol Company of Morton, Pennsylvania, was also actively pursuing the development of VTOL aircraft technology. In 1956, they built a tilt wing research aircraft, the Vertol Model 76, later designated the VZ-2 (figure 24). Although the major focus at Vertol throughout the 1960s remained on the higher disc loading tilt wing vehicle, evaluations of variants included lower disc loading tilt wing aircraft, and the low disc loading tilt rotor for certain applications.

Figure 24.
Boeing VZ-s tilt wing research aircraft.
(Boeing-Ames Photograph AD98-0209-15)

By 1967, preliminary designs for transport-size tilt rotor aircraft had been developed (Vertol had been producing at that time the heavy payload CH-46 and the CH-47 helicopters) and a concentrated effort at Vertol to develop and validate methodology for all relevant VTOL technologies had begun. The leading advocates for this work were Kenneth B. (Pip) Gilmore, V/STOL Technology Manager, and David (Dave) Richardson, Chief of Preliminary Design. To support these efforts, during the mid-1960s, Boeing Vertol recruited engineers with technical expertise in the key areas and toward the end of the decade had established a fully staffed Research and Development organization devoted to the development of VTOL aircraft technology. Appendix B presents the key technical personnel involved in these activities at Boeing Vertol during the late 1960s and the early 1970s.

The Boeing Vertol Company's technical approach to tilt rotor aeroelastic stability employed a hingeless rotor hub (i.e. with no blade flapping or lead-lag hinges and no rotor-flapping gimbal) and structurally tailored blades. With the appropriate wing stiffness, $-\delta_3$, and the short-coupled hub/wing distance, wind tunnel tests would later show that this design approach allowed high speed airplane mode flight free of aeroelastic instability. While Boeing's rotor would contain fewer parts and would provide higher helicopter mode pitch and yaw control moments than the gimbaled rotor approach resulting in increased aircraft control responses, it produced higher blade, hub, and main transmission-component loads which could impose weight or life penalties on these structures.

Nevertheless, both the Bell and Boeing technical approaches offered some desirable attributes and Government-funded analytical and experimental investigations were continued to compliment work being done by both companies.

Figure 25.
Bell 25-ft. diameter propro-
tor on semi-span wing in the
Ames Research Center 40-
by 80-ft. wind tunnel.
Left: David Koenig, Ames.
Right: Kip Edenborough,
Bell Helicopter Co.
(Ames Photograph
AC70-3476)

Meanwhile, during the early 1970's, Dr. Wayne Johnson at Ames developed a comprehensive code[16] that would evolve into the accepted standard for rotor dynamics and stability analysis. This code would prove to be an important tool used by Ames and industry engineers to predict the aeroelastic stability margins of safety in later wind tunnel and flight test programs. In the same timeframe, a number of small-scale wind tunnel tests were conducted (largely by LaRC and industry) to produce the empirical databases for validating the analyses being developed. However, the small-scale model tests did not accurately represent the full-scale aircraft with respect to both the structural and the aerodynamic characteristics. Since the small-scale effects of these factors required analytical corrections to represent full-scale hardware, a large model test was deemed necessary. Therefore, in 1969 a contract was awarded to the Bell Helicopter Company for the Ames 40- by 80-foot wind tunnel tests of Bell's 25-foot diameter proprotor,[17] figure 25. This test was jointly sponsored by NASA, the Army, and the Air Force. While wind tunnel speed limitations prevented operation at the actual design maximum airspeed of the tilt rotor aircraft, the high speed operating condition was simulated by running the 25-foot diameter Bell Model 300 rotor at reduced rotational speeds. The test results confirmed the predicted stability margins and trends within the required accuracy level, and provided the needed confidence in the ability to adequately predict these critical tilt rotor aircraft characteristics.

---

[16] Between 1970 and 1974 independent work on analytical methodology to predict rotor motions, forces, and stability was also conducted by Dr. Raymond G. Kvaternik at LaRC (reported in "Studies in Tilt Rotor VTOL Aircraft Aeroelasticity," Vol. 1, NASA TM-X-69497, June 1, 1973, and Vol. 2, NASA TM-X-69496, June 1, 1973). The initial work by Dr. Wayne Johnson includes: "Dynamics of Tilting Proprotor Aircraft in Cruise Flight," NASA TN D-7677, May 1974, and "Analytical Model for Tilting Proprotors Aircraft Dynamics, Including Blade Torsion and Coupled Bending Modes and Conversion Mode Operation," NASA TM X-62369, August 1974.

[17] This proprotor was developed with IR&D funding for a small corporate tilt rotor aircraft called the Bell Model 300. This configuration benefited from numerous in-house and Government sponsored preliminary design studies led by Bell's John A. (Jack) DeTore and Kenneth (Ken) Sambell.

The Boeing technical approach was also evaluated for dynamic stability in the Ames 40- by 80-foot wind tunnel. In August 1972, under Army funding, Boeing conducted dynamics tests of its 26-foot diameter proprotor with the hingeless, soft-in-plane hub on the same semispan wing and rotor nacelle used for the Bell full-scale aeroelastic stability test (figure 26). Performance tests of that proprotor in the 40- by 80-foot wind tunnel were completed in December 1972.

Performance and Control

In a related effort, a folding version of the Bell 25-foot diameter rotor (figure 27) was tested in the Ames 40- by 80-foot wind tunnel in February 1972. The stop/fold tilt rotor eliminated the rotor/pylon/wing aeroelastic instability by stopping the rotor while in the airplane configuration. The aerodynamic drag of the stopped rotor blades was then reduced by folding them back along the nacelle while a convertible engine was used to produce the jet thrust required for airplane-mode flight up to higher speeds than would be attainable with a rotor as the thrust-producer. This

Figure 26.
Boeing 26-ft. diameter proprotor on semi-span wing in the Ames Research Center 40- by 80-ft. wind tunnel. (Ames Photograph AC72-5255)

Figure 27.
The Bell stop/fold tilt rotor in the Ames Research Center 40- by 80-ft. wind tunnel. (Ames Photograph AC85-024702)

23

Figure 28.
Performance tests of 5-ft. diameter proprotor in the Army 7- by 10-ft. wind tunnel at the Ames Research Center. (Ames Photograph AC98-0209-4)

test, also conducted with Bell Helicopter as the hardware and technical support contractor (jointly funded by the NASA, the Army, and the Air Force), demonstrated the feasibility of the airplane-mode rotor stopping and blade folding, and of the blade deployment and spin-up process.[18] The stop/fold tilt rotor, however, had the additional penalties of the increased complexity and increased weight of the stop/fold mechanism, and, with the lack of a developed convertible engine, it was put aside as a potentially feasible concept that would require further advancements to be an effective contender.

Another major deficiency revealed by the XV-3 was the poor propulsive efficiency of the rotor (frequently referred to as a "proprotor" when used on a tilt rotor aircraft) in the airplane (or cruise) mode as well as poor performance in hover. The tilt rotor design philosophy that evolved during this period was that the proprotor should meet stringent performance requirements in the hover and airplane modes of flight but should not be significantly compromised to meet helicopter-mode (edgewise flight) design conditions. This meant that the proprotor blades could be designed with considerable twist, similar to that of airplane propeller blades, instead of the moderate twist of helicopter rotor blades (to accommodate the edgewise operation). While the opportunity to use twist more freely as a design variable could improve performance, the significant differences in blade loading (both in distribution and level) and in the distribution of air inflow to the proprotor between the hover- and airplane-mode conditions provided a challenging problem for the design engineers. Furthermore, the large diameter (low disc loading) proprotor which allowed the tilt rotor aircraft to hover at helicopter-like low levels of horsepower, results in a proprotor that is much larger than is required for maximum efficiency in the airplane mode. A search of prior experimental reports for applicable airplane mode test results showed that insufficient empirical data existed at this unusually light airplane-mode loading. NASA Ames and the Army AMRDL, therefore, sponsored and conducted several analytical and test activities to investigate both the hover performance level and airplane mode efficiency achievable with a properly designed proprotor.

In 1968, Boeing Vertol was awarded a contract by Ames to investigate the effect of blade twist on the performance of model-scale proprotors. Under

---

[18] Anon., "Large Scale Wind Tunnel Investigation of a Folding Tilt Rotor," NASA CR 114464, Bell Helicopter Co., May 1972.

this and an additional contract, Boeing conducted analytical design studies and performance predictions for a range of tilt rotor hover and cruise operating conditions. A series of 5-foot diameter proprotors was tested in the Army 7- by 10-foot wind tunnel at Ames (figure 28). Also, to investigate the effect of model scale on measured performance, 13-foot diameter proprotors of the same blade configurations were fabricated. Between 1969 and 1973, these proprotors (as well as others having additional twist configurations) were tested in the ONERA (Office National d'Etudes et de Recherches Aerospatiales) 8-meter (26 feet) diameter S-1 wind tunnel in Modane-Avrieux, France (figure 29), the Ames 40- by 80-foot wind tunnel (figure 30), and at the Air Force Aero Propulsion Laboratory, Ohio. Test operations covered a range of axial-flow flight conditions including hover-mode and airplane-mode flight from slow speeds up to a high-speed flight Mach number of 0.85. These experimental investigations also examined the changes in blade twist due to the aerodynamic and rotational loads and the effect of this "live twist" on cruise performance. The resulting data[19] enabled the validation of analytical proprotor performance codes by Government and industry engineers.

Left:

Figure 29.
13-ft. diameter proprotor in the ONERA S-1 wind tunnel, France. (Ames Photograph A98-0905-5)

Right:

Figure 30.
13-ft. diameter proprotor in the Ames Research Center 40- by 80-ft. wind tunnel. (Ames Photograph ACD-98-0209-11)

---

[19] A summary of the results of these tests is provided in "A Summary of Wind Tunnel Research on Tilt Rotors from Hover to Cruise Flight" by W. L. Cook and P. Poisson-Quinton, presented at the AGARD- Fluid Dynamics Panel Specialists' Meeting on the Aerodynamics of Rotary Wings, Marseille, France, September 13-15, 1972.

Figure 31.
Bell 25-ft. diameter proprotor performance test in the Ames Research Center 40- by 80-ft. wind tunnel.
(Ames Photograph AC70-5390)

For large-scale performance characteristics, the Bell 25-foot diameter proprotor was tested in the Ames 40- by 80-foot wind tunnel in November 1970 (figure 31) as part of an earlier contracted effort. Ames also contracted with Bell and made arrangements with the Air Force Aero Propulsion Laboratory (AFAPL) for the March 1973 proprotor hover performance test at Wright-Patterson Air Force Base.

While the fundamentals of tilt rotor aeromechanics were being explored, another group of researchers and engineers were investigating the flying qualities, crew station, and control law aspects of this class of VTOL aircraft. Model-scale wind tunnel tests, analytical modeling, and piloted simulations were used to address these issues.

A series of tests was conducted with a 1/5- scale powered aeroelastic model of the Bell Model 300 tilt rotor aircraft design under an Ames contract. Hover tests conducted in September, October, and December of 1972 with this model examined the performance and dynamic characteristics for operations near the ground. It was discovered that, in the helicopter mode, the downward flow from the rotors impinging on the ground produced a strong upward-moving flow below the aircraft's longitudinal axis. This upwash, known as the "fountain," impacts the lower surface of the fuselage with increasing strength as the aircraft descends to the ground. Because this fountain is somewhat unsteady, the major portion of this air mass is seen to skip from one side of the fuselage to the other (particularly on round cross-section fuselages), causing this fountain-flow to impinge, alternately, on the lower surface of the right or left wing. This condition can contribute to the lateral darting observed during the XV-3 flight tests and lead to a considerably high pilot workload during the landing operation. Also, the occurrence of the unsymmetrical aerodynamic loading on the wing surfaces produces a rolling moment that increases in magnitude, i.e. is statically destabilizing, as the aircraft descends toward the ground.[20] Recognition of these phenomena contributed to the development of improved stability augmentation control algorithms for future tilt rotor aircraft.

Subsequent wind tunnel tests, conducted in the Vought Aeronautics low speed wind tunnel, Texas, from January through March 1973, documented the performance, static stability in yaw and pitch, and determined trimmed control positions in all flight configurations. These data were critical for the flight dynamics ana-

---

[20] R. L. Marr, K. W. Sambell, G. T. Neal, "Hover, Low Speed and Conversion Tests of a Tilt Rotor Aeroelastic Model." *V/STOL Tilt Rotor Study,* vol. VI, Bell Helicopter Co., NASA CR-114615, May 1973.

lytical models that were being developed in order to validate control systems designed to meet the handling qualities requirements throughout the flight envelope. The tests also included flow surveys which revealed the presence of rotor tip vortices in the vicinity of the tail surfaces. These vortices could influence the effectiveness of the tail surfaces and produce oscillatory loads and disturbing vibrations.

Aircraft Design and Simulation

With the tilt rotor technology efforts producing positive results, the managers of the joint AMRDL and NASA Ames activities could now justify the initiation of the next step, the development of a new tilt rotor proof-of-concept aircraft. As part of this plan, in August 1971 Ames awarded contracts to Boeing Vertol and Bell to conduct preliminary tilt rotor aircraft design studies. These efforts defined the characteristics and performance of a first generation military or commercial tilt rotor aircraft using a hingeless (Boeing Vertol) or gimbaled (Bell) rotor system, provided a preliminary design for a minimum size "proof-of-concept" aircraft, developed a total program plan and cost estimates for the proof-of-concept aircraft program, and developed a wind tunnel investigation plan for the aircraft.

In January 1972, with Air Force funding, Ames extended an existing Boeing contract to produce a preliminary design on an advanced composite wing and to define a gust and blade load alleviation feedback control system for the tilt rotor aircraft. This study addressed the concern that the low-disc-loading proprotor may experience significant thrust, torque, and blade load excursions due to a high sensitivity to gusts and turbulence.

Work under the Boeing and Bell contracts also included the development of a mathematical model for simulation and for participation by each contractor in a piloted flight simulation investigation. These models allowed the test pilots to evaluate the workload and the handling qualities of the basic aircraft, both without automatic control-enhancing systems and with various control configurations, employing Stability and Control Augmentation System (SCAS) control-enhancing algorithms. The simulation also enabled the pilots to evaluate the thrust/power management characteristics, the Force-Feel System (FFS), and failure mode design philosophy and aircraft behavior. The math models were developed not only as an evaluation tool for a particular aircraft control system design, but also as a device for the development of improved generic tilt rotor control law and crew station configuration. Initial piloted simulations were conducted in the Ames Flight Simulator for Advanced Aircraft (FSAA) in November and December of 1973. The math model created by P. B. Harendra and M. J. Joglekar of Bell during this period for the tilt rotor design selected for the flight program, through extensive development and refinement by Roger Marr and Sam Ferguson, became the basis for the generic tilt rotor math model used to evaluate various tilt rotor aircraft designs and related air traffic management issues in the Ames Vertical Motion Simulator in the late 1990s.

Tilt Rotor Research
Aircraft Project Office

Ames

In 1971, the Aeronautics and Flight Mechanics Directorate at NASA Ames, led by Dr. Leonard Roberts, established the V/STOL Projects Office, headed by Woody Cook, for the development and flight investigation of powered lift V/STOL (Vertical or Short Takeoff and Landing) aircraft. Woody's deputy and manager of the Advanced VTOL Projects Office at that time was Wally Deckert who, as an Air Force lieutenant, was the flight test engineer for the XV-3 evaluation conducted at Edwards Air Force Base in 1959. Deckert coauthored the XV-3 Flight Test Report with test pilot Major Robert Ferry. During the early 1970s, flight research at Ames was being conducted with the Rotating Cylinder Flap Aircraft (a modified North American YOV-10A), the Ryan XV-5B Fan-in-Wing VTOL Aircraft, and the X-14B Jet-Lift VTOL Aircraft. Also, the Augmentor Wing Aircraft (a modified deHavilland Buffalo) was under development for STOL research. Since the tilt rotor presented technical issues or embodied technologies not found in these powered lift systems, NASA Ames and the Army AMRDL set out to acquire both new employees as well as current Government employees to staff the V/STOL Projects Office with personnel having the technical and managerial skills necessary to develop a new-technology rotorcraft.

David D. Few was selected to lead the Tilt Rotor Research Aircraft (TRRA) Project Office on May 31, 1972. With a long background in experimental flight testing, including the supersonic, rocket-powered X-15 project at NASA's Dryden Flight Research Center (DFRC), he had recently managed the development of the Augmentor Wing aircraft. Dean C. Borgman, of the AMRDL, was appointed deputy project manager (technical), based on his demonstrated technical competence and leadership qualities. In later years, Borgman served as president of the McDonnell Douglas Helicopter Systems Division and then as president and chief operating officer of United Technologies' Sikorsky Aircraft Corporation. The Army and NASA personnel associated with the TRRA and related supporting technology activities are identified in Appendix B.

U.S. Army LTC Daniel (Dan) Dugan, attached to the AMRDL, was designated as the project pilot for the TRRA on December 18, 1972. While not assigned to the TRRA Project Office, Dugan was responsible for providing technical guidance in areas related to flight management, flight safety, and crew station design.

A number of project management changes were made both at Ames and at Bell during the course of the project. In 1974, Dean Borgman, Deputy Project Manager, (Technical) left the NASA/Army TRRA Project Office and was replaced by Army LTC James H. (Jim) Brown in September 1975, thereby maintaining the joint Army/NASA lead management positions. Wally Deckert was appointed as chief of the V/STOL Aircraft Technology Division in 1977, and Dave Few, formerly the TRRA project manager, was promoted to the position of deputy division chief. At that time, LTC Jim Brown took over as the TRRA project office manager, with Mike Carness serving as deputy manager. When the

Helicopter Technology Division was established at Ames in 1979, Kip Edenborough, chief assistant, became TRRA project engineer (deputy project manager, technical).

Shortly after that, John P. Magee, who had been a Principal Investigator in numerous tilt rotor studies and experiments while at Boeing Vertol (including the August 1972 tests of the 26-ft. diameter proprotor in the Ames 40- by 80-ft. wind tunnel) before joining the Government Project Office, became chief engineer (deputy project manager, technical) of the Tilt Rotor Aircraft Office. Following LTC Jim Brown's retirement, Dave Few again became project manager while remaining as deputy division chief until John Magee was named as the project manager in October 1980, and LTC Clifford (Cliff) McKiethan, who had served as deputy manager, Army liaison since 1978, became deputy project manager, Army liaison. John Magee joined BHTI (Bell Helicopter Textron, Incorporated) in 1984 where he became the manager of the Bell Eagle Eye Unmanned Aerial Vehicle (UAV) project, and later the engineering director of the 609 program (Bell's six- to nine-passenger executive tilt rotor aircraft). During the last few years of the XV-15's operation at Ames, the flight research was conducted under the Rotorcraft Flight Investigations Branch led by William (Bill) Snyder.

In 1989, some of the initial TRRA Project Office staff and management who were still at Ames gathered in front of the XV-15 for a group picture (figure 32).

Bell

Sadly, the person most responsible for promoting the development of tilt rotor technology would not live to see the tilt rotor research aircraft project. Bob Lichten, Bell's director of advanced engineering and chief engineer for the XV-3 project, died on September 18, 1971, following an automobile accident. Through his steadfast confidence in the ultimate success of the new technology, he provided the inspiration and kindled the dedication to the tilt rotor aircraft to Bell's management and research engineering staff that continues to this day.

Dick Stansbury, who survived the crash of the XV-3, became Bell's IR&D manager and continued to advocate for the development of tilt rotor technology with company funds. He also contributed to the development of tilt rotor crew station configuration and flight controls. Many of his initiatives were encompassed in Bell's tilt rotor aircraft designs.

Figure 32.
Members of initial Tilt Rotor Research Aircraft Project Office at Ames, 1989. (N=NASA, A=Army) Left to right, front row, Mike Bondi (N), Dan Dugan (A), Shorty Schroers (A), Wally Deckert (N), Marty Maisel (A), Violet Lamica (N), Robbie Robinson (N), Demo Giulianetti (N), Dave Chappell (A), Duane Allen (N). Back row: Jerry Bree (N), Gary Churchill (A), Dave Few (N), Jerry Barrack (N), Kip Edenborough (N), Jim Lane (N), Mike Carness (N). Not shown: Dean Borgman (A), Al Gaehler (N), John Hemiup (N), Jim Weiberg (N), Jim Diehl (N). (Ames Photograph AC789-0048-13)

During the late 1960s and early 1970s, Bell's Stanley (Stan) Martin (chief of advanced design) and Richard (Dick) Spivey (manager of applications engineering) actively promoted the continuation of tilt rotor aircraft research and development to NASA and to the military services research organizations. This effort, coupled with the progress made in related analytical and experimental areas, helped to keep the tilt rotor alive during that period as a contender for future Government-funded development programs.

With the loss of Bob Lichten, Ken Wernicke became the lead design engineer for tilt rotor aircraft at Bell. When the RFP for the design of the tilt rotor research aircraft was released by NASA, Bell Vice President for Program Management Charles (Chuck) Rudning assigned Henry (Hank) Smyth as proposal manager and Tommy H. Thomason as his deputy. Ken Wernicke was the chief engineer during the proposal phase.

After contract award for the TRRA project, the Bell management team consisted of Hank Smyth, Jr. (program manager) and Tommy Thomason (deputy program manager). Troy Gaffey was the chief technical engineer for the project from 1972 to 1975. In 1975, Hank Smyth was assigned to a major Bell international program and Tommy Thomason took over the top position. His new deputy was Lovette R. Coulter. From 1974 until 1981, Mike Kimbell served as the engineering administrator for the Bell Project Office. Thomason left the project in 1981 to lead the new JVX military transport aircraft project (later called the V-22 Osprey), and Lovette Coulter was appointed as program manager. When Coulter became deputy V-22 program manager in 1984, Ron Reber was assigned as XV-15 program manager. In 1999, after serving in senior management posts at Bell and Rolls Royce Allison, Thomason became vice president of civil programs at Sikorsky Aircraft Corporation under President Dean Borgman. In 1994, the XV-15 test activity at Bell was placed under the technical direction of Colby Nicks.

Getting Started

Initial activities of the Project Office at Ames focused on the previously described Government-sponsored contractual efforts as well as several in-house activities devoted to tilt rotor technology data base development and validation. With increasing confidence in the ability to design a tilt rotor aircraft free of the problems and limitations encountered with the XV-3, a new agreement for the joint development and operation of tilt rotor proof-of-concept research vehicles at the Ames Research Center was signed on November 1, 1971, by Robert L. Johnson, Assistant Secretary of the Army, R&D, and Roy P. Jackson, NASA Associate Administrator for Advanced Research and Development. This document would be the cornerstone in the development of the proof-of-concept tilt rotor research aircraft project that was about to emerge and it came about through the hard work and dedication of many Army and NASA managers.

As the leader of the V/STOL Project Office, Woody Cook recognized that the tilt rotor would have a niche for military and civil applications between the helicopter (with good hover efficiency, low speed, and short range) and higher disc loading concepts such as the Harrier jet lift VTOL aircraft (with poor hover performance, high speed and longer range). With the critical analytical tools for this concept being honed and validated by the on-going industry and Government work, he began to advocate the development of the proof-of-concept aircraft to management at Ames and NASA Headquarters.

Figure 33.
Rotor Systems Research Aircraft (RSRA). (Ames Photograph AC82-0089-17)

Woody's colleague on the Army side was Paul F. Yaggy, the director of the Army Air Mobility Research and Development Laboratory (AMRDL). Yaggy provided a high level of support for the development of tilt rotor technology by co-funding the research and by sharing in the staffing requirements. While Woody promoted the TRRA project to NASA management, Paul advocated the activity to his command organization, the U.S. Army Materiel Command.

After Paul Yaggy retired in September 1974, Dr. Irving C. Statler was appointed as the director of the Ames Directorate, U.S. Army AMRDL, and became an enthusiastic and effective supporter of the tilt rotor research aircraft project.

Project Advocacy

By late 1972, the Director of Ames Research Center, Dr. Hans Mark, recognized that the technical "homework" had been done and done well, and that the tilt rotor aircraft was a unique utility that could well serve the civil and military user. Dr. Mark, therefore, strongly advocated continuing development of the tilt rotor aircraft and carried this position to NASA Headquarters. During this time, Langley Research Center, in a NASA/Army activity similar to the joint effort at Ames, had been investigating the rotor systems research aircraft (RSRA).[21] This aircraft was a compound helicopter with a changeable configuration that was flown with and without wings and auxiliary turbofan jet engines. Figure 33 shows the RSRA in flight with the rotors, the wings, and the turbofan engines installed. It was also flown as a fixed-wing turbofan aircraft with the rotor removed. The use of the additional lift and propulsion devices would enable flight research to be conducted on the rotor system and airframe over a broad range of loading conditions and up to and beyond the high speed capability of current helicopters. The leveraging of the equal sharing of both Army and NASA financial and human

---

[21] C. White, Jr., G. W. Condon, "Flight Research Capabilities of the NASA/Army Rotor Systems Research Aircraft," NASA TM-78522, September 1, 1978.

resources made work on both projects at their respective centers feasible. These two major NASA/Army efforts, the TRRA at Ames (West Coast) and the RSRA at Langley (East Coast), satisfied the competitive interests of both centers in working on the leading edge of rotorcraft technology. Also, the tilt rotor project was consistent with NASA's charter of maintaining world leadership in civil aeronautical vehicle technology and of advancing military aeronautical capabilities. The tilt rotor project was therefore an appropriate activity for Ames.

At NASA Headquarters, convinced of the validity of the approach taken by the tilt rotor advocates at Ames, C. W. (Bill) Harper, Director of the Aeronautics Division, A. J. Evans, Director of Military Programs, and M. Adams, Associate Administrator of OART (Office of Aeronautical Research and Technology) promoted the tilt rotor project to NASA Administrator Dr. James C. Fletcher and Deputy Administrator Dr. George M. Low. In addition, the long association of the former NACA aeronautics cadre at NASA Headquarters with their Army counterparts in rotary wing research provided an important ingredient in the advocacy of the tilt rotor project. It was decided that if Army support could be obtained, approval would be granted for the project.

Meanwhile, obtaining Army funding for this project was a formidable task. The Army's assistant chief of staff for force development, Lieutenant General Bob Williams, who set policy for aviation research, had openly stated after the XV-3 activity was completed that he would not support the development of the tilt rotor aircraft. With the favorable results of the technology activities in hand, Dave Sharpe and Dean Borgman of the AMRDL prepared a briefing advocating a joint Army/NASA tilt rotor research aircraft project. This briefing was then presented to Lieutenant General Williams at the Pentagon by Paul Yaggy, who was soon to receive a surprising response. Shortly after that meeting, Lieutenant General Williams issued a letter stating that he was reversing his prior opposition to tilt rotor research and requested his staff provide full support to the tilt rotor effort. Funding for the Army's participation in the tilt rotor research aircraft project was subsequently made available and additional funds were programmed into succeeding year Army budget plans. This decision was the final gate which led to the November 1971 Army/NASA agreement, cited earlier, for the joint development and operation of tilt rotor research aircraft.

Even with the groundwork established, NASA Headquarters required additional documentation and planning prior to final approval of a new project of the complexity, risk, and magnitude of cost for the proposed tilt rotor effort. This documentation consisted of 20 items including a Project Development Plan, a Risk Assessment, an Environmental Impact Statement, a Safety Plan, a Reliability and Quality Assurance (R&QA) Plan, and a Procurement Plan.

Initial planning presented an activity with four elements. The first element consisted of establishing the technology base (essentially done by this time). The next focused on program formulation and the third element was a competitive

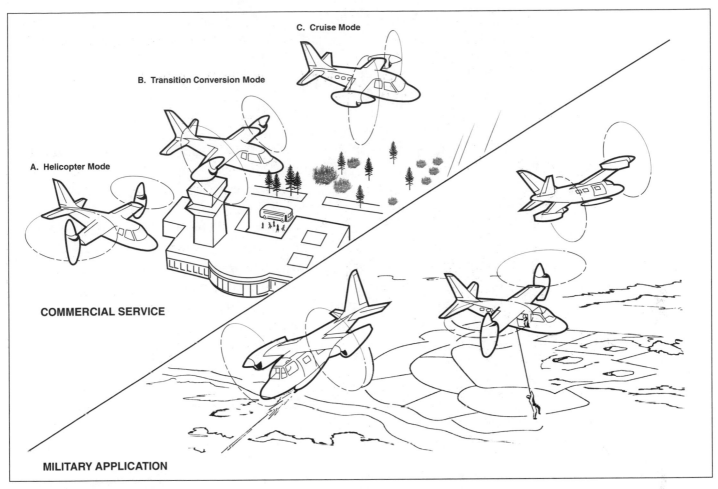

C. Cruise Mode

B. Transition Conversion Mode

A. Helicopter Mode

COMMERCIAL SERVICE

MILITARY APPLICATION

design and proposal activity. In the fourth element, one contractor would fabricate and test two research aircraft.

Figure 34.
Illustration from 1974
Tilt Rotor Research Aircraft
Project Plan.

Project Plan Development

The TRRA Project Office began to prepare several of these key documents toward the end of 1971. The initial version of the NASA/Army Project Plan for development of V/STOL tilt rotor research aircraft was released in April 1972. This document described the technical objectives of the project and defined the program elements, the management plan, the Government funding, facilities and manpower requirements, and the schedules. While the term "dual use" had not yet come into vogue, it was clear that the tilt rotor project would have to meet both civil and military needs to garner the necessary support. This dual use capability was highlighted in the Project Plan with the first illustration to appear in the document (figure 34). As the project took shape and underwent management reviews, the Project Plan would undergo two major revisions (once in April 1973 and again in September 1974) to change the scope and cost of the project, and to include, among other things, the review and reporting plan and the system and flight safety plan.

The initial projected cost of $48 million to complete two aircraft was rejected by Ames and AMRDL management as unacceptably high, leading to a reduction of scope to achieve a projected $40 million program cost. After several iterations, the TRRA Project Plan was approved by Bruce K. Holloway, NASA's Acting Associate Administrator for the Office of Aeronautics and Space Technology, and Norman R. Augustine, assistant secretary of the Army for research and development.

The System Safety Plan document identified the safety objectives of the TRRA project. It described the approach the Government and contractor organizations were required to take to meet the airworthiness goals and to implement the required industrial plant safety, reliability and quality assurance, and the ground- and flight-test safety programs. The plan also called for extensive subsystem, system, and operating hazard analyses. The principal safety objective of the TRRA project is concisely stated as: "the completion of all project activities without personnel injury or loss of life and without significant property damage or loss." To accomplish this, the following design philosophy was defined for the research aircraft: "As a goal, a single failure in any system or component should not result in loss of the mission. Also, a double failure should not result in the loss of life. The rotor blades and associated drive components are recognized exceptions to this and special attention and conservative design will be applied to these elements." Crew safety would be enhanced through the inclusion of a crashworthy crew station structure, the use of crashworthy (damage-resistant) fuel cells, a bird-proof windshield, and the installation of zero-zero crew ejection seats.

The technical objectives cited in the Project Plan for the two research aircraft programs were presented in two groupings and are worth noting here. The first set of objectives addressed fundamental tilt rotor proof-of-concept tasks. These were to:

a) verify rotor/pylon/wing dynamic stability and aircraft performance over the entire operational envelope;
b) conduct an initial assessment of handling qualities;
c) investigate tilt rotor aircraft gust sensitivity; and
d) investigate rotor downwash and noise.

In addition, advanced flight research program goals were defined as the secondary objectives and were not part of the contracted effort. These are summarized as follows:

a) evaluate gust and load alleviation systems;
b) perform thorough handling qualities evaluations and identify where additional V/STOL research in this area is required;
c) develop and investigate terminal area operational methods and procedures to reduce congestion and noise and increase safety;
d) determine V/STOL navigation/guidance requirements and evaluate automatic landing systems;

e) evaluate potential benefits of applying tilt rotor capabilities to Army missions;

f) provide data for development of design and operational criteria for potential civil and military tilt rotor aircraft; and

g) investigate alternate or advanced rotor concepts or configuration modifications.

Another key Project Office effort in late 1971 and early 1972 was the preparation of the Statement of Work that would lead to the research aircraft program. As noted earlier, this portion of the work was to be accomplished in two phases. Phase I would fund two parallel "competitive" preliminary aircraft design studies and the development of a program plan for a minimum-size tilt rotor research aircraft that could meet the proof-of-concept objectives. The research aircraft would be required to produce technology information that would be applicable to, or could be reasonably extrapolated to, first generation military or commercial tilt rotor aircraft defined in the initial part of these studies. The results of this effort were used as an industry-generated basis for determining the requirements of the research aircraft and for detailed planning for the Phase II aircraft development program, performed by one of the two Phase I contractors.[22]

Phase I - Studies

Following an open solicitation for bids, four proposals were received for the Phase I effort. Submittals from Grumman Aerospace, Sikorsky Aircraft, Boeing Vertol, and Bell were evaluated. On October 20, 1972, Ames awarded two fixed-price contracts of $0.5M each to the selected bidders, Boeing Vertol and Bell. Phase I generated analytical studies of performance, noise, stability and control, structural loads, and dynamics. Design efforts performed under these contracts addressed major structural and dynamic system components and assemblies, and included subsystem integration. In addition, outlines of the maintenance and inspection plans, tooling and fabrication plans, and component and integrated test plans were prepared. A model specification for the experimental aircraft project was also created. On January 22, 1973, as a product of the Phase I efforts, proposals from Bell and Boeing Vertol for the aircraft fabrication and testing activity were delivered to Ames Research Center. Each set of proposal documents consisted of 12 volumes weighing about 30 pounds.

The Bell proposal, as expected, was based on the IR&D-developed Model 300, now called the Model 301. It utilized the 25-foot diameter gimballed proprotor design that had been extensively wind tunnel tested at Ames. The engines, mounted in wing-tip nacelles, tilted with the proprotors as a unit. Also, as a result of earlier wind tunnel test results, the Model 301 now incorporated an "H"

---

[22] A description of the management approach used for the TRRA project is provided in "A Guide to Management of Experimental Shop Programs at Ames Research Center ("Experimental Shop" Concept)," NASA TM X-62,427 by David D. Few, April 1975.

Figure 35.
Illustration of the Boeing
Model 222 tilt rotor aircraft.
(Boeing-Ames Photograph
AC86-0140-1)

empennage configuration to improve the directional stability characteristics.

Boeing provided a proposal based on the new Model 222. This design used the Boeing-developed 26-foot diameter soft-in-plane hingeless proprotor on nacelles that tilted only the proprotors. The engines of the 222 were mounted in fixed horizontal wing-tip nacelles. To minimize research aircraft development costs, the Boeing 222 was to use the fuselage, landing gear, and empennage of the Mitsubishi Mu-2J twin turboprop executive transport aircraft. The 222 wing incorporated leading edge "umbrella" flaps and large deflection trailing edge flaps to reduce download. An artist's illustration of the Boeing 222 in flight is shown in figure 35.

A Source Evaluation Board (SEB) was convened to evaluate the proposals. In accordance with procurement regulations, the outcome of the competition was to be determined by the Evaluation Criteria defined in the RFP. These consisted of the Mission Suitability Factors which were scored, and "other factors" which were evaluated but not scored. The Mission Suitability Factors were comprised of Design, Implementation, and Management components. The other factors that were rated but not scored were: cost, company past performance, financial capability, and the new-technology plan.

To support the SEB in determining the attributes and deficiencies of the proposals, a number of technical and management specialist committees were established to provide written assessments to the Board. Most of the Project Office staff was involved in the SEB activity in the capacity of either Board members, committee members, or consultants. While both proposals were found to be competitive, the Bell proposal offered significant technical and cost risk reduction based on their successful demonstration of a flight simulation on the FSAA, their development and demonstration of a flightworthy rotor system, and their development of a main transmission gearbox. The findings of the SEB were presented to NASA and Army top management on April 12, 1973. The next day, the Bell Helicopter Company, Fort Worth, Texas, was selected for negotiations which would lead to a contract for the design and fabrication of two tilt rotor aircraft. It is interesting to note that this procurement, for the first time in the selection of a flight research aircraft, used a piloted simulation "fly-off" as part of the evaluation and selection criteria.

These negotiations, initiated in late April 1973, engaged the Government and Bell in debates over a series of difficult issues for three months. One of the most contentious areas was the Government's requirement for either a cost ceiling or a negative fee approach to motivate the contractor to control costs. After a meeting between Bell President James F. Atkins and Ames Director Dr. Hans Mark in June, the possible use of company funds to share the cost of an overrun was accepted by Bell. With that important decision made, other issues such as cost reduction items were soon resolved and a contract for the Phase II-A effort was awarded on July 31, 1973. This was to be a 60-day planning level of effort (not to exceed $0.2M). Following a Government assessment of the plans presented at the end of that period, a "go-ahead" for the Phase II-B for the design, fabrication, and test of two V/STOL tilt rotor research aircraft was given on September 30, 1973.

Phase II - Program Formulation

The work was to be performed under cost-plus-incentive-fee (CPIF) contract. The incentive fee was based on the ability to meet the target cost of $26.415M. If the contract was completed at the target cost, the contractor would earn a 6 percent fee. The fee would be increased to 12 percent if the final cost fell to $23.2M, and would be decreased to a negative fee of about -5.6 percent if the cost grew to $32.4M. This arrangement resulted in the contractor and the Government sharing equally in any overrun or underrun from the target cost.

During the Phase II-A period, the Government Project Office worked with the contractor to refine the Model Specification. This document defined the performance goals as well as the operational and design features and the structural design standards for the new aircraft. With this Model Specification as the guide, the TRRA would become the first experimental aircraft to be developed "from scratch" to meet Ames research requirements. The Model Specification became part of the Phase II-B contract and was revised, when necessary, to reflect

changes that evolved during the detailed design process.

Preparations for the Model Specification and program planning were made in late summer of 1972 when Shorty Schroers (a Project Office member) and two other engineers from the Ames Aeronautics and Flight Systems Directorate staff conducted a fact-finding mission to establish possible future military tilt rotor research and technology requirements. Their visits included the Aviation Systems Command, St. Louis, Missouri, the Naval Air Development Command, Johnsonville, Pennsylvania, the Army Electronic Command, Ft. Monmouth, New Jersey, and the Ft. Eustis Directorate of the Army AMRDL at Ft. Eustis, Virginia. The trip report addressed takeoff, transition and cruise requirements, descent and approach issues, and precision hover requirements for military applications. The findings identified both desirable or required characteristics and areas of research that would be included in the Model Specification and future flight test program of the TRRA.

The Ames Tilt Rotor Research Aircraft Project Office requested an experimental designation for the new aircraft from the Air Force office that assigned designation numbers for Department of Defense experimental aircraft. The TRRA was to carry the prefix XV (for experimental, vertical takeoff). The initial response from the Air Force was XV-14. This was perceived to be a problem, since Ames was still operating the X-14B VTOL aircraft and the similar designations might cause confusion. The designation was therefore changed to XV-15 and a proof-of-concept aircraft that would make aviation history was named.

In the 1970s, the tail numbers of aircraft flown by NASA under "public law" contained three digits, the first digit indicating the research center, with Ames being assigned the 700 series. At the start of the aircraft development program tail numbers N702NA and N703NA were designated for the tilt rotor research aircraft.

Figure 36.
1/5 scale XV-15 model in 7-by 10-ft. wind tunnel.

Top:
Small landing gear housings.
(Ames Photograph
AC98-0204-2 (6-A))

Bottom:
Large landing gear housings.
(Ames Photograph
AC98-0202-1)

Shortly after the start of the Phase II-A work, Bell began to focus on TRRA design issues and identified two options for the main landing gear configuration. One approach retracted the gear into the fuselage. The retracted gear would occupy a substantial amount of cabin space, but required only a modest-sized housing (landing gear pod) to enclose the mechanism in flight. Another arrangement utilized the main landing gear hardware developed for the Canadair CL-84 Tilt Wing VTOL Aircraft. To achieve the necessary distance between the outboard wheels, the landing gear would be mounted so that it would retract outboard of the fuselage contour, resulting in a clear cabin space but requiring a larger landing gear pod. While this approach offered a lower development risk and could be implemented at a lower cost than the internally retracting configuration, it would produce a higher drag that would reduce the maximum airspeed in the airplane mode. To evaluate and compare the drag of the two pod configurations, an unpowered 1/5 scale force-model was tested in the AMRDL 7- by 10-foot wind tunnel at Ames in August 1973. Figures 36a and 36b show a front view of the model installed in the wind tunnel with the different landing gear housings. This brief test showed that using the larger pods would result in a 5-7 knot reduction in maximum airspeed. This performance loss was considered acceptable in light of the cost and risk reduction benefits from using an already flight-qualified landing gear. Therefore, the existing CL-84 landing gear design was selected for the XV-15.

With the work on the aircraft design underway, a Government Resident Project Office headed by Jim Lane (from the Ames TRRA Project Office) was established at the main Bell engineering plant in Hurst, Texas. The major function of this Office was to interact with the Bell staff to monitor technical progress and to understand technical issues. Additionally, this Office tracked the level of effort and the periodic labor hour and cost reports, served as representatives of the Ames Project Office in certain activities that required Government observation, coordinated with the Army Defense Contract Audit Agency (DCAA) in matters related to Government inspection activities, and coordinated pertinent information with the TRRA staff and management. The Resident Office issued weekly reports which documented the key events of each week and the technical and administrative status of the project from the time it initiated operation in 1973 until it shut down after completion of the aircraft proof-of-concept flight test at Bell, nearly a decade later.

The tilt rotor research aircraft project (called Level I) was to be managed by a Work Breakdown Structure approach. This management tool[23] divided the planned activity into its major parts, or "Elements" (Level II). These Work Breakdown Structure Elements (WBSE) were further divided to the level required for adequate project management and control. For the TRRA project, the WBSE's were the major hardware subsystems and the major focused activities to be worked on

[23] James J. Diehl, "Application of a Cost/Performance Measurement System on a Research Aircraft Project," NASA TM 78498, June 1, 1978.

under the contract. To accomplish this, a Statement of Work was prepared so that these work areas and activities were clearly identified. It was also critical that the WBSE's be consistent with the work categories in the contractor's internal operating system, and this was verified during the Phase II-A period. The TRRA project utilized 50 key work elements as shown in figure 37.

In the Phase II-A effort, the Government Project Office and Bell each assigned lead individuals, or element managers, to each Level II element. This was intended to assure that direct communications would be maintained between the Government and Bell in every key work area. Initial Government and Bell assignments to major WBSE lead positions are presented in Appendix B.

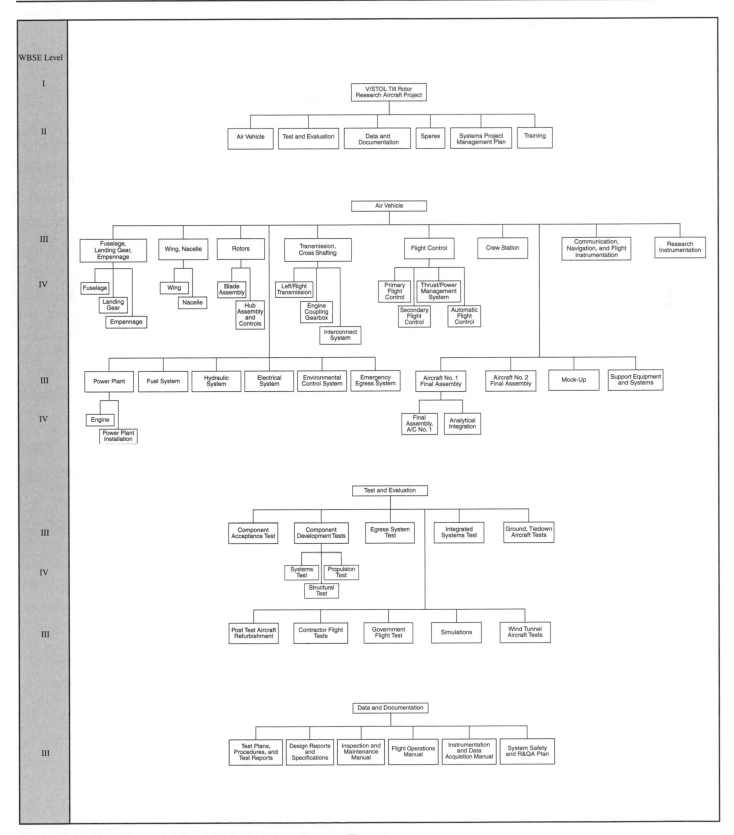

Figure 37. Tilt Rotor Research Aircraft Work Breakdown Structure Elements.

Aircraft Development

The primary task of designing the TRRA was placed clearly and directly in the hands of the very capable Bell team. The Bell chief engineer for the tilt rotor research aircraft contract activity was Ken Wernicke. George Carter led the design effort. Bell operated their aircraft programs with a matrix approach wherein specialists from the various Bell technology and design organizations were assigned to the project as required to meet the technical needs and schedule. These individuals were identified as the Bell Element Managers referred to earlier. A few examples of the engineering and design activities they and the Army/NASA TRRA Project Office staff were involved with during the development of the XV-15 are reviewed here. Appendix A provides a description of the design characteristics and features of the TRRA.

Engines

One of the early areas of focus in the development activity was the qualification of the engines. Prior to the award of the TRRA contract, the NASA/Army Project Office had determined that the Government furnished powerplant would be a variant of the Lycoming T53-L-13B turboshaft engine. The factors leading to this decision were that the T-53 was available in large numbers in the Army inventory, it produced more than the required power to handle the projected weight growth of the XV-15 above that of the Bell Model 300 (i.e. 1550 SHP vs. 1150 SHP of the Model 300 Pratt and Whitney PT-6 engine), and it had previously been operated in the vertical mode on the Canadair CL-84 tilt wing VTOL aircraft. The selection of the T-53 eliminated the need to conduct an extensive engine development program required to qualify a vertical-running PT-6, and therefore reduced the associated costs and program risk. To prepare the T-53 engines for the TRRA, Lycoming modified oil sumps and seals, changed the first stage turbine disc to provide overspeed capability, replaced the first stage gas producer turbine blades to provide a two-minute contingency rating, removed the nose gearbox to provide for direct drive, and conducted ground qualification test runs in the vertical and horizontal modes at their Stratford, Connecticut, facility. The modified engine was designated the LTC1K-4K.

Three negative aspects of the use of the T-53 to replace the PT-6 were the need to redesign the nacelle configuration and the transmission interface, the increase in engine weight (and its spillover effect on aircraft-structure installation weight), and its higher fuel consumption. Nevertheless, the modified T-53 was the Government's choice to power the TRRA and this choice would prove to be a good one.

Transmission

The Bell Model 300 technology demonstrator main-gearbox was considered by the Government to be in an advanced state of development at the time the TRRA contract was awarded. This transmission included a new gear design developed by Bell to reduce weight and cost. The new technology gears, of a "herringbone" tooth configuration, were fabricated by grinding two halves of the herringbone as separate components, and then joining them using a recently developed electron beam welding technology. The manufacturing process required extremely accurate alignment, and distortions due to welding were unacceptable. When Bell started fabricating the gears for the XV-15 TRRA, the process proved to be more difficult than expected. These difficulties which led to schedule slippage and cost increases were eventually resolved and the required parts were produced.

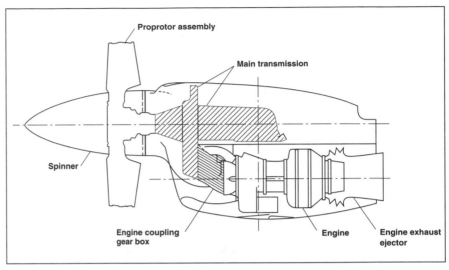

Figure 38.
XV-15 nacelle arrangement.

The use of the Lycoming engine imposed significant changes to the transmission arrangement. As previously noted, the Bell Model 300 main transmission had been designed based on the use of the PT-6 engine. Since the PT-6 output drive shaft operated at 30,000 RPM (at hover power) and the LTC1K-4K output speed was about 22,000 RPM, an "engine-coupling gearbox" (ECGB) was required if the designed main transmission was to be used. This engine-coupling gearbox would have the unusual function of increasing the RPM provided by the engine output to match the higher input speed of the existing design for the main gearbox. The main transmission then reduced the RPM to the rotor speed. An illustration of the new nacelle arrangement, showing the location of the engine-coupling gearbox is provided in figure 38.

Fabrication problems surfaced during the development of the engine coupling gearbox. The ECGB case and cover plate were made of magnesium furnished by a specialized casting vendor. Initially, the complex parts yielded from the casting process had a level of porosity, flaws and voids that were not acceptable. Ultimately, satisfactory parts were produced after incurring a further cost increase and a schedule slip.

By mid-1976, the problems that continued to occur during developmental testing of the transmissions became a serious concern to the Government Project Office. In May, NASA and Army Headquarters management established an ad hoc review committee to provide an assessment of the design adequacy, manufacturing procedures, and qualification testing for the TRRA transmissions. The committee was composed of Government and industry transmission experts and was chaired by John Wheatly, a renowned NACA rotorcraft pioneer and former Army rotorcraft scientist and consultant. The final report issued by this committee validated the design and manufacturing approach but recommended a pre-flight qualification test of not less than 50 hours duration.

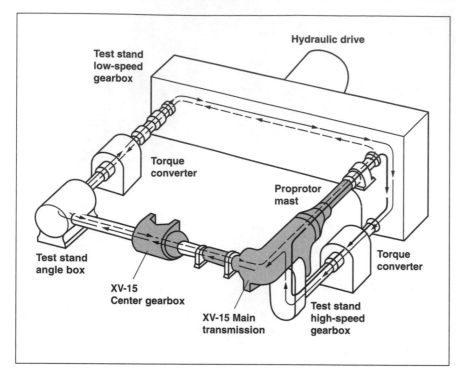

Extensive qualification test operations were then conducted on the Bell transmission test rig illustrated in figure 39. This apparatus placed the transmission elements in a continuous drive linkage that simulated the engine-input and the proprotor drive-output shafts flight loads. The test apparatus drive system was assembled so that a prescribed torque was applied to the XV-15 TRRA transmission which was then operated for a specified number of hours at a selected RPM. During these qualification tests a range of torque levels and RPM's was applied to the left and right main transmissions, the engine coupling gearboxes, and the center gearbox.

Figure 39.
Bell test apparatus used for transmission qualification testing.

Over the next two years the qualification test program revealed problems that required modification of gear designs, gear and shaft welding processes, bearing designs, and lubrication and cooling arrangements.

The transmission ground tests also included an evaluation and calibration of the output torque sensing system which was to provide the input to the torque indicator on the instrument panel. This sensing system consisted of concentric cylindrical shafts affixed to each other at one end. The inside shaft transmitted the torque while the outside shaft remained unloaded. The torque was measured by determining the magnitude of the deflection of the loaded (inside) shaft and comparing it to the undeflected, un-torqued (outside) shaft. This torque sensing device, however, did not provide output data of sufficient accuracy for a primary flight instrument. After considerable effort to correct the problem, Bell suggested a rather unusual approach. This was to make an exception to a standing XV-15 TRRA Project Office and Bell policy and allow the use of research instrumentation system data for primary flight instrument data. The Project Office agreed and the transmission output torque indication in the cockpit was now to be obtained from research instrumentation strain gages mounted on the proprotor drive shaft (called the proprotor mast). The research instrumented proprotor mast had a calibration resolution of two to three percent, sufficient for the management of the aircraft. Despite concerns by Bell and Government engineers about the reliability and durability of this instrumentation-based torque indication system, it served the XV-15 well during many years of flight operations.

Fuel Cells

During the formulation of the TRRA Program Plan, a prime focus of many discussions among members of the Government Project Office was the need to build "safety" into the design. In the 1960s, the Army and civil rotorcraft operators were experiencing loss of life and property due to post-crash fires. Studies that examined the statistics from these crashes showed that injuries and fatalities were significantly reduced when rupture and tear resistant fuel cells were installed. The fuel cells, basically flexible rubberized fabric bladders that held the fuel, were less likely to burst and release fuel upon impact with the ground than rigid metal tanks or fuel-containing wing structures that did not include the bladders. By the early 1970s, the use of fuel cells, in particular in Army helicopters, had dramatically reduced the incidence of post-crash, fuel-fed fires.

The original Bell Model 300 design (predecessor to the XV-15) incorporated a "wet wing," which used the volume within the wing to hold the fuel. While crashworthy fuel bladders would significantly increase the cost and weight of the fuel system and would reduce the available fuel volume by about five percent, the potential safety benefits were believed to be high enough to accept penalties, and the fuel cells were made part of the XV-15 design.

Bell then contracted with Uniroyal Inc., of Mishawaka, Indiana, the manufacturers of fuel cells for Army helicopters and Air Force fixed-wing fighters, to fabricate the cells for the XV-15 TRRA. With no background in the design of fuel cells for a research aircraft, a method for the selection of the thickness of the rubberized fabric (i.e. the number of the rubberized fabric laminates used in the bladder material) had to be defined. Thinner fabric would be lighter and easier to install in the wing (through small openings in the aft wing spar) but it would be more susceptible to impact damage than the thicker-wall material. To resolve the issue, a standard test was conducted at the Uniroyal facility on December 3, 1974. Two test bladders, in the shape of cubes measuring three feet on each side were fabricated, one with a light gage material and one with a thick wall material. The bladders were filled with water and dropped from a height of 65 feet onto a concrete surface. The lighter-gage material bladder ruptured on impact, while the thicker-walled bladder material did not. This not-so-scientific method, along with the previously qualified seam and fitting designs and validation of acceptable tear and puncture material characteristics, provided the basis for the qualification of the thicker-wall fuel cells for use in the XV-15.

In addition to the fuel bladders intended to provide fuel containment in the event of damage to the wing structure, the interconnecting fuel lines between adjoining cells (there are two cells in each wing) were provided with breakaway fittings which sealed in fuel when the lines were broken on impact.

The fuel system, like all other critical XV-15 TRRA systems, was designed with adequate redundancies (such as dual fuel pumps with the capability to feed both engines) so that a single failure would not result in the requirement to terminate the flight.

Flight Controls

One of the more difficult technical challenges in the development of the XV-15 TRRA was the design of the flight control system. The XV-3 had revealed various degrees of flying qualities, handling qualities, and pilot work load deficiencies in nearly all flight modes. It was the job of the engineers to address these problems and produce a flight control system that could meet existing and pending handling qualities and stability and control requirements from military and Federal Aviation Administration (FAA) standards. While normal operations would be conducted by a crew of two, the XV-15 control system was designed to permit a single pilot to perform all normal and emergency procedures from either seat.

The controls effort was divided into four categories: Primary Flight Controls, Secondary Flight Controls, Thrust/Power Management System, and Automatic Flight Controls.

Figure 40.
Proprotor response to cockpit control input.

Because the tilt rotor aircraft combines the flight characteristics of a conventional helicopter and those of a fixed-wing airplane, its flight control system had to blend the basic elements of these two vehicle types. The flight deck of the TRRA was configured so that each pilot station had complete controls for pitch, roll, yaw, and thrust in all modes of flight. They consisted of control sticks, rudder pedals with brakes, and power levers (for proprotor collective pitch and engine throttle functions). A single set of airplane-type throttles, rpm governor, flap, and landing gear controls were located in the center console.

In the helicopter mode, the controls apply collective or cyclic blade pitch changes to the rotors to produce control moments and forces. Fore and aft cyclic pitch (produced by moving the center control stick fore and aft) provides longitudinal control, and differential cyclic pitch (in response to rudder pedal motion) produces directional control. Collective pitch commanded by collective lever input is used for vertical control, and differential collective pitch, resulting from center

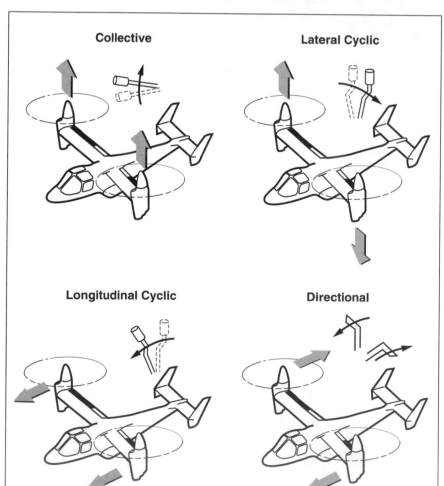

Collective

Lateral Cyclic

Longitudinal Cyclic

Directional

stick lateral input, controls roll. Figure 40 illustrates the helicopter mode control functions and the resulting proprotor forces that control aircraft motion.

Conversion or reconversion can be made within a corridor having a wide range of airspeeds, conversion angles, and fuselage attitudes. While the fixed wing control surfaces (ailerons, elevator, and rudder) remain active in all flight configurations, the rotor controls are automatically phased out in two "mixing boxes," as the nacelles are tilted toward the airplane configuration. This system is designed so that the need for control inputs during conversion is minimized, the primary requirement being a longitudinal input to maintain attitude as the large mass of the nacelles is tilted. The phasing of the controls through conversion is smooth and not apparent to the pilot and the process effortless.

In the area of automatic flight controls a stability and control augmentation system (SCAS) was incorporated in the aircraft design. It consisted of actuators which were connected to the longitudinal, lateral, and directional fixed control linkages in the fuselage. The SCAS makes automatic control inputs with these actuators to effect rate damping, control augmentation, and pitch and roll attitude retention. SCAS actuator motions are in series with the pilot's control inputs. Force-feel system (FFS) actuators prevent SCAS actuator motions from feeding back motions or forces into the control stick or pedals. These actuators are installed in parallel to the longitudinal, lateral, and directional control linkages and are effective in all flight modes. The SCAS and FFS control laws (i.e. the equations built into the automatic control system) are hard-wired on circuit cards which can be changed to alter the control characteristics of the aircraft. This feature would later be used for tilt rotor aircraft flight controls research.

Another unique and flight-critical element of the TRRA was the conversion system. This electro/hydraulic/mechanical system was designed by Bell with functional redundancies to provide fail-operate and fail-safe features. After extensive testing using production hardware, all operational and performance goals were met and the system was qualified for flight.

Emergency Egress System

The safety goal of the TRRA project stated that two simultaneous failures should not result in the loss of life. However, in the event of a catastrophic situation, emergency protection for the crew was to be provided with the installation of ejection seats. This was possible because the tilt rotor aircraft, unlike conventional helicopters, provides a clear crew ejection path without the need to remove the proprotor blades. The Government-furnished LW-3B seats were developed by North American Aviation (later Rockwell International) of Columbus, Ohio, for the OV-10 aircraft used by the Marines and the Air Force. These seats, termed "zero-zero" seats, were designed to be capable of ejecting a crew member and deploying the parachute for a safe landing with the aircraft in a normal attitude while on the ground and at zero airspeed. These seats were propelled out of the

cockpit by a rocket fired by a crew member activated ignition system. The inclusion of these seats dictated several aspects of the cockpit design. The seats had to be oriented to allow simultaneous ejection of the pilot and copilot with adequate clearance from the instrument panel, center console and side panels, and the overhead window frame had to be large enough to permit the seat and crew member to pass through without interference. In addition the flexible oxygen and communication lines had to have breakaway fittings to permit separation upon ejection.

To verify the operation of these ejection seats in the XV-15 cockpit, a functional test was conducted using the forward section of the N703NA fuselage, fabricated by Rockwell International at their Tulsa, Oklahoma, site. The test would determine if a simultaneous (pilot and copilot) seat

Figure 41.
Simultaneous static test firing of XV-15 ejection seats.
(Ames Photograph
AC75-1602)

ejection could be safely performed. Shorty Schroers was the principal Government investigator for this evaluation and Rod Wernicke, brother of Bell Program Manager Ken Wernicke, was the test director for the contractor.

Two 95 percentile (large-size) anthropomorphic test dummies were dressed in flight suits and helmets and strapped into the seats. The cockpit interior structure, control panels, and windows were marked with a pattern of various colors and shades of lipstick so that any contact made by the simulated pilot and copilot with the aircraft would be identified by the transferred markings. One of the project's more unusual moments was when Schroers and his team of engineers and technicians went to a local cosmetic store to purchase the large quantity of lipstick required for the test, being careful to select as many distinguishable colors and shades as they could find. It is hard to imagine what the salesperson must have been thinking.

In July 1975, the forward fuselage section mounted on a flatbed truck was moved to the designated test area at the Tulsa International airport. An array of still- and movie-cameras were set up around the site and two high-speed cameras were mounted inside the cabin to capture the ejection in slow motion. Aerial movies of the test were taken from a helicopter piloted by Ron Erhart, Bell's XV-15 chief test pilot. Figure 41 shows the nearly simultaneous ejection just after both seats left the fuselage and figure 42 shows the parachutes deployed after seat separation. After the test it was concluded that the ejection system operated satisfactorily (although prevailing winds caused the deployed parachutes to contact each other) and that no XV-15 configuration changes were necessary.

In addition to the ejection seats, the overhead and side windows were provided with an emergency removal system (employing a mild detonator cord in the window frame) that could be activated from within the cockpit or from an external lever in the nose section. Markings were provided to indicate the location of the external emergency window release control lever.

Major Subcontractors

Critical to the development of the TRRA was the design and fabrication of numerous aircraft components and subsystems. These required the development of specification documents which detailed the configuration, performance, and functional definition during the early design phase. Bell's decision to "make or buy" based on Bell's in-house capability, the potential subcontractor's ability to meet these requirements, as well as the proposed cost and schedule, was submitted to the Government TRRA Project Office for review and approval. Bell elected to fabricate in-house the critical dynamic components of the tilt rotor aircraft which included the proprotors, the transmissions, and the wing. All components and subsystems, whether furnished by Bell or by subcontractors, had to be shown to be qualified in accordance with the requirements established by Bell and approved by the TRRA Project Office. This qualification was established either by similarity to previously tested components, by tests, or in some cases, by analysis. The major subcontractors noted in this section provided unique components and subsystems and were instrumental in making significant contributions to the development of the XV-15 TRRA.

The Rockwell International, Tulsa Division, was responsible for the detailed design and fabrication of the fuselage and empennage of the TRRA. The flight control hydraulic actuators and hydraulic reservoirs were provided by the Hydraulic Research and Manufacturing Company (HR&M) of Valencia, California, a long-standing and reliable supplier of hardware for many of Bell's

Figure 42.
Parachutes deployed during seat ejection test.
(Ames Photograph AC75-1605)

49

helicopters. For the conversion system, SPECO (Steel Products Engineering Company), a division of Kelsey-Hayes of Springfield, Ohio, modified Lockheed P2V ball-screw jack actuator components to meet the requirements of the XV-15 and also provide the flap drive system for the TRRA. Components for the automatic flight control system were developed by Calspan Corporation, Buffalo, New York, and the proprotor RPM electro-hydraulic governing system was developed by Decoto Aircraft Inc. of Yakima, Washington.

A critical requirement was the need to carry high pressure hydraulic fluids, fuel, and high temperature engine bleed air from the fixed airframe to the tilting nacelles. This required the use of swivel fittings. Furthermore, because of the design requirement to avoid the simultaneous loss of the critical hydraulic systems that provide power to the flight control actuators, each of the three hydraulic systems used a differently designed swivel fitting at the wing/nacelle joint. These components were designed by the Dumont Aviation Division of Litton Industries, Lakewood, California.

The later success of the TRRA is a tribute not only to the designers and engineers working directly on the project, but also to the subcontractors who were able to meet the technical needs of the XV-15 within stringent cost and schedule constraints.

Data Acquisition

Early in the design of the TRRA, attention was focused on defining the project's data system. As it evolved, the system was required to have a capacity for a large number of pressure, temperature, load, torque, and position data parameters (containing a range of oscillatory levels from steady values to high frequencies), an onboard flight-crew controlled data recorder to ensure the collection of complete, high quality data records, and the capability to transmit critical data to a ground monitoring station. At the start of the development of the data system for the XV-15, the use of state-of-the-art digital technology was recommended by Ames instrumentation experts and accepted by the TRRA Project Office.

While Ames had been using digital data acquisition systems in its wind tunnels for several years, the XV-15 would be the first research aircraft at Ames to use such a system for primary (safety-of-flight) data acquisition. Furthermore, the XV-15 would become the first new rotorcraft to utilize digital "pulse code modulation" (PCM) technology for the expansion of its flight envelope.

By the early 1970s, the Teledyne Controls Division in El Segundo, California, had completed the NASA DFRC-sponsored development of a versatile, high speed, high capacity digital data acquisition system small enough to fit a remotely piloted vehicle or a small-size piloted flight test vehicle. Unfortunately, the DFRC-developed system did not meet the requirements of the TRRA, so a larger, next-generation system was developed by Teledyne with NASA Ames funding under the technical guidance of Herb Finger of the Ames Instrumentation Branch.

The advantages of the digital PCM system over prior state of the art analog instrumentation were many. The onboard digitization of the measured values preserved data accuracy, the system was relatively compact, set-up and data calibration values were retained in the records, and the digital data allowed both rapid "near-real-time" computerized data reduction (for safety or experiment monitoring), and efficient digital computer data processing after the flight.

The timing for the application of a digital PCM system in the TRRA project was right. Recent developments had demonstrated that these systems were capable of handling the high frequencies (up to 10 Hz) required for the analysis of the proprotor dynamic data generated by the TRRA. For higher frequency needs (such as acoustic or engine vibration data) and for cockpit voice recordings, a few channels of wideband FM (frequency modulated) tape recording were provided.

The consideration of the TRRA's instrumentation needs at the beginning of the project resulted in a significant cost benefit by having access-limited sensors and instrumentation wiring installed as the aircraft was being built. As part of a plan to facilitate major maintenance or modifications, the large components of the data acquisition system were mounted on a pallet in the cabin. If required, this allowed the entire pallet to be removed (with difficulty) and brought to the instrumentation shop.

For the planned wind tunnel test of the XV-15, provisions for connecting the aircraft's digital data to the control room were incorporated and consisted of two coaxial cables (compared to hundreds of wires that would be required for an analog instrumentation system), thus saving considerable installation time. A further feature of the digital system that proved to be useful during the test was the ability of the wind tunnel engineers to change the selection of the parameters being monitored in real time during the test runs. This provided the versatility needed to enable on-line trouble-shooting or anomaly assessments during the running of the test.

The XV-15's data system consisted of two Remote Multiplexer/Digitizer Units (RMDU's), signal conditioning and filtering components to process various types of sensors (such as strain gauges, pressure transducers, thermocouples, and potentiometers), a wide-band twelve-channel flightworthy magnetic tape recorder (that provided almost one hour of data acquisition), and a telemetry system. The wires from the various sensors were fed into the system using a large patch-panel (similar to an old-fashioned telephone operator's switchboard). While the system was reasonably robust, this element proved to be the source of many of the reliability problems that did occur.

Prior to the start of flight operations at Ames, the Government Project Office initiated the development of the data acquisition system for the TRRA. The requirement to monitor numerous structural load parameters in real-time at a ground station dictated the need to improve the acquisition, processing, and display of the digital data. This enhanced capability was developed, with the input of TRRA project funding, by the Ames Avionics Systems Branch. Since some of the test operations would be performed at the remote Crows Landing Naval Landing Field, a duplicate data acquisition and processing capability was developed at that site. To allow the ground safety monitoring crew to be located at either location during testing, a telemetry data "repeater" was installed on 3900-foot Mount Diablo, one of the higher topographical features in the San Francisco Bay area. For tests that called for the XV-15 to fly near Crows Landing or over the adjacent San Joaquin Valley, while the monitoring crew remained at Ames, the aircraft's telemetered data would be initially received by the Crows Landing data station. This signal was then sent to the repeater where it was transmitted to the telemetry receiver at Ames. With the addition of video coverage, the remote management of flight tests at Crows Landing became as routine and efficient as if the aircraft was flying at Ames.

The NASA Ames ground data acquisition group developed and maintained the control rooms at Moffett Field and at Crows Landing, from where the Test Director communicated with the flight crew and the ground test-support personnel. Each control room had a monitor that displayed aircraft status and critical parameter values (such as loads or moments) and had four strip-chart recorders that provided time histories of a total of thirty-two key items (selected for each test) in engineering units in real time. These strip-chart recorders were monitored by engineers or technicians familiar with the behavior of the items being monitored, and who would alert the Test Director if allowable-limit values were approached or exceeded. In addition, the ground data acquisition group would process all data from the flight tapes for post-flight review, and would calculate the accumulated "fatigue damage" to structural components due to oscillatory loads in excess of the "infinite-life" limit.

In addition to working with the group developing the ground data acquisition and processing capabilities, Mike Bondi of the TRRA Project Office was also responsible for the development of an interactional database program which could be used by engineers to analyze the flight test results. This program would be capable of storing a large volume of data, retrieving data sets within constraints defined by the engineer, providing a variety of data processing options, and generating data tables or plots in a number of user-defined formats. This work was contracted to Analytical Mechanics Associates of Sunnyvale California in 1980 and the resulting program was called the Tilt Rotor Engineering Database (TRENDS). In addition to the TRRA, TRENDS was also successfully used for other Ames flight research activities such as the JUH-60A Black Hawk Airloads project and the Quiet Short-Haul Research Aircraft (QSRA) Jump-Strut project.

In 1979, the need to conduct XV-15 flight tests at the Dryden Flight Research Center in southern California presented logistics problems for the TRRA Project Office engineering team at Ames. With the small project staff having responsibilities at both Ames and Dryden within the same time period, it was apparent the team could not be relocated frequently to meet the test schedules. The solution was the use of satellite communications technology and the installation of a satellite dish at Ames. With this equipment, flights at DFRC were controlled and monitored by the Army/NASA crew at Ames.

The Ames-developed data systems were installed in both XV-15 aircraft and remained in use for several years. For aircraft N702NA, Bell changed to a new onboard data acquisition system in 1988 to match the data acquisition system being used on the V-22 Osprey aircraft. The original system remained in N703NA until 1994 when the aircraft was bailed to Bell.

Figure 43.
Bell XV-15 ground tiedown facility. (Ames Photograph AC76-1518-115)

Ground Tiedown Test

Following the completion of the Integrated Systems tests, each XV-15 was subjected to a series of operational tests at Bell on an elevated ground tiedown facility (figure 43) that Bell had constructed for that purpose. The facility had a moveable tripod structure that attached to the wind tunnel "hard points" under the wing to secure the aircraft while enabling the proprotors to be run in all flight modes. The purpose of these tests was to evaluate the performance of all systems within the limitations of the static operation.

During the initial runs, for pilot protection, a set of thick steel shields were placed along the sides of the cockpit (figure 44). Also, for early tiedown operations, a rescue ramp was moved into position over the nose of the aircraft to facilitate exit of the crew through the overhead windows, if that should become. When sufficient running had been completed to gain confidence in the proprotor structure and RPM control system, the shields were removed, but the rescue ramp remained throughout the test series.

One of the primary elements examined was the transmission system. With an external fuel supply, the tiedown facility permitted continuous operation of the proprotors at various power levels and RPM's (as in the initial qualification of the

Figure 44.
Initial Bell tiedown showing metal protective shields. (Bell Photograph 240178)

transmissions in the Bell Transmission Test Laboratory). Functional checks of the aircraft's electrical system, hydraulic system, proprotor RPM governor, and other systems were also conducted.

First Flight

With the completion of the integrated systems test and with substantial progress being made in the ground tiedown runs, the Bell and Government TRRA project offices initiated discussions addressing the start of the flight test program. While each was anxious to explore the new technology, the Government approach, as defined in the TRRA Project Plan, called for a wind tunnel test prior to flight to "be certain all critical mode analyses are valid and that the (analytical) methods properly assess the dynamic characteristics, capabilities, limitations, and operating behavior of the tilt rotor flight research aircraft." Bell, however, argued for the initiation of a limited flight program as soon as practical, which would have been their usual practice, in order to reveal issues that may require further analytical investigations or additional attention during the wind tunnel test. The early detection of problems would allow more time for their resolution and could ultimately accelerate the program. This rationale for an early flight evaluation had sufficient technical merit for the Army/NASA TRRA Project Office to present the plan to the Ames Airworthiness and Flight Safety Review Board (AFSRB).[24]

After establishing the readiness and airworthiness of XV-15 N702NA located at the Bell Flight Test Center, and examining the test results from the ground-based operations, the Ames AFSRB approved a limited hover and air-taxi flight test activity. Since the Ames 40- by 80-foot wind tunnel could not produce steady airflow at very low wind tunnel airspeeds, the AFSRB restricted flight speeds to 40 knots, where data at steady-state conditions could be obtained from flight tests. In addition, this hover and air-taxi evaluation was limited to a maximum of three flight hours and to low altitude operating conditions.

On May 3, 1977, following a series of ground-taxi and systems tests, the XV-15 TRRA became airborne for the first time. The initial liftoff, conducted by Bell test pilot Ron Erhart and copilot Dorman Cannon, was executed according to plan. With Bell Test Director Shep Blackman and a team of XV-15 project engineers carefully watching the critical flight parameters in the Bell Flight Test Center control room, the XV-15 was accelerated in helicopter mode along the runway by the application of power and the forward movement of the center control stick. After a short ground roll a slight increase in the power provided the additional thrust needed for liftoff. As planned, the power was immediately reduced, the aircraft settled back on the runway, and a rollout was performed. This first flight demonstrated satisfactory handling qualities and safe structural loads. In subsequent operations, longitudinal and directional controllability were verified and a hover over a fixed point was made. The initial flight pilot report stated "In general, the aircraft hovered almost exactly as predicted, based on the simulator evaluations," a clear validation of the extensive TRRA simulation program. Further testing performed by the Bell pilots at the Arlington, Texas, Municipal Airport during this initial test period included flights in the helicopter mode in hover and in forward, sideward and rearward flight. Testing also included an assessment of the SCAS

---

[24] The Ames Airworthiness and Flight Safety Review Board was a panel of senior members of the Ames staff, including technical/research specialists, who were charged with the evaluation of planned aircraft activities to ensure that adequate design, testing, planning, and training had been done in order to achieve proposed mission objectives safely. The AFSRB members were appointed by the Director of Ames Research Center and had no direct involvement in the project being reviewed.

and the FFS. For the first time in this flight program, the nacelles were tilted to 85 degrees[25] and a brief assessment was made of the handling qualities. During this period, NASA/Army project pilot Dan Dugan flew N702NA for his first tilt rotor flight. After completing the authorized three flight test hours, the aircraft was configured with a remote control system for wind tunnel operation, and operationally checked out on the Bell ground tiedown stand.

On March 23, 1978, after completing ground runs and repairs (to be discussed later), XV-15 N702NA, with the proprotors and wing removed, was transported to Moffett Field onboard an Air Force C-5A. At Ames, a Bell crew reassembled the XV-15 and prepared it for the wind tunnel test.

Wind Tunnel Tests

As noted earlier, prior to the expansion of the flight envelope, the TRRA was to be tested in the Ames 40- by 80-foot wind tunnel, both to check out the aircraft and its systems and to collect data that accurately described the aerodynamic characteristics of the XV-15. While the acquisition of a flight data base that could be reliably used for the development of larger tilt rotor transport aircraft clearly required the XV-15 to be as large as practical (considering factors such as the available powerplant), the 40- by 80-foot wind tunnel test called for the consideration of two conflicting issues. One of these issues was due to the well known effects that the wind tunnel walls have on the flow around the "test model" (in this case the XV-15). The wind tunnel "wall effect" phenomenon occurs because the flow at the wind tunnel walls is constrained to move in the wall surfaces of the test section, whereas in free flight, induced velocities occur that could have a component normal to the solid boundaries of the wind tunnel. A test model is considered too large if the wall constraint on the flow has a measurable influence on the desired test data such as the magnitude of wing lift or proprotor performance. The other major consideration in selecting the dimensions of a wind tunnel model is the effect that the size of a body moving through viscous air has on the behavior of the flow, particularly in the vicinity just over the surface called the "boundary layer." On very small models the airflow, traversing through regions where local pressure changes occur, would not develop the turbulence and resulting drag changes that would appear with larger models. To represent "full-scale" aerodynamic characteristics, therefore, the test model needs to be large enough to adequately represent the viscous effects.[26] While the size of the XV-15 was sufficient to properly represent "large-scale"

---

[25] The position of the proprotor shaft indicates the flight mode configuration of the tilt rotor aircraft. The convention adapted by the Government TRRA Project Office and Bell referred to the airplane mode position as 0 degrees and the helicopter position as 90 degrees.

[26] An aerodynamic term called "Reynolds Number" indicates the degree of influence that the flow viscous effects have on the boundary layer for a selected model size and airspeed. For most full-scale aircraft, Reynolds Numbers exceed three million. The aerodynamic behavior of the wings and propellers are usually significantly different for small scale models having Reynolds Numbers below one million.

aircraft aerodynamics and proprotor performance in flight, it was about as large as could be accepted for tests in the 40- by 80-foot wind test section.

The wind tunnel test of the XV-15 was made a required part of the TRRA project in the first Project Plan that was issued in 1972. This requirement was carried forth in later revisions of the Plan and through execution. The technical rationale for this test was strong. It provided an opportunity to evaluate the loads, performance, and aerodynamic characteristics, as well as the function of the mechanical, electrical, and hydraulic systems under operational conditions in the controlled environment of the wind tunnel and without risk to a flight crew. Yet there were arguments against the wind tunnel test. These detractors questioned the wisdom of exposing the aircraft to the risks associated with a tied-down wind-on experiment.[27] They were also concerned about the impact of the additional costs to conduct the test as well as delaying flight activity. There were even discussions questioning whether the real motivation was to show that the 40- by 80-foot wind tunnel was still a viable tool for developing new types of aircraft. In any event, the wind tunnel test was a critical milestone that needed to be reached before embarking on the flight evaluation program.

The ability to operate the XV-15 N702NA as an unmanned wind tunnel model was provided as the aircraft was designed and constructed. Mounting locations for the wind tunnel struts (called "hard points") were built into the aircraft's structure at the lower surface of each wing and the tail. Provisions were made for the installation of remote operation devices for the engines and flight controls. The external supply source connections were installed for hydraulic and electrical power used to operate the control systems during wind tunnel testing with the engines not operating. For tests with the engines running, the aircraft's engine-driven electrical and hydraulic systems were used.

Prior to entering the tunnel, the aircraft's fuel tanks were drained and filled with nitrogen (to reduce the risk of an explosion), and the fuel lines capped (the wind tunnel "external" fuel supply was connected directly to the engines, bypassing the fuel tanks). Actuators for the remote operation were installed. The landing gear was retracted and the gear doors were closed during the test.

Figure 45 shows the XV-15 mounted on the three-strut support system in the Ames 40- by 80-foot wind tunnel. To assure safe operation, crew training was conducted during the ground tiedown tests at the contractor's facility with the remote control systems installed. At Ames, the TRRA simulation math model was modified to represent operation in the wind tunnel and remote operations were simulated to evaluate emergency operating procedures. The only failure identified that could cause a dangerous condition was a simultaneous dual engine failure in high-speed helicopter mode flight (with the nacelles above 85 degrees).

---

[27] An aircraft constrained by a wind tunnel mounting system might be subjected to operating conditions not normally encountered nor sustained in flight. These unusual conditions could produce airloads, moments, and torques that exceed allowable design limits and result in structural failure.

Figure 45.
XV-15 in the Ames Research
Center 40- by 80-ft.wind
tunnel. (Ames Photograph
A78-0579-3)

The emergency procedure required to avoid potentially destructive loads called for the reduction of the nacelle incidence angle within five seconds of a dual engine failure.

During the two-month test period, 54 hours of wind-on time were logged. Of this, 19 hours were with the rotors operating. Static aerodynamic forces and moments data were acquired from the wind tunnel balance (scales) system and structural loads and aircraft systems data were obtained from the XV-15's onboard instrumentation system. Critical temperature, pressure, and static and dynamic load parameters were monitored in "real-time" in the control room. Testing was conducted over a range of nacelle angles and airspeeds and included the baseline aircraft configuration and various combinations of vortex generators, pylon strakes, and wing fences. A report titled "Wind Tunnel Tests of the XV-15 Tilt Rotor Aircraft"[28] containing summary data and photographs was issued in April 1980.

In general the aircraft's components and systems performed well. The few exceptions to this were: a failed nacelle downstop[29] (the "hard-point" that limits the nacelle position when operating in the airplane mode), nose boom and antenna vibration,[30] and engine oil venting.[31] The most significant issue, however, was the high empennage loads that occurred in helicopter mode forward flight and in portion of the conversion envelope. In helicopter mode flight, the loads were caused by aerodynamic excitation of the vertical tail surfaces arising from the close proximity of the inboard proprotor tip vortices. At the 60 degrees nacelle-incidence conversion mode flight condition, a strong vortex emanating from the nacelle/wing juncture also was swept near the tail, causing a high oscillatory load condition. After the wind tunnel test program structural changes were made to accommodate these loads.[32]

---

[28] James A. Weiberg, M. D. Maisel, *Wind-Tunnel Tests of the XV-15 Tilt Rotor Aircraft,* NASA TM 81177 and AVRADCOM Technical Report TR-80-A-3, April 1980.

[29] Following the wind tunnel test, the downstop bracket failure problem was resolved by a bracket redesign and a change to the preload/rigging procedure to reduce impact loads.

[30] The vibration problems were later resolved by increasing nose boom stiffness and by repairing a structural failure (discovered after the wind tunnel test) at the antenna attach point.

[31] The problem of seepage from the engine oil scavenge lines was addressed by providing an angular (scarf) cut at the exposed end of the tube. The seepage, however, continued to occur in subsequent flights.

[32] Subsequent flight tests, however, showed that the empennage load problems were less severe than indicated by the wind tunnel tests.

Navy Participation

For a period of about eight years, starting in the mid-1970s, the USA experienced one of the longest sustained periods of high inflation of the century. This occurred, unfortunately, while the TRRA project was in its most active phase and required high levels of contractor labor and expenditures of large amounts of funding for subcontractor work. The completion of the wind tunnel test of aircraft N702NA, in June 1978, left it in a non-flightworthy configuration and a considerable effort was required to refurbish it for flight. In addition, resolution of technical problems in most of the aircraft-development WBSEs was taking a toll on the project's financial resources. The "joint" commitment to the TRRA project by the Army and NASA had, on numerous occasions, served to maintain the support of each of the parties. Throughout the early years of the project, neither agency was prepared to be first to walk away from their funding obligation while the other was seen to be preparing to step up to the challenge. However, by early 1979 costs had grown to the point where the TRRA Project Office was forced to reevaluate its plans for the completion of the project in light of its resource limitations. Among the solutions considered was the reduction of the contractor's flight program, a reduction of the procurement of needed spare parts, and the discontinuation of work on aircraft N702NA. Each of these approaches could have serious adverse effects on the ability of the TRRA project to complete its technical goals.

Meanwhile, starting in early 1978, the Naval Air Systems Command (NAVAIR) had been engaged in a congressionally-authorized Sea Based Air-Master Study (SBA-MS)[33] to assess the Navy's technology requirements. The report to Congress was to "evaluate the capabilities and cost effectiveness of current and future platform, aircraft and weapon system combinations." The aircraft to be considered included VTOL and V/STOL types (and, in fact, the original stimulus for the SBA-MS was the Navy's need to establish a basis for, or against, a future commitment to V/STOL aircraft). For the Navy's V/STOL Type "A" low speed application, including the ASW (Anti-Submarine Warfare), COD (Carrier Onboard Delivery), tanker, and SAR (Search and Rescue) missions, the tilt rotor under development in the NASA/Army TRRA project was a candidate aircraft type that warranted serious consideration. The XV-15 was seen by some

---

[33] The Navy's SBA-MS evolved from the Sea Control Ship (SCS) initiative established by Admiral Elmo Zumwalt after he became Chief of Naval Operations (CNO) in 1970. The SCS was to employ high performance V/STOL aircraft to perform various elements of the sea control mission. Subsequent NAVAIR studies indicated that the tilt rotor aircraft had significant advantages over other V/STOL concepts when applied to several Navy mission scenarios. In 1976, two years after relieving Admiral Zumwalt, CNO Admiral James Holloway initiated a new V/STOL aircraft study under which the fighter/attack missions were to be performed by the V/STOL "B" aircraft, and the assault/support (helicopter replacement) vehicles were designated V/STOL "A." During this period the Marine Corps was also investigating replacement aircraft for their aging fleet of CH-46 helicopters under a program called HMX. Lieutenant General Thomas Miller, USMC Deputy Chief of Staff, and Rear Admiral C. P. Ekas, Naval Materiel Command (NAVMAT) Chief of Naval Development directed their subordinates to explore and demonstrate, if feasible, new aircraft technology that could have potential for future Marine assault transport applications. This provided the impetus for the Navy's participation in the XV-15 project.

NAVAIR managers as a means of determining the tilt rotor aircraft's readiness and suitability for Navy missions. One of the leading advocates for Naval VTOL capability, and a strong proponent for the tilt rotor aircraft within NAVAIR at that time, was Harold (Hal) Andrews.

By March 1978, discussions had been initiated between NAVAIR and the NASA/Army TRRA Project Office for the participation of the Navy in the XV-15 activity. This new collaboration provided for the infusion of $4.0M of Navy funds into the program between 1979 and 1981. Of particular interest to the Navy was the timely opportunity to conduct concept feasibility flight testing of this unique aircraft type onboard a Navy carrier. The Navy funds permitted the Army/NASA TRRA Project Office to refurbish aircraft N702NA for flight, purchase the required spare parts, continue the contractor flight test activity, and initiate the Government concept evaluation (proof-of-concept) flight testing as planned. In addition, the use of the XV-15 for the Navy evaluation was consistent with the NASA goal of making available advanced aeronautical technology to the military. It was a "win-win" arrangement.

George Unger of NAVAIR was assigned to develop an agreement for Navy participation in the TRRA program with the Army and NASA. Coordination for this between NASA Ames and the Navy was provided by Clark White, of the Ames Aeronautics and Flight Systems Directorate, who was on assignment to the Naval Air Systems Command in Washington, D.C., John Ward, Rotorcraft Manager at NASA Headquarters, provided HQ support. The Army/NASA/Navy Memorandum of Agreement signed in July 1978 led to a request from Rear Admiral E. R. Seymour, Commander, Naval Air systems Command to the CNO for a shipboard evaluation of the XV-15.

The request cited key areas of interest as "gust and turbulence sensitivity, deck edge effect, handling qualities, pilot work load, and STOL performance." Within a short time, the request was approved and arrangements were made to conduct sea trials aboard an LPH class ship operating in the California coastal waters off of San Diego. The story of that evaluation will be covered later.

The timely funding provided by the Navy enabled the TRRA to be put back on its original plan.

Flight Envelope Expansion

With the initial hover/low-speed/low-altitude evaluation and the 40-by 80-foot wind tunnel test completed and all identified technical issues addressed, authorization was provided by the Government to initiate Phase I of the Contractor Flight Test activity. This phase involved the initial venture into the full flight capabilities of the XV-15 TRRA. It became apparent that the Government Project Office and the Ames Airworthiness and Flight Safety Review Board (AFSRB) had a conservative view on the approach to envelope expansion. Bell, on the other hand, having had more recent experience in the development of new flight vehicles was anxious to more aggressively explore the flight capabilities of the XV-15. The directives from the Ames TRRA Project Office prevailed and Bell was required to accept the more cautious approach to envelope expansion. Expansion would be performed in small airspeed and nacelle angle increments and a thorough analysis of the test data would be conducted prior to the next configuration and airspeed test condition.

The first flight of XV-15 N703NA (the aircraft available at Bell for the Contractor Flight Tests) occurred on April 23, 1979, at the Bell Flight Test Center, Arlington Municipal Airport, Texas. The Bell pilots assigned to the envelope expansion were Ron Erhart and Dorman Cannon, and the Bell test director was Shep Blackman.

In mid June, when the XV-15 had explored flight regimes from the helicopter mode to a nacelle angle of 60-degrees, LTC Dan Dugan, the NASA/Army project pilot, made an evaluation flight. In his report to the Ames AFSRB, he recommended that the envelope expansion be continued, and permission was granted.

After a total of 15 hours of flight testing and more than three months of expanding the flight envelope with carefully planned incremental steps, a major milestone was reached when, on July 24, 1979, the first full in-flight conversion from helicopter-to-airplane mode was accomplished. During that initial airplane mode flight lasting about 40 minutes, the crew evaluated climbs, descents, turns, accelerations, and decelerations and reached an airspeed of 160 knots. The Bell flight crew and test engineers were quite pleased with the results and envelope expansion in the airplane mode continued.

The success of the Phase I effort now opened the door for the Proof-of-Concept Flight Tests, Phase II of the contractor's XV-15 flight activity. This phase of the flight program involved a closer examination of the flight characteristics of the XV-15 and of the performance and operation of its systems. It also presented an opportunity for the Bell test pilots to train the Government flight crew and permitted an initial Government evaluation of the XV-15.

In accordance with the Project Plan, the completion of the Proof-of-Concept phase was to be conducted at a Government test site. Because of the level of risk associated with the flight test of a low-time research aircraft, it was decided that

this work should be conducted at the NASA Dryden Flight Research Center (DFRC) at Edwards Air Force Base near Mojave California, instead of the heavily populated area around Ames. To accomplish this, the proprotors and wing of XV-15 N703NA were removed and the disassembled aircraft, along with support equipment, were airlifted to DFRC from Bell onboard an Air Force C-130 on August 13, 1980. Following reassembly and ground tests at DFRC, the proof-of-concept flight activity resumed on October 6, 1980, and continued through May 1981. During this period, the Government and Bell team members gathered in front of N703NA for a group picture (figure 46).

Government Acceptance of N703NA

A formal Government acceptance ceremony for XV-15 N703NA was held on October 30, 1980, at Dryden. The program schedule called for the arrival of Ames senior NASA and Army personnel onboard the ARC/DFRC shuttle aircraft at precisely 11:00 am, followed by the immediate XV-15 takeoff and fly-over demonstration by a Government flight crew. The aircraft was then to land and taxi to the area where the presentations were to be made. The Project Office staff had established a crisp schedule to reflect the precision and efficiency of the TRRA project.

Once again we learned that things do not always work as planned. The shuttle flight landed on time, but as soon as the Ames dignitaries deplaned, one of them anxiously asked where the nearest men's restroom was located... and the "crisp" schedule rapidly evaporated.

At the end of the ceremony, Bell flight test crew Ron Erhart and Dorman Cannon provided a plaque to Government pilots LTC Dan Dugan and Ron Gerdes illustrating the XV-15 in various flight modes. This symbolized the turning over of the "keys" of the new research aircraft to the Government (figure 47).

Ames Flight Preparations

Wherever the XV-15 was maintained special facilities were required. In preparation for planned future XV-15 operations at Ames, the Ames VTOL tiedown pad, developed years earlier for static tests of VTOL aircraft, was modified to allow the proprotors of the TRRA to be operated in the airplane mode, providing similar ground run capabilities as the one developed at Bell. A hydraulic lift platform, under the main and nose wheels (figure 48), elevated the XV-15 so that hinged tripod structures could be attached to the wing hard-points. In addition, a tubular strut pinned at ground level was attached to the tail hard-point to stabilize the tail section. With the supports in place, the hydraulic lift platform under the main and nose wheels was lowered to ground level, leaving the area under the elevated aircraft clear and resulting in a 6-ft wheel height.

When mounted on the tiedown stand, the proprotors could be operated in any nacelle position. As a safety measure, for early operations of the XV-15 on the Ames tiedown stand, a ramp was positioned over the nose of the aircraft to enable emergency pilot egress and rescue (figure 49).

Prior to its first flight at Ames, it was necessary to remove modifications made to the aircraft for the wind tunnel test in order to restore it to a flightworthy status. This refurbishment was delayed several months while project funding issues were being resolved. The provision of Navy funding at this point provided the contractor support necessary to refurbish XV-15 N702NA. A Bell team of engineers and technicians arrived at Ames in mid-1980 to work with NASA and

Top:

Figure 47.
XV-15 plaque being presented to Government pilots by Bell pilots at the acceptance ceremony. (Bell Photograph 309835)

Bottom:

Figure 48.
Ames tiedown test facility showing rescue ramp. (Ames Photograph AC80-0686-1)

Figure 49.
Tiedown test facility at the Ames Research Center showing the hydraulic lift. (Ames Photograph AC80-0686-3)

Army personnel on the restoration of the aircraft to the flight configuration. Following the reassembly, ground tie-down operations for XV-15 N702NA were initiated in August 1980 and completed in October 1980. The first flight of this aircraft at Ames occurred on November 20, 1980.

With one XV-15 aircraft permanently stationed at Ames, NASA contracted with Bell to provide ongoing on-site support. Bell's Jerry Pickard performed this support and remained at Ames, providing logistics between the Government and Bell, until the task was terminated in 1988. This support was essential for the successful operation of the XV-15 at Ames. The long periods away from Bell presented an occasional dilemma (sometimes humorous) for Pickard. One example of such an occurrence was when Pickard requested his manager at Bell to provide a few Bell baseball caps to give to visiting dignitaries. After considerable time had passed, and with no hats delivered to Pickard at Ames, his manager requested a photograph of Pickard and the Government XV-15 pilot standing near the XV-15. The picture sent back to Bell by Pickard was exactly what was requested, except that Pickard was wearing a Hughes Helicopter Company hat and Dan Dugan, the NASA pilot, wore a Sikorsky hat. Within one week the Bell hats arrived at Pickard's desk. His manager never again ignored his requests.

Flight Research

In 1981, after a number of maintenance test flights, the Project Office began a series of ground and flight investigations to acquire a comprehensive data base to meet the fundamental and advanced technical goals of the TRRA project. These test activities would eventually address structural loads, handling qualities, flight dynamics, structural dynamics and stability, acoustics, performance, and proprotor downwash.

Figure 50.
XV-15 hovering in-ground-effect during 1984 performance and downwash test. (Ames Photograph AC81-0165-152)

Hover Performance

One of the first experiments at Ames explored several characteristics of the TRRA in the hover mode. The scope of this hover test included an evaluation of performance, acoustics, and the documentation of the "outwash" (the flow parallel to the ground generated by the proprotor downwash) at various hovering heights. These data were required by the Navy for the planned operational evaluation of the XV-15 onboard an aircraft carrier. To measure the proprotor wake flow in the vicinity of the hovering aircraft, the Naval Air Test Center of Patuxent River, Maryland, provided data acquisition equipment and a supporting research team. The outwash test apparatus consisted of a remote-controlled motorized cart that carried an array of sensitive electronic (ion-beam) anemometers (to measure the low-speed airflow) mounted on a 10-foot high pole. While the aircraft hovered (figure 50) over a point on the hover pad at a selected height, the instrumented cart was moved to various predetermined positions along a track radiating from the point below the XV-15. To survey the region around the hovering aircraft, the heading orientation of the TRRA was varied 180 degrees in 30-degree increments, thereby documenting the outflow from the region directly forward of, to the region directly aft of the aircraft.

The outwash test required that the aircraft hover at a precise height, heading, and position for a 15- to 20-second data acquisition period. The method devised to accomplish this involved the use of sets of visual targets mounted on tall poles around the hover pad. By lining up two sets of selected targets, the aircraft was positioned at the desired point in space (figure 51). Hover conditions for these tests ranged from an in-ground-effect (IGE) 2-foot wheel height to an out-of-ground effect (OGE) 50-foot wheel height. In addition to the outwash data, these steady hovering operations conducted in near-zero wind conditions enabled the simultaneous acquisition of excellent performance data.[34,35]

---

[34] M. Maisel, D. Harris, "Hover Tests of the XV-15 Tilt Rotor Research Aircraft." Presented at the 1st Flight Testing Conference, Las Vegas, Nevada, AIAA Paper 81-2501, November 11-13, 1981.
[35] D.J. Harris, R.D. Simpson, "Technical Evaluation of the Rotor Downwash Flow Field of the XV-15 Tilt Rotor Research Aircraft." NATC Report No. SY-14R-83, July 28, 1983.

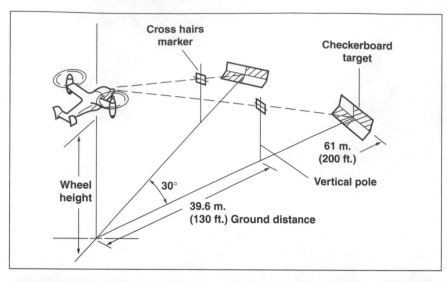

Also during this period, an evaluation of electromagnetic interference (EMI) effects on the XV-15's electronic systems was conducted at Ames to ensure compatibility with Navy shipboard operations.

An associated test to measure download performed during the same test period was conducted with the XV-15 N702NA mounted on the tiedown stand at Ames. Load cells placed between the aircraft's two-wing and one-tail support "hard" points and the tiedown structure provided a means of determining the net vertical force of the aircraft. This information was then coupled with the aircraft weight and the free hover performance data to determine the download, the downward force acting on the aircraft due to the impingement of the proprotor wake on its wing and fuselage surfaces.

The magnitude of the download deduced from this test series turned out to generate a technical dilemma.

Top:

Figure 51.
Method used to position the aircraft for the downwash and acoustics hover test at the Ames Research Center.

Bottom:

Figure 52.
XV-15 proprotor on the propeller test apparatus at the Ames Outdoor Aerodynamic Research Facility. (Ames Photograph AC84-0473-100)

Previous estimates of the download for a tilt rotor aircraft using deployed plain flaps ranged from 7 percent to 8 percent of the rotor thrust.[36,37,38] This, combined with the estimates of rotor hover efficiency obtained from earlier hover tests of an isolated proprotor, appeared to properly account for the thrust produced and the wing-in-proprotor wake (interference) losses. Now the download obtained from the hover/tiedown tests indicated that the interference loss was twice the expected value.

The question would not be completely resolved until nearly three years later when several full-scale rotors were tested at the Ames Outdoor Aerodynamic Research Facility (OARF, figure 52). Further investigations of the proprotor wake interaction with the aircraft in 1985 provided a better understanding of the

[36] R. L. Lichten, "Some Performance and Operating Characteristics of Convertiplanes," SAE National Aeronautical Meeting, Los Angeles, California, October 1957.

[37] Anon., "V/STOL Tilt Rotor Aircraft Study - Task I - Conceptual Design," Bell Helicopter Company, NASA CR-114441, Bell Helicopter Co., May 1972.

[38] Anon., "V/STOL Tilt Rotor Aircraft Study - Volume I - Preliminary Design of Research Aircraft," NASA CR-114438, Boeing Vertol, March 1972.

flow phenomenon that caused the higher than expected download. These tests involved the use of a new "balance" designed to provide highly accurate proprotor thrust and torque data. The balance, mounted between the proprotor and the drive motors, was developed by Boeing Helicopters (previously Boeing Vertol) under the contract that provided for the development of new composite-material proprotors for the XV-15 aircraft. The original XV-15 metal blades obtained from Bell for performance and stability wind tunnel tests in the early 1970s were one of the full-scale configurations tested. Data obtained from this test showed that the XV-15 proprotor performance was, in fact, better than the earlier estimates. The somewhat mixed blessing that came out of these investigations was that highly twisted proprotor blades could be designed to produce high performance, but the high download generated by the proprotor wake consumed all of the unexpected performance gains. It was clear that the hover performance, and therefore the effectiveness of the tilt rotor aircraft, could benefit from an understanding and reduction of the download loss.

Aeroelastic Stability Evaluations

Of all of the technical areas to be explored in the TRRA test program, none would be as important as the investigation of the aeroelastic stability of the XV-15 in high-speed airplane-mode flight. The future of the tilt rotor aircraft depended on the outcome of these tests.

The instability problem encountered by the tilt rotor aircraft is caused by elastic deformation of the wing, pylon, and proprotor which oscillate when disturbed. The flexing of the wing and pylon imposes a pitching and/or yawing motion on the proprotor. This produces a proprotor in-plane force acting in the same direction as the original motion. Under some circumstances these in-plane forces are sufficient to make the displacements in amplitude grow with each oscillation, in effect acting as a powerful negative spring, producing an aeroelastic instability.

Both Bell and the Army/NASA TRRA project offices produced predictions of the structural dynamic stability of the XV-15. Bell used a company-developed method and the Government used predicted values determined from the analysis generated by Dr. Wayne Johnson. Both analyses indicated satisfactory stability throughout the envelope of the XV-15 except for one operating condition. The predicted instability occurred only at high airplane mode airspeeds and at the high RPM that was used for the hover and helicopter mode flight. The solution was to set an airplane mode speed limit above which the proprotor RPM had to be reduced to a level where the "one-per-rev" excitation of the natural mode could not occur. Fortunately, this RPM reduction was planned during the design of the XV-15 to improve the performance of the proprotor so that it became standard procedure to reduce RPM just after converting to the airplane mode.

To evaluate the aeroelastic stability of the TRRA in flight it was necessary to create rotor/pylon/wing displacements at the frequencies that corresponded to the various

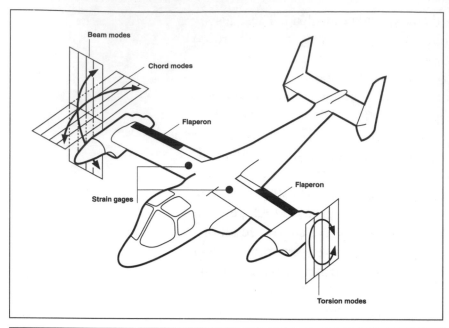

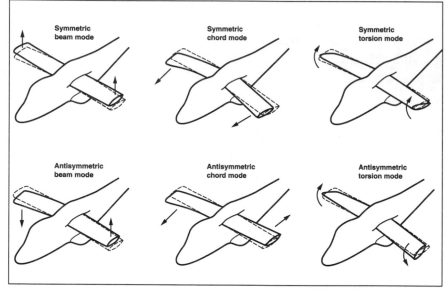

natural "modes" of the tilt rotor structure (as illustrated in figures 53 and 54) and to measure the response of the aircraft's structure to these deformations. Diminishing oscillation amplitudes following the excitations occurred for a stable system (called "positively damped"), while potentially dangerous increasing amplitude oscillations indicated an unstable (negatively damped) structure at that operating condition.

The initial approach taken by researchers at Ames and Bell involved the installation of limited-authority (i.e. limited-motion) electrohydraulic actuators in the flaperon and collective-pitch control linkages on the right side of the aircraft. These "excitation" actuators were controlled from the cockpit where amplitude and oscillatory rates (frequency) were set.

The flight tests required special care. While confidence was high in the predictions of stability within and beyond the XV-15's flight envelope, this evaluation was treated as having a significant risk because of the potential for a catastrophic failure if the predictions were wrong. Testing was initiated in airplane-mode level flight. When steady, level flight conditions were established, the crew activated the excitation system in accordance with the test plan. To minimize hazard, the series of test operations were initiated at lower airspeeds where the risk of encountering an instability was very low. After a thorough analysis of the data and a projection that the next test condition would be stable, the airspeed was increased in small increments and the test cycle was repeated.

Early flight tests involved oscillating the right-hand excitation actuators (one at a time) at a fixed frequency to drive a selected structural mode at resonance. The oscillations were then abruptly turned off and the resulting rate of decay of the structural vibrations was measured to determine the level of damping (an indication of stability). Since the resonant frequency for each of the modes was not precisely known in advance, the test had to be repeated several times to excite the desired mode. Another early method used to excite the various structural modes of the tilt rotor aircraft involved natural (or wake) turbulence excitation. The results of these initial structural dynamic evaluations are presented in reports by Bell and Government researchers.[39,40]

An extensive series of airplane mode aeroelastic stability tests were conducted in March and April of 1987 by Wally Acree, the Ames TRRA principal investigator. The analysis of these test results revealed several problems. Many of the important mode-shape natural frequencies were closely spaced and some modes were not easily excited, especially with the natural turbulence excitation. Most significantly, the resulting damping-estimate scatter, although always indicating positive stability, was too extensive for meaningful correlation with, and validation of, the analytical predictions. The addition of left-hand flaperon and collective-pitch actuators similar to those on the right side of the aircraft enabled the excitation of specific symmetric and anti-symmetric mode shapes but the damping level scatter remained too large.

Another modification to the excitation system provided the capability to input "frequency sweeps," the continuous variation of the excitation frequency from a pre-selected low setting to a pre-selected high setting (over a period of 23 seconds), at a chosen amplitude. Each test point required the test pilot to maintain the flight condition for about 30 seconds. Again, using the prior analytical methods, the damping level for many modes was poorly defined.

The search for improved aeroelastic stability test and data analysis technology led to the application of frequency-domain methodology by Dr. Mark B. Tischler of the Army Aeroflightdynamics Directorate at Ames.[41] This work improved the quality of the flight test results, improved the identification of the modes and, coupled with the frequency sweep excitation, was demonstrated to reduce the total flight time required for flight envelope expansion stability evaluation.

The aeroelastic stability flight program at Bell, led by Jim Bilger, evaluated various experimental methods and conducted extensive investigations of two configurations of titanium proprotor hub yokes and one steel hub. No significant effects on stability were detected for the three hub configurations.

An important result of the aeroelastic stability flight test evaluations[42] done at Ames and Bell was that positive damping (i.e. positive stability) was verified for

---

[39] J. M. Bilger, R. L. Marr, Ahmed Zahedi, "Results of Structural Dynamic Testing of the XV-15 Tilt Rotor Research Aircraft," Presented at the 37th Annual AHS Forum, New Orleans, Louisiana, May 1981.
[40] L. Schroers, "Dynamic Structural Aeroelastic Stability Testing of the XV-15 Tilt Rotor Research Aircraft," AGARD Paper No. 339; also NASA TM-84293, December 1982.
[41] C. W. Acree, Jr., M. B. Tischler, "Using Frequency-Domain Methods to Identify XV-15 Aeroelastic Modes," NASA TM-100033, Nov. 1987, and; C. W. Acree, Jr., Mark B. Tischler, "Determining XV-15 Aeroelastic Modes from Flight Data with Frequency-Domain Methods," NASA TP-3330 and ATCOM Technical Report 93-A-004, 1993.
[42] W. L. Arrington, M. Kumpel, R. L. Marr, K. G. McEntire, "XV-15 Tilt Rotor Research Aircraft Flight Test Report," Vol. I-V, NASA CR 177406 and USAAVSCOM TR-86-A-1, June 1985.

all identified elastic modes at all airspeeds and altitudes examined. The most significant and technically difficult objective of the TRRA project and the goal set nearly 30 years earlier during the XV-3 project had finally been achieved.

Short Takeoff Investigations

In August, 1982, the Ames TRRA Project Office continued performance and handling qualities evaluations of the XV-15, aircraft N703NA. This included investigations of the tilt rotor's short takeoff performance (STO) characteristics. To vary the weight and center-of-gravity (c.g.), lead shot-filled bags were placed in the fuselage and lead plates were affixed at the nose and tail of the aircraft. Following a series of evaluations at various c.g. locations, a number of flights were conducted to assess STO performance at high gross weights. Because of the high risk involved, these tests were performed at the sparsely populated and remote Crow's Landing Naval Auxiliary Landing Field (NALF), located about sixty miles from Ames. With the aircraft at or near the maximum takeoff gross weight, and the nacelles positioned at a preselected angle, the pilot released the brakes as the proprotors were brought to the desired torque level. The aircraft was then rotated for liftoff at a target ground speed and an attitude for maximum rate-of-climb was established (see figure 55). The aircraft position was measured using a laser operated by Ames Flight Operations Division personnel and contractors. The tracker utilized a laser retro-reflector mounted on the landing gear pods of the aircraft and the data was recorded for later correlation with aircraft data. Even at the maximum gross weight of the XV-15, the short takeoff operation was a rapid and very dynamic maneuver. This investigation enabled the effect of nacelle angle on STO performance to be evaluated. Too high an angle (at reduced torque to simulate a condition for which only STO and not vertical takeoff was possible) resulted in lower rates of acceleration, therefore extending the ground roll before liftoff could occur. Too low a nacelle angle provided improved ground roll acceleration, but the reduced vertical lift vector from the proprotors delayed the liftoff. It was determined (for the XV-15 at its maximum takeoff gross weight, and at approximately 60 percent of the normal power) that the optimum nacelle position for minimum ground roll to clear a 50-foot obstacle was 75 degrees. Evaluations of this type verified the capability of the tiltrotor aircraft to perform short takeoffs at gross weights well above its vertical takeoff gross weight, adding an important performance capability to this new aircraft type.

As often happens in developmental work, a totally unforeseen incident involving a critical proprotor hub

Figure 55.
XV-15 during short takeoff performance test.
(Ames Photograph AC82-0723-22)

component occurred during the STO tests. This component, called the "yoke," to which the blades are attached, was manufactured of Titanium because it afforded valuable weight saving over steel while still providing the required fatigue life.

On October 1, 1982, while performing STO operations at the Crows Landing NALF, at the XV-15's maximum takeoff gross weight, a telephone call was received by the Ames test director Shorty Schroers, from engineers at the Bell facility in Texas. They informed Schroers that they had just discovered that the strength of Titanium material used for the rotor yokes was significantly lower than that used in their design. The flight crew was informed about this new and somewhat disturbing development while in flight. They landed the XV-15 safely and removed the weights added for the STO tests. After further consultation with Bell engineers, it was decided to "gingerly" fly the aircraft back to Ames taking special care to keep the hub yoke oscillatory loads at a low level.

The full story regarding the Titanium fatigue strength anomaly emerged later. While performing design work for another project, a Bell engineer came across a published fatigue strength allowable load level for Titanium that was lower than that used for the design of the XV-15 yokes. Although the Titanium identified by the Bell engineer and the Titanium used for the proprotor were the same, a difference existed in their fatigue strength because of heat treatment (a process by which the strength and other properties of metals are altered by exposure to specific thermal conditions). As luck would have it, the heat treatment for the Titanium used for the XV-15 yokes was the one which resulted in the lower fatigue strength. This meant that aircraft N703NA had been operating at significantly higher loads than the lower strength Titanium could bear for the duration of the flight program.

Operation of both XV-15 aircraft was continued but with the installation of a new set of Titanium yokes and with the allowable loads reduced until a better solution was found. The solution was replacement of the Titanium yokes with steel yokes of the same design. Steel yokes were installed on aircraft N703NA in July of 1985 and have been used continuously since then without incident.

Flow Visualization Studies

In the early 1980s, a number of tilt rotor technical issues remained unexplained. One of these was that acoustic measurements in the hover mode of flight revealed that noise, rather than being at about an equal intensity around the aircraft, was greater behind the aircraft than at an equal distance along its sides. Another issue was that, although the magnitude of the download was now accepted as being greater than initially estimated (based on recent performance investigations), verification of the reason for this was needed. In an attempt to answer these questions and to better understand the airflow around the tilt rotor

aircraft in general, in-flight flow visualization studies were made using tufts taped to the wing and flaperon upper surfaces.[43] Flow direction was recorded in flight with a movie camera mounted at the tail of the XV-15. These studies surprisingly showed a spanwise inboard flow over the wing instead of the expected chordwise flow from hover through low-speed helicopter flight mode.

Another simple but unusual test was set up on the Ames tiedown test stand to investigate the flow conditions above the wing. The approach involved video taping smoke ejected over the wing while the aircraft was operated in the hover mode. Since the XV-15 was full-scale with accompanying high airflow velocities through the rotor, a high volume smoke source was required. Nontoxic, non-corrosive, smoke grenades of the type usually used by downed aircrew were selected.

The test apparatus consisted of a heat-insulated "smoke" box into which the smoke grenade would be dropped, a blower at the outlet of the box, and ducting leading from the blower to the top of the wing. Since this was a low budget test operation, an electrically powered leaf blower, generously provided by TRRA project engineer Jim Weiberg, was used to pump the smoke. To everyone's satisfaction, the first test of this system (without the aircraft in position) was a resounding success. When a smoke grenade was ignited and dropped into the smoke box everything looked fine. A thick jet of colored smoke emerged at high speed from the duct exhaust accompanied by the comforting roar of the blower. However, success was short lived. In very short order the sound of the leaf blower changed from a roar to a high pitched squeal and smoke started flowing from the box instead of from the end of the duct. Clearly something was not right. Following a fast shutdown, it was discovered that the leaf blower was equipped with a plastic fan which had melted from the heat generated by the smoke. Thus,

Top:
Figure 56.
Flow visualization near the XV-15 wing tips.
(Ames Photograph AC85-0804-49)

Bottom:
Figure 57.
Flow visualization near the XV-15 wing mid-span position.
(Ames Photograph AC85-0804-35)

---

[43] Tufting is a flow visualization technique using small lengths of yarn affixed to a surface to indicate directions and patterns of surface flow.

Jim Weiberg's leaf blower became a casualty in the quest for advancement of tilt rotor aircraft technology. The leaf blower was replaced with a commercial blower having metal fan blades and an electric motor. This new smoke generating system functioned well and provided the smoke needed for the flow visualization study.

Figure 58.
Inboard flow visualization showing "fountain flow" above fuselage. (Ames Photograph ACD-0804-3.1)

The flow visualization data revealed that near the wing tips, as expected, the proprotor wake impinged on the wing upper surface and spilled over the leading- and trailing-edges of the wing in a chordwise direction (figure 56). As the smoke was moved to the wing midspan position, it showed that the proprotor wake was also moving in a spanwise direction toward the fuselage (figure 57). With the smoke source moved further inboard, it was seen that the flows from the two proprotors moved spanwise toward each other and combined above the fuselage centerline, turning vertically upwards to form a "fountain flow" above and along the aircraft's longitudinal plane of symmetry (figure 58).

These observations confirmed the inboard flow observed from the tuft study mentioned earlier. Furthermore, the large air mass involved in the over-fuselage fountain flow created a large downward force which accounted for the higher than expected download in the hover mode of flight. As explained later, this fountain flow was also found to contribute to the nonuniform distribution of noise around the hovering tilt rotor aircraft.

Sidestick Controller

Among the many decisions made early in the development of the TRRA was the cockpit control configuration. Simulation and flight evaluations by Bell and Government pilots resulted in the selection of a helicopter-type power lever for rotor control and a conventional center stick and rudder pedals for longitudinal, directional, and pitch control inputs. The tall center stick, however, with its mass-center several inches above its pivot point, introduced undesirable dynamic effects (called "bobweight" motions) during maneuvers. This issue, coupled with the possible interference of the center stick with crew station structure (instrument panel), problems with cockpit ingress or egress, and the general interest in conserving limited cockpit "real estate," led researchers to investigate the use of a sidestick controller as the principal flight control for the developing military JVX tilt rotor aircraft (later called the V-22 Osprey). The principal concerns with this type controller were whether it would be able to provide the same level of control as the conventional center stick, and whether it could perform adequately during "degraded" flight control system conditions (such as a malfunctioning or battle-damaged control system).

To answer these questions, it was decided to perform a piloted simulation evaluation and a full flight investigation of a 3-axis sidestick controller on an XV-15 TRRA for both normal and "degraded" flight control system conditions. Gary Churchill, senior controls engineer with the TRRA Project Office, developed the control laws and was the primary investigator.

The XV-15 TRRA was ideal for the installation of the sidestick controller because it had bulging side windows (designed into the aircraft for better visibility) and an uncluttered side console which provided room for a functional installation, including an adjustable arm rest. A control and status panel for the sidestick controller was added to the instrument panel.

Initial sidestick control system gains and sensitivities were established using the Ames Vertical Motion Simulator (VMS) and a refined simulation math model based on the one originally developed in the early stages of the XV-15 project. These control law parameters were adjusted during XV-15 installation/hangar checks, and the resulting configuration was taken into the flight program.

In July 1985, an intensive flight evaluation of a three-axis sidestick controller was performed in XV-15 N703NA. During a nine day period, a total of 13 flights were flown with eight pilots from six agencies (the NASA, Army, Navy, Marine Corps, Bell Helicopter Textron, and Boeing Helicopters). Control characteristics of the center stick and the sidestick controller were compared. Each pilot received a familiarization flight in the left seat using a conventional center stick control and flew an evaluation flight in the right seat which was equipped with a sidestick controller. Without exception, all of the evaluation pilots found the sidestick to be a viable controller and that the aircraft was safe to fly with a degraded control system (i.e. with the SCAS turned off). The pilots even reported that some tasks could be performed with more precision with the sidestick controller than with the conventional center stick.

While the sidestick investigation successfully achieved its objectives, the V-22 Osprey was nonetheless configured with a center stick control. However, the sidestick controller continues to be considered by the V-22 Project Office for future application to the tilt rotor aircraft.

Acoustics

By the late 1970s, communities adjacent to airports and heliports had become quite sensitive to the noise generated by aircraft operations, in particular, to the disturbing character of the sound of rotorcraft noise. Therefore, if the tilt rotor were to be used as a civil transport aircraft, it was important to document its noise in the terminal area. In addition, it was necessary to establish a tilt rotor noise database for various flight modes and operating conditions for use in the development of prediction methodology. The XV-15 became the test bed for a wide range of tilt rotor acoustics studies.

Some very limited initial noise data were obtained with the XV-15 at Bell and consisted of only a few data points acquired during early hover tests. The next opportunity to measure tilt rotor noise occurred during hover performance testing at Ames in February and March 1981. An array of 16 microphones was distributed around a selected hover point to fully document the noise around the aircraft. The resulting acoustic data (refer to footnote 34) surprisingly showed that the noise varied by a few decibels around the aircraft, rather than remaining nearly constant. An explanation was later provided by Professor Al George of Cornell University who postulated that this was caused by the reingestion of the turbulent fountain flow (revealed during the flow visualization test) into the proprotor over the root end of the wing.[44]

Several subsequent tests were conducted to explore the sound generated during flyover or terminal approach conditions. The first was conducted at Crows Landing in September 1982 by a NASA/Army team and again in April 1986 with support from Bell. The NASA operated radar-coupled laser tracker was used at the isolated Crows Landing NALF to measure the track of the XV-15 during approach and flyover operations. This allowed the researchers to relate the exact position of the aircraft with respect to each microphone with the recorded noise data. The initial evaluation[45] of these data was reported by John Brieger, et al. Later analysis of this and other acoustic data was reported[46] by Bell's Bryan Edwards.

Another area of interest was the proprotor noise at the external fuselage walls of the aircraft (which would affect cabin acoustics). The cabin noise, especially for civil transports, would have to be at or below acceptable comfort levels. Furthermore, if large amounts of noise-reducing insulation were required, it would impose a significant weight penalty and impact the economic viability of the civil tilt rotor aircraft. Measurements of the distribution of sound pressure along the side of the XV-15 fuselage and at two locations within the cabin were obtained for various flight conditions during tests of N703NA at Ames. Later tests focusing on cabin interior noise were conducted by Suzanna Shank[47] of Bell.

---

[44] C. D. Coffen, Albert. R. George, Analysis and Prediction of Tilt Rotor Hover Noise, AHS 46th Annual Forum and Technology Display, Washington D.C., May 21-23, 1990.

[45] John T. Brieger, Martin D. Maisel, Ronald Gerdes, External Noise Evaluation of the XV-15 Tilt Rotor Aircraft, AHS National Specialists' Meeting on Aerodynamics and Aeroacoustics, Arlington, Texas, February 25–27, 1987.

[46] Bryan D. Edwards, "XV-15 Tiltrotor Aircraft Noise Characteristics." Presented at the AHS 46th Annual Forum and Technology Display, Washington, D.C., May 21–23, 1990.

[47] Suzanna S. Shank, "Tiltrotor Interior Noise Characteristics." Presented at the AHS and Royal Aeronautical Society, Technical Specialists' Meeting on Rotorcraft Acoustics/Fluid Dynamics, Philadelphia, Pennsylvania, October 15–17, 1991.

Figure 59.
Hover acoustics tests
during low wind conditions
at sunrise.
(Ames Photograph
AC90-0448-31)

A further series of noise measurements was made during hover tests at Ames in December 1990, and during terminal area and flyover tests at the Crows Landing NALF in August and September 1991, with the new composite blades installed on XV-15 N703NA. These were the first such experimental measurements from flight data with a proprotor blade configuration other than the original metal blades. The data were acquired to validate acoustics analyses being developed by researchers at the Langley Research Center, under the NASA Short-Haul Civil Tiltrotor (SHCT) program. These tests were a joint effort between the Langley acoustics engineers and technicians and the Army/NASA TRRA team at Ames. Operations were conducted just after sunrise (shown in figure 59) to ensure low wind conditions (usually less than 3 knots) during noise data measurements.

Additional investigations of the terminal area noise generated by the XV-15 with metal blades were conducted by Bell at a remote site near Waxahachi, Texas, in October and November of 1995. The relatively level, undeveloped terrain, far from major roads and undesirable background noise, provided an ideal environment for this work. A large microphone array was set up around the target landing point while a mobile laser tracker from Ames was placed nearby to measure the position of the XV-15 during the tests. This study focused on the effect of approach profile on the intensity of the noise propagated to the ground, and utilized approach conditions examined earlier during simulation evaluations of terminal area operations in the Ames Vertical Motion Simulator. Bill Decker, the NASA Ames principal investigator for the simulation studies, participated in the terminal area test planning and test operations. To provide flight path guidance, the XV-15 used a Global Positioning System (GPS) monitoring research flight director which was developed by Mark Stoufflet and Colby Nicks of Bell. A Langley team acquired acoustic data from an array of 33 microphones covering an area of five miles long and 1.25 miles wide. The test results confirmed that appropriate combinations of aircraft configuration and flight path profile could be used to significantly reduce the noise level and footprint area during tilt rotor approaches.

In December 1995, with plans being developed for an acoustics test of the XV-15 metal-bladed proprotor in the acoustically treated test section of the Ames 80- by 120-foot wind tunnel, a special flight investigation was required to obtain comparable free flight noise data to determine the effect of the wind tunnel walls on the measured sound. The evaluation involved flying the XV-15 behind, and in

close formation to a quiet research aircraft (the Lockheed YO-3A) which was equipped with microphones and recording equipment. By maintaining the YO-3A microphone location at a fixed distance and position with respect to the XV-15 proprotor (shown in figure 60) corresponding to a microphone location in the test section of the wind tunnel, and by operating at the same proprotor operating condition, a direct comparison (with corrections for the second proprotor) between the flight data and wind tunnel test data was obtained. This experiment was conducted by Ames researchers. The tests[48] involved a Bell flight crew in the XV-15, and a NASA flight crew in the YO-3A.

Figure 60.
The XV-15 flying in close formation with the YO-3A for acoustics data. (Ames Photograph AC95-0438-15.1)

Composite Proprotor Blades

From the very beginning of the TRRA project the proprotor blades were of special concern to the Government Project Office. The metal blades used on the XV-15 were designed in the late 1960s under Bell's IR&D funding for the predecessor tilt rotor aircraft, the Bell Model 300. This aircraft had a design gross weight of 12,400 pounds, 600 pounds lighter than that of the XV-15. The concern was

---

[48] The results of the 1995 terminal area and in-flight acoustics tests are presented in: Michael A. Marcolini, Casey L. Burley, David A. Conner, C. W. Acree, Jr., "Overview of Noise Reduction Technology in the NASA Short Haul (Civil Tiltrotor) Program," SAE International Powered Lift Conference, Jupiter, Florida, November 18-20, 1996.

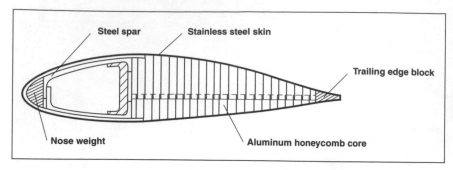

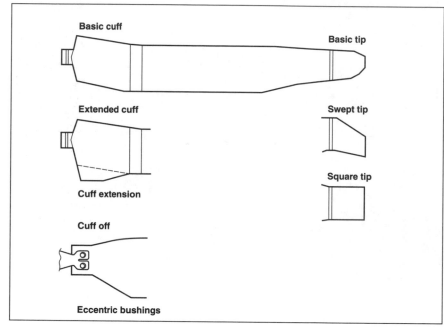

that the proprotors would be too highly loaded, i.e. operating too close to aerodynamic stall, to provide adequate reserve thrust for control when operating in hover at high gross weights. This could result in a reduction of control effectiveness or the need for a substantial increase in power when operating at the high gross weight condition.

Flight tests of the XV-15, however, did not indicate deficiencies. The metal bladed proprotor, although sized for a smaller aircraft, performed well at all XV-15 operating weights and flight conditions. While performance was satisfactory, another problem emerged that could threatened the future of the XV-15. This was the possibility that one or more blades could become unserviceable or unflightworthy due to mishandling or deterioration of the blade's structural integrity.

Top:

Figure 61.
Typical cross section of the XV-15 metal blades.

Bottom::

Figure 62.
XV-15 Advanced Technology Blades configuration variations.

Concern centered on the aft blade section, an aerodynamic fairing constructed of a lightweight aluminum honeycomb core covered with a thin steel skin (figure 61). Over the first few years of aircraft operations, minor surface damage was incurred due to ground handling. More significantly, small areas of separation of the bond between the skin and the honeycomb was detected on several blades. While the size of these "voids" was monitored during frequent inspections, the discovery of a rapid growth in size or an unacceptably large separation area could render the blade unusable for flight. The limited number of spare blades (two right and one left) meant that the loss of two left flightworthy blades would ground an aircraft.

Part of the TRRA Project Office advanced flight research program goals was the "investigation of alternate or advanced proprotor configurations." This was consistent with the Project Office's perceived need to replace the blades, both to assure the continuation of flight testing and to explore the application of new materials technology. The activity, to design, build, and flight test a new set of proprotor blades for the XV-15, was known as the Advanced Technology Blade (ATB) project.

Although there were no immediate prospects for funding an upgraded transmission that would allow a larger amount of the installed engine power to be used (providing a significant enhancement of the XV-15's performance), the ATB project was considered the first step in this direction. Therefore, on August 12, 1980, an RFP was issued by the TRRA Project Office for the procurement of the ATB's. The design objectives called for the development of "a blade design compatible with the XV-15 tilt rotor research aircraft which improves static stall margin and cruise speed performance using advanced structural materials and design techniques to improve the strength and service life of the tilt rotor blades." Proposals in response to this RFP were received from Bell and Boeing Helicopters, and were evaluated by an SEB comprised of NASA and Army technical and procurement specialists. While both proposals were determined to be acceptable, the decision was made to award the contract to Boeing. Among the factors that influenced this decision was the significant experience Boeing had acquired with composite rotor blades provided for the Army's fleet of CH-47 helicopters. Also, the Boeing blade design provided the ability to alter blade sweep and incorporate removable tip and cuff (inboard fairing) sections which allowed them to propose alternate blade configurations for research purposes. These features are illustrated in figure 62. It was noted that the Boeing blade had a larger solidity (effective area) than the Bell blade which contributed to the desired improvement in the stall margin. This would prove to have an unexpected effect on the XV-15/ATB flight program. A contract to develop the composite proprotor blades was awarded to Boeing Helicopters on July 9, 1982.

Figure 63.
Advanced Technology Blades proprotor mounted on the test apparatus at the Ames Research Center Outdoor Aerodynamic Research Facility. (Ames Photograph AC84-0498-2)

As part of the ATB qualification and evaluation program, a series of hover performance tests were conducted on the OARF at the Ames Research Center between February and April of 1985. These tests, evaluated three tip configurations and two cuff configurations on the ATB, as well as the XV-15 metal bladed proprotor, and an approximate 2/3-scale model of the proprotor designed for the JVX military tilt rotor aircraft. Figure 63 shows the ATB on the OARF Prop Test Rig.

This test series produced a large amount of high quality performance data.[49, 50] The isolated proprotor hover data validated the predicted ATB performance and showed that the XV-15 metal blades actually performed slightly better than previously expected.

[49] F. F. Felker, M. D. Maisel, M. D. Betzina, "Full-Scale Tilt-Rotor Hover Performance." Presented at the AHS, 41st Annual Forum, Fort Worth, Texas, May 15–17, 1985.
[50] K. Bartie, H. Alexander, M. McVeigh, S. Lamon, H. Bishop, "Hover Performance Tests of Baseline Metal and Advanced Technology Blade (ATB) Rotor Systems for the XV-15 Tilt Rotor Aircraft," NASA CR-177436, 1986.

Following the completion of controllability flight evaluations at Ames with modified SCAS components installed in N703NA, efforts began to prepare the ATB for flight tests. XV-15/ATB ground runs on the ramp and on the tiedown stand were conducted between September and early November of 1987 and the first hover flight with the new blades was performed on Friday, November 13, 1987.

From the first operations with the ATB there were problems. The initial difficulties surfaced during the runs required to obtain a satisfactory proprotor track and balance. Balance of the two interconnected proprotors presented problems on the XV-15 since a change on one proprotor provided an excitation that resulted in a change in the dynamic behavior of the other proprotor. Obtaining a proper balance with the ATB presented a special problem which stemmed from the frequent addition or removal of small weights from a fiberglass weight block located at the tip of each blade within a removable tip cover. The frequent removal of the tip covers to alter the weights resulted in the failure of the metal screw-retention inserts installed in the fiberglass weight blocks. Other problems included the deformation of the skin material under the retention screws at the fiberglass tip requiring the installation of metal washers, the failure of the bonds within the tip-weight assembly, and the delamination (unbonding) of the blade skins from the underlying nomex honeycomb material. Many of these material issues continued to cause problems during operations with the ATB.

When the expansion of the flight envelope in the helicopter mode with the ATB began in June 1989, higher than expected oscillatory blade control loads were measured at airspeeds as low as 40 knots. These loads increased with airspeed and reached the allowable limit at about 65 knots, too low to allow a safe envelope for initiating conversion. At that point, efforts were intensified to analyze test results and initiate analytical studies in order to determine the cause of the high loads. In addition, the loads investigation, headed by John Madden from Ames, included a series of tests on the XV-15 control system to determine stiffness characteristics as a function of the rotational (azimuthal) position of the proprotor. The results of this evaluation revealed that a major mechanical rotor control component, called the swashplate inner ring, did not provide uniform stiffness at all azimuthal positions. The lower than expected stiffness, coupled with the increased blade mass and inertia of the ATB (due to the larger solidity than the metal blades) resulted in lowering the natural frequency of the control system to the 3/rev (3 vibrations per proprotor revolution). When the three-bladed proprotor was flown in forward helicopter mode flight, the 3/rev aerodynamic excitation coupled with the system's natural frequency to produce high structural loads.

A temporary remedy was proposed by John Madden and was subsequently implemented. A set of shims was installed between the inner ring and the transmission housing which locked out the lateral cyclic input to the rotor (used for flapping reduction in helicopter mode flight) and provided the required increase in the control system stiffness. A permanent modification to change the inner swashplate ring material from aluminum to steel was planned if the shims proved effective.

After another series of ground runs, tiedown tests, envelope expansion flights and tip repairs, the XV-15 with the ATB achieved airplane mode flight on December 14, 1990. The oscillatory control loads were sufficiently reduced by the shims to allow full conversion. Then another problem appeared.

The ATB, having a larger solidity than the metal blades which the control system was designed for, required greater steady control forces to hold the blade at the collective blade angles required for high-speed airplane mode flight. The dual hydraulic collective actuator was, in fact, capable of providing this force, but since only one of the dual units was equipped with an automatic switchover to the backup hydraulic system in case of a primary hydraulic system failure, flight operations had to be limited to loads within the capability of one half of the dual actuator. This imposed a restriction on the maximum airplane mode airspeed with the current control system configuration. To correct this limitation, Bell was tasked to develop a design for the automatic hydraulic backup for the unprotected side of the dual collective actuator. The task order, under the XV-15 support contract, also required Bell to provide steel swashplate inner rings to correct the low control system stiffness and restore the lateral cyclic control.

With the dynamics and loads issues associated with the ATB understood and with corrective actions taken, the Army/NASA TRRA team once again focused on tilt rotor research. In a cooperative program with acoustics experimenters from Langley Research Center, ATB noise surveys in the hover mode were conducted at the Ames Research Center in December 1990. Starting on August 21, 1991, a series of flyover and terminal area noise measurements were also performed at Crows Landing.

On September 6, at Crows Landing, while NASA test pilots George Tucker and Rickey Simmons were on a downwind leg of the traffic pattern prior to setting up another test approach, they heard a loud noise in the cockpit followed by a sudden and violent increase in the vibration level. At the same time, in the control room at Ames, the normally narrow traces on the strip chart recorder showing safe, within-limit, oscillatory loads and moments instantly blossomed to the full width of the bands, indicating that the safe load levels had been greatly exceeded. In the cockpit, the vibration was so severe that the instruments were not readable. George Tucker reduced power and turned toward the runway while Rickey Simmons contacted the control tower requesting an immediate landing. The tower asked if emergency vehicles were required and the response was affirmative. With fire and rescue trucks rolling, the aircraft was brought to a safe landing about 80 seconds after the high vibration started, followed by a rapid shut-down.

After the proprotors stopped, the problem became obvious. The cuff fairing on one of the left proprotor blades had moved outboard about eight inches. Analysis revealed that the displacement of the cuff was due to the failure of metal retaining clips to carry the cuff's centrifugal loads to the blade structure, as intended by the design. Instead, because of tolerance buildup and poor workmanship and assembly, the loads were borne by the fiberglass flange rather than the metal retaining clips. This eventually led to the failure of the fiberglass flange. Following inspection, the aircraft was disassembled with the assistance of a Bell crew, and transported to Ames onboard flatbed trucks.

After reassembly, a structural dynamics "shake test" was performed at Ames with aircraft N703NA. This activity was conducted by Wally Acree to provide accurate aircraft resonant frequency characteristics for aeroelastic stability analyses. Upon completion of the shake test in January 1991, the aircraft entered a 100-hour major inspection.

Meanwhile the high oscillatory loads imposed on the aircraft's structure were analyzed to determine the amount of fatigue life consumed by the sliding cuff incident. While the fatigue damage was considerable for a single event, it was determined that aircraft N703NA was safe to fly again.

Before the ATB could be used again, however, the cuff retention configuration would have to be redesigned to prevent a reoccurrence of the failure. An improved cuff retention was designed and fabricated by Ames and successfully proof tested. Changes in NASA Ames' role in flight research soon occurred and altered plans for further flight testing of the XV-15.

Incidents

Door Strike

On September 2, 1977, during the start of a ground run the test pilots noticed that the door lock caution light was illuminated as the normal engine start procedure was initiated. This caution light, which was connected to a sensitive microswitch, indicated the position of the door bolt. This had previously been the source of numerous nuisance indications which were suspected to be due to the improper setting of the microswitch position. Because of this, the position of the door handle was visually checked, found to appear to be in the correct position, and the engine start procedure was continued.

After less than three minutes following engine start, with the proprotors in the airplane mode and while increasing power, the cabin door opened and was struck by the proprotor blades, scattering pieces of aluminum over the aircraft. The crew immediately began to convert back to the helicopter mode, shut down the engines, and cut off the fuel supply. There were no injuries.

The incident which damaged the three right hand blades (one beyond repair) and destroyed the cabin door, was a classic example of ignoring a troublesome caution light that was, in fact, providing valid information.

Because the XV-15 airframes were essentially hand crafted, the door from N703NA would not fit the N702NA fuselage satisfactorily, so a new door was fabricated. Modifications to reduce the probability of a repeat of this incident included a small window in the frame to allow visual inspection of positive latching of the door bolt and the installation of a short cable inside the cabin for the crew to connect to the door after entry.

In-Flight Engine Failures

After the initial XV-15 flight envelope expansion activities demonstrated the predicted favorable handling qualities and performance capabilities, the Government Project Office began to plan for the second phase of flight tests with the tilt rotor aircraft in support of potential military applications. To better understand military application requirements, and to inform key civil and military aviation planners of the capabilities offered by tilt rotor aircraft, a Tilt Rotor Experiments Planning Workshop was held on December 4 and 5, 1979, in Arlington, Texas.

The meeting was attended by about 100 senior military and civilian personnel from each of the U.S. armed services. Presentations were made by Government Project Office personnel, senior Government and Bell managers and test pilots. During the second day of the meeting, the managers were informed that XV-15 aircraft N702NA, on approach to Arlington Municipal Airport, only a few miles away from the meeting site, experienced an engine failure. It was reported that the chase aircraft had observed smoke trailing from the right nacelle at about the same time that the XV-15 flight crew heard a screeching noise, followed by the sudden stoppage of the right engine. The flight crew declared an emergency and were cleared for immediate landing as emergency vehicles were positioned along the runway. The failed engine was immediately disengaged from the drive system by the automatic clutch, allowing the operating left engine to drive both proprotors by transmitting power through the cross-shaft to the right proprotor. The drive system and flight controls worked as planned and a single engine run-on landing was completed with the nacelles set at 70 degrees without further complications. This unplanned event, although poorly timed because of the workshop, demonstrated both the benign impact that an isolated, single engine failure would have on the tilt rotor aircraft, and the proper functioning of the cross-shafting during an engine-out emergency.

A subsequent analysis and evaluation by Lycoming determined that the cause for the failure was a fatigue crack in one of the aft bearing support struts which caused interference of concentric counterrotating shafts. This resulted in the sudden engine stoppage. The strut failure was brought about when, during numerous startups over the life of the engine, it was operated at a particular RPM that corresponded to the resonant frequency of that structure, momentarily producing excessively high loads. The approach employed to avoid this problem in the future was to monitor engine housing vibrations during startup to ensure that when high "g" vibration levels occurred that could lead to a fatigue failure of the aft bearing support, the high loads would be reduced by changing RPM.

Another engine failure occurred on September 7, 1983, while XV-15 N702NA was hovering at a wheel height of about 15 feet. A fuel control unit failure induced fuel starvation, and the low initial height did not allow sufficient time for the power on the operating engine to be brought to the necessary level to arrest the rapid descent. In spite of the hard landing that followed, the cross-shaft system again worked as it was designed to and no damage to the aircraft was incurred.

Tree Strike

The XV-15, like all aircraft of any type, at one time or another, was exposed to inadvertent hazardous conditions, even while in the hands of the very capable pilots. One such incident occurred on July 30, 1979, at the Arlington, Texas, Municipal Airport, the base for Bell's flight test operations. The flight plan called for a maximum acceleration from a low hover over the runway. As the nacelles were continuously tilted forward at the maximum conversion rate, the aircraft speed began to increase. But when the end of the airfield was reached the XV-15 was still below the level of the tree tops just beyond the perimeter of the airport. With barely enough speed to climb, the XV-15 passed through the tops of the trees. After circling back and landing, the ground determined that the aircraft had survived the "tree strike" essentially unscathed. The only damage being the green stains on the proprotor blade tips, the shattered nerves, and the embarrassment of the crew.

It turned out that once again a set of unusual circumstances caught the experienced pilots by surprise. The maximum rate conversion was previously performed at a greater altitude, usually from a helicopter mode with some airspeed. A conversion from hover to airplane mode can be completed in 12 seconds. While this routinely does not present a problem at altitude, it did in this case. The rapid conversion lowered the rotor thrust vector before adequate speed for wing lift was achieved, resulting in a slight settling of the aircraft. However, the settling was not detected by the flight crew until they approached the end of the airfield boundary. The XV-15 on that flight came within a few feet of disaster. Good fortune is a wonderful thing to have.

Gear Down Conversion

The NASA flight crew continued to have good luck on their side. During a busy flight test at the Crows Landing NALF, the XV-15 was converted from the helicopter mode to the airplane mode in view of the photo/chase helicopter. The ground monitoring station personnel at Ames noticed that many of the critical structural loads that were usually reduced following conversion remained seriously high. In the cockpit, the pilots were alerted by the unusually high noise level. After an anxious call from the Test Director to the XV-15 to report the high load levels, the loads suddenly were reduced to the expected levels. It turned out that the conversion to the airplane mode was inadvertently made with the landing gear down (and, of course, with the landing gear doors open). Besides resulting in increased aerodynamic drag that could have adversely affected the control characteristics of the aircraft, the landing gear doors were structurally limited to flight speeds below 90 knots. The loss of these doors in flight could have damaged the aircraft's tail surfaces. On that flight, the landing gear doors were inadvertently "test-qualified" to an airspeed of nearly 160 knots without a failure. While the XV-15 was definitely the product of good, sound engineering, it did benefit from a large measure of good luck on that day.

Oil Vent Incident

Sometimes lessons are learned the "hard way." This was the case when what appeared to be a minor configuration change turned out to have a major effect. During the initial flights of the XV-15 in 1977 and the 40- by 80-foot wind tunnel test in 1978, seepage from the engine oil vent was noticed. After putting up with the annoying, but unimportant seepage for about eight years, on December 19, 1986, Bell engineers decided to make a minor modification to the left engine oil vent tube in an attempt to reduce or eliminate the problem. If the modification worked, then they would apply it to the right engine vent tube. The modification consisted of nothing more than rotating the beveled end of the vent tube by 90 degrees. During the first flight with the modification in place, and after converting to airplane mode, the chase aircraft reported seeing excessive oil venting from the left engine while the flight crew simultaneously noted fluctuating left engine oil pressure. These conditions precipitated a shut down of the left engine. A reconversion to the helicopter mode was followed by a safe single engine roll-on landing within three minutes of shutting down the left engine. The engine oil system was thoroughly checked and nothing amiss was found. The excessive oil venting could only be attributed to the "minor" change made to the oil vent tube resulting in a change in vent pressure. The engine oil level was restored, the oil pressure transducer was replaced, and the vent tube returned to its original configuration and position. The important lesson re-learned was that all aircraft configuration changes, no matter how minor, should be thoroughly evaluated before implementation.

Bird Strike

The "unexpected" can be expected at any time while flying in an aircraft. This occurred on May 1, 1991, when Bell pilot Ron Erhart was demonstrating aircraft XV-15 N702NA to USAF Gen. Schmaltz. Shortly after converting to the airplane mode, while performing a high speed flyby at Bell's Arlington Flight Research Center, a large hawk passed through the right proprotor disc and collided with the leading edge of the right wing at midspan. The impact was so severe that it collapsed the leading edge fairing and cracked the wing's aluminum forward spar. No damage was incurred by the proprotor blades. The aircraft was slowed and a reconversion and an uneventful landing was made immediately after the impact incident. The crack in the spar seriously damaged the integrity of the wing. The repair took over five months and the aircraft was returned to flight on October 8, 1991.

How a bird the size of a large hawk could have passed through the proprotor turning at about 500 rpm and not touch any of the blades was nothing short of miraculous. Such an occurrence could easily have seriously damaged the proprotor with catastrophic results.

This event was remembered by Ron Erhart's friends from the Federal Bureau of Investigation (FBI) when he retired in October of 1998. At his retirement party a bogus but official-looking "Wanted by FBI" poster was displayed that claimed Ron Erhart was sought for allegedly "stalking, hitting, and killing a red tailed hawk," leaving its chicks to starve, all casualties of the tilt rotor project.

Blade Cracks

Because of the limited budget of the TRRA project, the critical structural components of the XV-15 were subjected to the minimum number of structural tests required to establish safe operating loads and to define the fatigue life. During ground and flight operations, these critical parameters were constantly monitored and the data analyzed to assess the portion of the allowable fatigue life that was consumed due to high loads. For many components, such as the metal proprotor blades, the requirement for frequent inspections was also established.

The metal blades were constructed of a steel spar, the main load-carrying component, with light-weight aluminum honeycomb aft of the spar to provide the airfoil trailing-edge fairing. The entire surface of the blade was covered with a thin steel skin as illustrated in figure 61. Early in the flight test program evidence of delamination (i.e. the loss of the bond) between the honeycomb and the skin was detected in small areas on several blades. The method for determining the delamination area was called the "tap test" and was performed by a skilled inspector or engineer with a "good ear." A small tool or coin was lightly tapped along the surface of the blade and the characteristics of the sound revealed the integrity of the bond. Delamination areas were outlined on the blade and any growth in the size of this area was documented. Ernie Schellhase, the Bell blade designer, defined acceptable (i.e. "not-to-exceed") delamination areas and a frequent blade tap test was instituted as part of the standard XV-15 inspection program.

On October 22, 1987, during a routine inspection, Bell technicians discovered chordwise hairline cracks in the skins of two left proprotor blades near the 60 percent blade radius. These cracks, which ran from just aft of the spar to just forward of the trailing edge, were at first thought to be a defect in the surface paint, but were confirmed by use of an electrical "eddy current" testing device and by x-ray analyses to be a complete skin separation.

Metallurgical studies of skin samples from the vicinity of these cracks revealed the presence of severe intergranular corrosion. It was determined that the cause of the corrosion occurred during the manufacture or processing of the blade skin material. An inappropriate "pickling" or chemical surface cleaning treatment produced the corrosion on some of the material used in the manufacture of the blades. The severity of the intergranular corrosion on the two damaged blades rendered them unrepairable, leaving only two flightworthy left blades (the remaining undamaged flight blade and a spare) for N702NA. Further analyses determined that the fatigue failures were due to the reduced effective skin thickness resulting from the corrosion combined with the local stress increase caused by the proximity to the edge of an internal doubler (below the skin).

Shortly after the determination of the probable cause of the cracks, Bell and the Government TRRA Project Office initiated an inspection of all XV-15 metal blades. The blades from N703NA at Ames were removed from the aircraft and shipped to Bell. While all of the remaining blades did not show signs of the severe intergranular corrosion (probably because of variations in the pickling process), it was decided to install the N703NA blades on the N702NA XV-15 at Bell and to initiate the investigation of the composite Advanced Technology Blades on XV-15 N703NA at Ames. The use of the N703NA shipset by Bell was driven by the fact that these blades had about half of the flight time as those of the N702NA blades, and by the desire to maintain a balanced set of blades. On May 16, 1988, N702NA was returned to flight.

Paris Air Show

By early 1981, the XV-15 had sufficiently explored the flight envelope in all flight modes to provide at least a first-order verification of the validity of all design-critical analytical methods. This included performance, loads, and structural-dynamic stability. While much work remained to be done to document the accomplishment of the initial proof-of-concept goals and to complete the advanced research objectives of the TRRA project, it was becoming apparent that the significance of the technical success of the project was recognized only by a small core of people close to the activity. The NASA/Army Project Office and Bell, therefore, decided that the emerging tilt rotor technology should be demonstrated before a wider aviation community. The venue for this public debut would be the renowned Paris Air Show.

The successful participation of the XV-15 at the Paris Air Show at Le Bourget from June 4 to June 14, 1981, would prove to be one of the key nontechnical moments in the history of this aircraft. While operation of the XV-15 at the Paris Air Show was primarily managed by Bell, the presence of this aircraft at this event marked two "firsts" for NASA. It was the first time that NASA has ever participated in flight demonstrations of any experimental aircraft at an event having public international exposure such as the Paris Air Show in France. It also marked the first public flight demonstration of an aircraft of this type. Its success paved the way for participation of yet another NASA Ames aircraft, the QSRA, at the 1983 Paris Air Show.

Participation of the XV-15 TRRA at the Paris Air Show was a cooperative effort between the NASA, the Army, the Air Force, and Bell. Dr. Irving Statler, director of the Army AMRDL, enthusiastically supported this activity. Further support was provided by then Secretary of the Air Force Dr. Hans Mark, (previously Director of the Ames Research Center when the TRRA project was initiated) who arranged USAF Military Airlift Command (MAC) transport of the XV-15 and support equipment. The logistics of such a venture were complex.

The schedule for the next few weeks was carefully planned to meet the critical requirement to arrive at Le Bourget within the assigned time period. This involved not only the preparations required to return the XV-15 to flight after shipment to Europe, but the movement of high-value items (including the XV-15, the spare engine, sophisticated support equipment, tools, and instrumentation) into and out of foreign countries. The achievement of this important task, tightly controlled by foreign regulations, was handled by Demo Giulianetti of the Ames TRRA Project Office.

Working with an international freight company, the necessary documentation (including a U.S. Department of Commerce-issued International Carnet[51]) was prepared that permitted the transport of this equipment into and back out of

---

[51] The Carnet documents the items to be shipped and provides an official permit to cross international borders.

England and France. As a result, transport of the XV-15 and all associated equipment into and out of England and France was accomplished as planned and the Paris Air Show arrival schedule was met without a problem.

On March 6, 1981, just after the completion of the hover, tiedown, and outwash investigation, XV-15 N702NA was ferried from Ames to the DFRC. From the time of the arrival of N702NA at DFRC, until it departed less than two months later, both XV-15 aircraft, in flight status, were stationed at the same site (figure 64). This rare event would occur only one more time during the TRRA project. At DFRC, the XV-15 TRRA, along with a complete set of spares (including an engine), ground support equipment, and a mobile telemetry data van, was prepared for shipment to Europe. On April 28, 1981, the aircraft (with its wing and proprotor blades removed) and related equipment were flown to Farnborough, England, onboard a MAC C-5A and a C-141 aircraft.

At Farnborough, the XV-15 TRRA was reassembled and the flight routine

Top:
Figure 64.
XV-15 N702NA co-located with XV-15 N703NA at the Dryden Flight Research Center, October 1981. (Ames Photograph AC84-0498-2)

Bottom:
Figure 65.
The XV-15 enroute to the Paris Air Show in 1981. (Bell Photograph 027781)

designed to exhibit the unique capabilities of the aircraft at the Paris Air Show was practiced by Bell pilots Ron Erhart and Dorman Cannon, and by NASA Ames pilot Dan Dugan. This flight routine demonstrated vertical takeoffs and landings, hovering turns, transitions to and from the cruise mode of flight, backward and lateral translations, rapid climb-outs, and airplane- and helicopter-mode fly-bys. The 10-minute demonstration consisted of flight conditions selected to minimize fatigue damage to the aircraft's structural components in order to preserve the structural life of the XV-15 for further flight experiments. On May 27, the aircraft was ferried from Farnborough, with a refueling stop at Manston, England, to a staging airfield at Melun, France, near Paris. Figure 65 shows the XV-15 with the assigned Paris Air Show number "53" on its fuselage while enroute from Farnborough to France. After clearance was received from the French authorities, the aircraft was flown from Melun to Le Bourget on June 1.

During the 10-day air show, the XV-15 was the only aircraft to perform flight demonstrations daily and on schedule. Inclement weather caused the cancellation of all flight demonstrations on one day, except during the time period assigned to the tilt rotor aircraft. On another morning, the wheels-up landing of a transport aircraft resulted in the closure of the airfield's only runway for the remainder of the day. The only aircraft that could perform its demonstration routine with the restricted operating conditions was the XV-15 which simply took off vertically from the ramp. This high level of operational readiness was the result of a sustained cooperative effort by the Government and Bell teams. When not flying, the aircraft was on static display. To say that it "stole the show" would be an understatement. The successful first public appearance of this new aircraft type before a crowd which included U.S. and foreign dignitaries, journalists, and people representing the international aircraft community, greatly enhanced U.S. prestige around the world.

Aircraft N702NA was then ferried back to Farnborough on June 15 where a demonstration flight was performed for British Government officials and members of the Royal Aeronautical Society on June 17. The aircraft was disassembled and airlifted to the Ames Research Center onboard a MAC C-5A transport on July 1, 1981. On arrival and for the last time, aircraft N702NA was co-located with aircraft N703NA which had been ferried to Ames after completion of Government flight tests at the DFRC.

Turning Point

By this time it was clear to the Army/NASA Project Office that it would not be possible to continue with a funded two-aircraft flight test program. During the next few weeks, negotiations were conducted between the Government and Bell. A contract modification provided for the operation of aircraft N702NA by Bell and performance of military evaluations at no cost to the Government. Co-location of the two XV-15 aircraft was therefore ended on October 26, 1981, when aircraft N702NA was ferried back to the Bell Flight Test Center at Arlington, Texas. The operation of N702NA by Bell under contract was later converted to a bailment agreement. This was motivated by the Government's concern that while it still retained airworthiness responsibility for the aircraft, it had no direct oversight of its use. Under the bailment, ownership of the aircraft remained with the Government, while the day-to-day airworthiness accountability was Bell's. With this arrangement, Bell would be able to demonstrate the capabilities of the tilt rotor aircraft to military and civil aviation decision makers in an attempt to seek and develop potential markets. These demonstrations of the XV-15 may well have been the catalyst that turned a successful proof-of-concept research aircraft program into a cornerstone for a new type of future civil and military aircraft.

Evaluations and Demonstrations

Evaluations

Under the agreement for Navy participation in the Army/NASA XV-15 TRRA program, the first military pilot familiarization and preliminary assessment of this aircraft type for Navy and Marine Corps applications was arranged at the Bell Flight Research Facility. The first military pilot flight in the XV-15 was made by Major William S. "Bill" Lawrence, USMC (later Commander of the Rotary Wing Division, Naval Air Test Center) on June 5, 1980. From June 5 through June 9, 1980, Major Lawrence evaluated the characteristics of the tilt rotor aircraft. The final Naval Air Test Center technical report (No. RW-44R-80) concluded that "... the tilt rotor concept exhibited excellent potential for a variety of Navy/Marine Corps V/STOL missions." During that test period, the first Army evaluation flight was conducted by Major Ron Carpenter (later Director of the Army Aeronautical Test Directorate (AATD), Ft. Eustis, Virginia).

A subsequent Navy flight test was conducted in May 1983 by LCDR John C. Ball, USN (who later joined Bell as a test pilot), to evaluate the potential of the tilt rotor aircraft to perform the combat search and rescue (SAR) and external lift applications. This was done to determine the suitability of the tilt rotor aircraft for the projected JVX (V-22 Osprey) missions. In the final Naval Air Test Center technical report for these tests (No. RW-29R-83), it was concluded that "the tilt rotor concept, as represented by the XV-15, exhibited excellent potential to perform the combat search and rescue and external lift missions."

One of the notable XV-15 events occurred when Ames test pilot Fred Drinkwater flew N703NA for the first time on January 13, 1984, almost 25 years after he became the first NASA pilot to perform a full conversion in the XV-3. Fred Drinkwater later participated in control system test flights in the XV-15.

Civilian pilot evaluation flights were also conducted. On March 12, 1985, pilot and writer David L. Green flew the XV-15 at Ames and issued the first widely distributed pilot report in the June 1985 issue of *Rotor and Wing International*. Other familiarization flights were performed by Sikorsky Aircraft test pilot Frank Gallagher on October 22, 1982, and by Boeing Vertol test pilots Dick Balzer on July 18, 1985, and A. Lynn Freisner on October 28 and 31, 1986. Later, with the initiation of a civil tilt rotor aircraft program in the late 1990s, a pilot evaluation of the XV-15 was conducted by Clay Lacy, an experienced test pilot and author, to assess the characteristics of this aircraft type from the commercial pilot's point of view.[52]

Over the 21 years since its first hover flight, the XV-15 has had more than 300 military and civilian guest pilots.

---

[52] Clay Lacy, "Tiltrotor Technology," *Professional Pilot*, September 1998.

Guest Pilots

One of the influential U.S. dignitaries who observed the performance of the XV-15 at the 1981 Paris Air Show and recognized its potential as a military aircraft was Senator Barry Goldwater (R-AZ), then Chairman of the Senate Armed Services Committee. Senator Goldwater, a former military pilot, requested and was granted a flight demonstration in the XV-15. On October 30, 1981, immediately after N702NA returned to Bell, Senator Goldwater became the first nontest pilot to fly in Bell's tilt rotor aircraft guest pilot program (figure 66). Following his flight he said that "the tilt rotor is the biggest advance in aviation in a quarter of a century."

On September 28, 1981, just prior to the Senator Goldwater flight, the Army/NASA TRRA team at Ames provided their first guest pilot demonstration for General Story Stevens, Commander, U.S. Army Aviation and Troop Command.

Another important early flight demonstration occurred on March 26, 1982, when Secretary of the Navy John Lehman, who also witnessed the demonstration at the Paris Air Show, flew the XV-15 at the Quantico USMC Air Station, Virginia (figure 67). The experiences of both Senator Goldwater and Secretary Lehman were instrumental in obtaining the support of Congress and of the administration for the future acquisition of the military tilt rotor aircraft, the V-22 Osprey.

Top:

Figure 66.
Senator Goldwater in the XV-15 with Bell pilot Dorman Cannon.
(Bell Photograph 02727)

Bottom:

Figure 67.
Secretary of the Navy John Lehman after flying the XV-15.
(Bell Photograph 023970)

Initial Demonstrations

Following return to the U.S. after a successful performance at the Paris Air Show, the XV-15 N702NA, painted in a desert camouflage color scheme, conducted nap-of-the-earth flight evaluations at Ft. Huachuca, Arizona, during June and July 1982 (figure 68). The evaluations were flown against simulated "enemy" ground-to-air threats employing then-current procedures for the location, identification, and "lock-on" of enemy aircraft. The simulated ground-to-air threats were located at ranges of 10, 20, and 30 kilometers from a simulated "enemy" command post. The procedure followed for these evaluations allowed a radar lock-on to the XV-15 at the simulated command post after which the XV-15 would attempt to break the radar lock through a combination of maneuvers which included hover, rapid altitude changes, quick transitions to cruise speeds and back again to hover or near-hover flight, and nap-of-the earth flying. In every case, the XV-15 was able to break radar lock and avoided further detection and lock-ons by the ground-to-air radar trackers. The results indicated an impressive capability of the tilt rotor aircraft to avoid being captured by the ground-to-air tracking systems used for these flight tests.

Figure 68.
Nap-of-the-earth flight demonstrations at Ft. Huachuca, Arizona. (Ames Photograph AC82-0612)

In July of 1982, immediately following the Ft. Huachuca evaluation, a flight demonstration was performed at a Marine Harrier flight facility in Yuma, Arizona. Once again, the XV-15 performed faultlessly. It exhibited precision hover control, transition and cruise capability, and maneuvering capability in all flight modes. Demonstrations such as this were effective in convincing potential users that the tilt rotor aircraft was ready for serious consideration.

One of the significant military applications issues was the ability of the TRRA to perform shipboard operations. With the tilt rotor surfacing as a candidate for Navy and Marine shipboard vertical assault and replenishment missions, questions had arisen concerning what was known as the "deck-edge effect." The issue addressed the condition that occurred as the tilt rotor aircraft moved laterally on to or away from the deck of an aircraft carrier. During that operation, one proprotor would be "in the ground-effect" (IGE) of the deck while the other proprotor would be in an "out-of-ground–effect" (OGE) condition. The concern was that this would cause an unacceptable control problem or a high pilot workload issue. While the results of the Ames hover test conducted in 1981 indicated that a slight lateral displacement of the control stick would be adequate to compensate for the "deck-edge effect" (so small that it was expected that the pilots would probably not notice the required control motion), it was clear that only a flight demonstration would satisfy tilt rotor critics. In addition, proprotor noise and downwash effects on flight deck personnel during launch and retrieval operations of tilt rotor aircraft needed to be assessed.

Figure 69.
Shipboard evaluations of
the XV-15 onboard the
USS Tripoli.
(Ames Photograph
AC82-0612)

Therefore, in order to evaluate tilt rotor aircraft suitability for operations on an
aircraft carrier, arrangements were made with the U.S. Navy under the terms of
the NASA/Army/Navy agreement, to perform shipboard evaluations with the
XV-15 on the U.S. Navy amphibious assault ship *USS Tripoli* (LPH 10) during
the first week of August 1982. This class of ship is designed to launch and
retrieve helicopters in support of the vertical assault phases of amphibious landing operations. The Navy's purpose in performing these tests was to "...evaluate
the XV-15 as a representative future tilt rotor aircraft in the Navy shipboard
environment... ." To accomplish this, the XV-15 was to launch daily during the
test period from North Island Naval Air Station near San Diego and rendezvous
with the *USS Tripoli* to perform the shipboard operational assessments.

The XV-15 TRRA arrived at North Island on July 9, 1982 ,after completing evaluations at Ft. Huachuca in Yuma, Arizona. While at North Island, the aircraft was
prepared for the upcoming sea trials.[53] Takeoffs and landings were practiced in a
designated area marked to represent the flight deck of an LPH. LCDR John Ball,

---

[53] The XV-15 was painted in a desert camouflage color scheme with water soluble paint for the
Ft. Huachuca, Arizona, flight tests. After arrival at North Island, California, and prior to the shipboard evaluations, the camouflage colors were washed off to reveal a Navy gray paint scheme.

from the Naval Air Test Center, Patuxent River, Maryland, and Dorman Cannon of Bell, performed the Navy's flight evaluations of the XV-15.

During the week of the evaluations (figure 69), the XV-15 TRRA once again performed faultlessly. It completed a total of 54 operations which included short- and vertical-landings and takeoffs with the LPH headed into the wind as well as with crosswinds over the deck. It successfully performed all shipboard operations that helicopters would normally have performed including shipside hover at various distances over water during simulated air-sea rescue.

Figure 70.
XV-15 during nap-of-the-earth flight demonstration at Ft. Rucker, Alabama. (Ames Photograph AC86-0140-25)

There were no adverse effects with one rotor positioned OGE and the other IGE. Pilot evaluations during such conditions were that the XV-15 was stable and easily controllable as predicted based on data from the prior ground-effect performance evaluation at Ames. Jim Lane, Demo Giulianetti, and Mike Bondi were the Ames project personnel assigned to the support the operations onboard the *USS Tripoli* during all phases of the XV-15 shipboard evaluation flights. Following the carrier operations, LCDR Ball reported that he "was struck by how easy and just plain fun it was to control."[54] Postoperation interviews with deck personnel indicated that deck-handling of the XV-15 was quite manageable; that tiedown operations after retrieval and preparations prior to launch were no worse than, or, as some deck personnel reported, were easier and quicker than with helicopters.

Later Flight Demonstrations

While Ames continued flight tests to expand the evaluation and documentation of the XV-15's characteristics with aircraft N703NA in accordance with the objectives of the TRRA project, Bell flew aircraft N702NA for a wide range of missions as was permitted by the contract modification executed in October 1981. These included assessments of engineering enhancements, aircraft evaluations by guest pilots, and flights demonstrating military and civil tilt rotor applications. Therefore, in September of 1984, the Bell XV-15 team embarked on a tour to demonstrate the civil and military potential of this aircraft type. This would become one of the highlights of the project and was to be known as the "Eastern U.S. Tour." This three-week adventure was managed by Ron Reber, Bell's Program Manager and LTC Cliff McKiethan, Department of Defense liaison for the Government Project Office.

---

[54] John C. Ball, "Tilt-Rotor Memories," *Naval Helicopter Association Rotor Review,* Number 19, November 1987.

Figure 71.
XV-15 at the New York
Port Authority
downtown heliport.
(Bell Photograph 02704)

The first destination was Ft. Rucker, Alabama, where the XV-15 was evaluated in nap-of-the-earth (NOE) flying, that is, following the contour of the terrain at low flight levels (figure **70**). In addition to the Army Aviation Development Test Activity (ADTA), pilots (including one marine pilot) who flew the XV-15 NOE course, several other Army aviators, including the Commanding General of Ft. Rucker, Major General "Bobby" Maddox, were given guest pilot evaluation flights. The timing of this series of evaluations was important in that it allowed the attributes of the tilt rotor aircraft to be considered for the Army's new LHX program, although a later decision influenced by aircraft cost and weight resulted in the selection of a conventional helicopter for the program.

After the Ft. Rucker demonstrations, the XV-15 was ferried to the U.S. Navy flight test center at Patuxent River, Maryland, where it was evaluated in air-to-air maneuvers against a jet (A-4 Skyhawk), a turboprop (OV-1 Mohawk), and a helicopter (CH-46). In each case the XV-15, with its ability to maneuver by vectoring the proprotor thrust independently of the fuselage attitude, demonstrated that the tilt rotor aircraft had effective evasive maneuver capability against these aircraft types at a range of speeds up to 450 knots. Also while at Patuxent River, the XV-15 made sloped landings at up to 14-degree nose-up attitude and simulated refueling operations, all without difficulty.

The next series of demonstrations used the Quantico Marine Corps Air Station (MCAS), Virginia, as a base for operations. Flight demonstrations for the Washington, D.C., area military and congressional personnel were then performed at Bolling Air Force Base, Ft. Belvoir, Virginia, the Pentagon, and at Quantico.

The XV-15 was then flown to the New York Port Authority downtown heliport at the base of the World Trade Center in Battery Park, Manhattan (figure 71), where it was placed on static display. The return flight, from downtown New York to downtown Washington, D.C. was completed in 66 minutes with Bell's President Jack Horner flying co-pilot. This demonstrated tilt rotor city center-to-city center capability as a civil transport. After landing at the Bolling AFB heliport, Bell conducted a briefing for congressional and news media personnel gathered for the event. The XV-15 was subsequently ferried back to Arlington, Texas.

In all, 55 flights in 20 flying days were accomplished, including 21 evaluation flights by five military pilots, 19 guest pilot flights, and demonstration flights in five different locations. All flights were made on schedule, without difficulty, and with a "proof-of-concept" research airplane. The XV-15 performed faultlessly.

The success of the "Eastern U.S. Tour" proved to be typical of later events of this type conducted by Bell and supported introduction of the tilt rotor concept to military planners and a curious public. In following years, Bell demonstrated and displayed the XV-15 at locations such as Chicago, Illinois; Dayton, Ohio; McDill AFB, Tampa, Florida (Special Operations); and to commercial users such as Petroleum Helicopters International, Lafayette, Louisiana. The exposure generated the desired widespread interest in the potential of this unique aircraft.

Figure 72.
XV-15 in formation flight at Ames Research Center with the NASA QSRA and AV-8B aircraft.
(Ames Photograph AC87-0180-454.1)

Air Shows and Demonstrations

The first opportunity to show the XV-15 to the public in the U.S. occurred on September 1, 1981, when N703NA, stationed at Ames, was demonstrated at the NASA/APA (Airport Planners Association)/HAI (Helicopter Association International) Community Benefits Conference in Monterey, California. Because of the low noise level produced during the takeoff and landing operations, the XV-15 was seen to be a community-friendly aircraft by the many conference participants.

For many years during the Navy's operation of Moffett Field, an open house and air show was held annually during the spring or summer months to allow the community to enjoy an interesting close look at local aviation activities. By 1982, the XV-15 was becoming a familiar sight in the sky over Moffett Field. On May 15 and 16, 1982, the NASA/Army TRRA performed air show demonstrations on each day of the event and was then placed on static display before an overflow crowd of approximately 200,000 people. This popular exhibition of the XV-15 was repeated at the July 1983 and the July 1985 Moffett Field air shows. The last public appearance of XV-15 N703NA at Moffett Field occurred on March 9, 1987, when NASA pilots Ron Gerdes and Grady Wilson flew in formation with the NASA QSRA and the NASA AV-8C Harrier during the dedication of the NASA Ames Numerical Aerospace Simulation (NAS) computational facility (figure 72).

Public flight demonstrations of the tilt rotor aircraft by Bell included appearances of XV-15 N702NA at the Wright-Patterson AFB air show (July 19-22, 1990), the Ft. Worth air show (October 9 and 10, 1991), and the Dallas air show (October 16 and 17, 1991).

Crash

For about 10 years, Bell effectively promoted the tilt rotor aircraft concept by using the bailed XV-15 N702NA to demonstrate flight capabilities to guest pilots from various military, civil, and governmental organizations. One of these guest pilot flights was conducted on August 20, 1992, for M. Guy Dabadie, the chief experimental test pilot for Eurocopter, France.

Prior to the flight, Bell test pilots Ron Erhart and Tom Warren performed a short flight with the XV-15 both as a check of the aircraft, which had not been flown for a while, and to maintain pilot proficiency. During the check flight each pilot made three uneventful landings after which the aircraft was declared ready for the demonstration flight. The pilot in command for that flight was Ron Erhart, chief pilot for BHTI.

A briefing for the guest pilot was conducted the day before by Bill Martin, the Bell flight test engineer, and was continued by Ron Erhart just prior to the flight. The briefing covered the configuration and operation of the aircraft's systems, flight controls and safety features, as well as emergency procedures. The planned flight profile and communications procedures were also reviewed.

The demonstration, with Guy Dabadie at the controls, lasted about 30 minutes and included hover, conversion, and airplane mode operations. After returning to the Bell ramp at the Arlington Municipal Airport, the XV-15 was lifted to a low hover by Dabadie to perform another landing before terminating the flight. As he initiated the descent for landing, the aircraft began to roll to the right. Dabadie put in correcting roll control as Ron Erhart reached up to provide the input. By that time the control stick was on the stop but the aircraft continued to roll to an inverted attitude and struck the ground. The rapid roll, inverted attitude, and proximity to the ground prevented the use of the ejection seats.

The right nacelle engine exhaust ejector and the steel proprotor blades broke upon contact with the ground. The impact also fractured the left wing at the root, swinging the still rotating spinner with only blade stubs attached against the inverted left side window. The right nacelle separated at the wing tip and came to rest next to the wing. Except for a crushed nose section, collapsed vertical fins and a gash from a rotor blade, the fuselage and cockpit area received little damage. The flight crew, Ron Erhart and Guy Dabadie, hanging upside-down by the seat harnesses, initiated emergency egress procedures. However, the cabin door was blocked by the damaged wing and attempts by Ron Erhart to activate the side window removal system failed. By this time, the Bell ground personnel who had reached the aircraft, were able to remove broken sections of the thick side window plexiglass in order to rescue the crew. Both pilots received only minor injuries.

No fire occurred after the crash, due in part to the low fuel level onboard at the time of the accident, but also attributable largely to the crashworthy fuel cells which contained most of the remaining fuel, thereby providing the added safety for which they were designed.

An accident investigation was conducted by the National Transportation Safety Board (NTSB). Their findings revealed that the loss of control was due to human error and was not due to any inherent characteristics of the tilt rotor aircraft. It was found that the proprotor blade collective angle mechanical linkage had disconnected from the hydraulic actuator when a critical nut backed off because it had not been secured by a cotter pin as required.

Further, failure of the window removal system to operate properly was found to be due to improper procedures noted in the XV-15 tilt rotor research aircraft flight manual. These procedures had been extracted directly from the flight manual for the Army AH-1S which used the same device. Following the discovery of this major procedural problem, both the XV-15 and AH-1S manuals were changed to include the correct operating instructions for the window removal system.

The End of an Era

By the mid 1990s, the flight research situation in the Government was changing. NASA Administrator Daniel Goldin, in an attempt to reduce the operating costs of the Agency, directed that all flight activities were to be consolidated at one research center, the Dryden Flight Research Center (DFRC). For nearly two years following that directive, heated debates raged between NASA Headquarters (for consolidation) and the Centers, local officials, and members of Congress (from affected congressional districts) who argued for the continuation of flight activities at the Centers. Ultimately the decision was made to move all NASA flight test activity to DFRC by January 1, 1998.

Meanwhile, XV-15 N703NA was undergoing a major inspection at Ames. In addition to the scheduled transmission overhaul, the composite blade cuffs were modified to prevent a reoccurrence of the failure that resulted in the emergency landing in September 1991, and modifications to the proprotor control system were designed to correct the dynamic problems and load limitations encountered during the initial flights with the advanced technology blade (ATB). When the final decision was made by NASA Headquarters to terminate XV-15 operations at Ames in early 1994, the inspection and modification work ceased and the XV-15 TRRA was placed in temporary storage at Ames.

Starting Over

The availability of XV-15 N703NA was seen as an unexpected opportunity by Bell. Having lost N702NA in the unfortunate accident in August 1992, and with an ongoing requirement to conduct tilt rotor research, demonstrations, and applications evaluations in support of the V-22 program, Larry Jenkins, Bell's director of technology, requested that a new bailment be established for N703NA. The NASA/Army owners of the XV-15, with no funding and no prospects for continuing the XV-15 flight test program, consented to a new agreement. The terms of the new bailment, described in a Memorandum of Agreement effective April 21, 1994, were approved by the NASA Ames Director, Dr. Ken Munechika; the NASA Associate Administrator for Aeronautics, Dr. Wesley Harris; the Director of the Army Aeroflightdynamics Directorate, Andrew W. Kerr; the Executive Director of the Army Aviation Research, Development, and Engineering Center, Thomas L. House; and Bell President Webb Joiner. The aircraft was again disassembled and was shipped from Ames to Bell's flight test center onboard flatbed trucks immediately after the bailment was authorized.

The delivery of that aircraft with the Boeing Helicopters composite blades (ATB) presented a problem for Bell. The unplanned cost of refurbishing the aircraft during the current fiscal year represented a large portion of Bell's tilt rotor discretionary research funds. With inadequate funding for the development of the control system improvements, and with low confidence in compatibility of the ATB with the XV-15 and in the integrity of some of the ATB's composite components, Bell sought an alternate approach. Bell's preferred solution was to return to the use of their metal blades fabricated for the XV-15.

A review of the availability of flightworthy metal blades brought the plan to an immediate halt. It turned out that when the NASA/Army TRRA team at Ames initiated the ATB evaluations on the XV-15, the metal blades from N703NA were sent to Bell to replace the higher flight-time blades on N702NA, some of which had become unserviceable due to skin cracks. When N702NA crashed, all of its proprotor blades (from N703NA) were destroyed leaving only two usable left metal blades and four usable right blades. Short of fabricating a new blade for the left proprotor at great expense, there was no hope of obtaining the required blade.

At this point another of those remarkable events that have periodically rescued the program from a seemingly unsolvable situation occurred. The Ames long-term hardware storage facility, located at Camp Parks near Oakland, California, requested the aircraft projects to remove or dispose of the aircraft-related items in storage since, under the new flight activities consolidation plan, the Ames aircraft assets were now to be moved away, primarily to DFRC. While searching through the large warehouse, a crate containing a left XV-15 metal blade was discovered. The blade, still in primer paint was apparently unused. The documents indicated that this blade was fabricated for structural fatigue testing under the TRRA contract, but funding limitations at that time caused that test to be eliminated. After inspection at Bell by Ernie Schellhase, who had designed these blades in the late 1960s under Bell's IR&D funding, the blade was declared flightworthy. It was refinished and installed on N703NA, completing the required proprotor "shipset." Once again, lady luck smiled on the TRRA.

With the proprotor blade problem question resolved, Bell stepped up the refurbishment of N703NA. At the completion of this refurbishment, the aircraft had the original metal blades, a new data acquisition system (similar to the system being used on the V-22), and had the Ames-modified automatic flight control system restored to Bell's control laws. Because of the extended time period since the last operation of the XV-15, arrangements were made for the Bell pilots to perform training sessions in the Ames simulator as the aircraft was nearing flight readiness. On March 3, 1995, test pilots Ron Erhart and Roy Hopkins returned this aircraft to flight at the Bell Flight Test Center, Arlington Texas, nearly 16 years after its initial flight at the same location.

Deja Vu

After a brief checkout period, XV-15 N703NA was pressed into action as the tilt rotor technology demonstrator, this time in executive transport colors including painted-on simulated windows. On April 21, 1995, it became the first tilt rotor to land at the world's first operational vertiport, the Dallas Convention Center Heliport/Vertiport (figure 73). In June, when the Bell-Boeing V-22 Osprey made its first international public debut at the forty-first Paris Air Show, the XV-15 was also present (figure 74), marking a triumphant return 14 years after its initial appearance. With both aircraft performing flight demonstrations on the six days of the air show, the tilt rotor aircraft, once again, was the star of the event.

Onward/Back to Work

Following the return of the XV-15 to the United States (the round trip this time was made onboard a cargo ship) Bell performed additional demonstrations before flying N703NA back to its base. These included the first tilt rotor flight demonstration in Canada, made on July 10, 1995, at the Bell Helicopter Mirabel facility near Montreal, Quebec, and the first tilt rotor operation at the Indianapolis Heliport on the following day. During the next few years, in addition to the continuation of the guest pilot program, the aircraft was utilized in numerous tilt rotor research activities sponsored by Bell, Boeing Helicopters, NASA Ames and NASA Langley, and the National Rotorcraft Technology Center (NRTC) located at Ames. At the time of this writing, investigations of tilt rotor flight controls, crew station displays, terminal area operations, certification issues, and other technical areas continue to be planned for this aircraft.

XV-15 Project Summary

This review of approximately 45 years of Government and industry efforts to develop a VTOL tilt rotor aircraft reveals the unique research activities that were accomplished and the magnitude of the technical challenges that had to be overcome.

The large diameter rotor required for the desired low speed characteristics produced serious dynamic instabilities at moderate cruise speed conditions. Initially, the lack of understanding of the cause of these instabilities, as well as the absence of a valid mathematical model to analyze the multiple degree-of-freedom elastic tilt rotor aircraft structure, made the search for a solution a slow and costly trial and error process. For about 20 years, starting with the XV-3 program in the early 1950s, extensive experimental work ultimately resulted in breakthrough analyses which made possible the identification of solutions to the high speed aeroelastic stability problem.

Other significant problems that surfaced in the early XV-3 tilt rotor flight work included poor performance and handling qualities. Once again, many hours of wind tunnel tests provided the empirical data required to support the development of new analytical codes necessary to address these problems. By the late 1960s, the results of these methodology developments were being applied to the design of tilt rotor aircraft that could effectively perform various civil and military missions. Also, improvements in the flight control system, which provided the desired handling characteristics, were demonstrated through the use of real-time piloted flight simulations.

This new understanding of the tilt rotor's complex problems was achieved through focused studies conducted by Government and industry researchers, largely directed by a single joint Army/NASA office. Each major problem was addressed and solved by a planned series of experimental and analytical investigations leading to the highest level of confidence possible, short of actual flight test validation.

This ever-expanding technology base, coupled with the validation of new analytical codes completed in the early 1970s, provided the evidence needed to proceed confidently with the development of a new proof-of-concept tilt rotor research aircraft.

A Tilt Rotor Research Aircraft Project Office was created at Ames in the early 1970s to develop and flight-test two tilt rotor research aircraft. The Office was staffed by both Army and NASA personnel knowledgeable in the critical disciplines needed to develop such an aircraft. The contractor, Bell Helicopter Textron Inc., likewise provided the necessary personnel and facilities to design and build the aircraft. Furthermore, a Government Resident Office was established at the contractor's facility to provide a high level of communication between both parties as well as close monitoring of technical status and costs. Despite significant technical and cost problems encountered during the conduct of the work, the management system was very effective for controlling costs and resolving technical issues and was instrumental in contributing to the overall success of the project.[55]

A lesson learned was the advantage of multiple or joint participation, in this case the Army and NASA. This became an important factor in maintaining the continuation of project funding when one agency was able to provide funds during a period that the other agency was experiencing a temporary funding shortfall. This was further emphasized when the Project Office was able to accommodate a request by the Navy for sea trial evaluations of the XV-15 tilt rotor research aircraft (TRRA) to evaluate it for Navy ship board applications. As it happened, this provided further funding at a time of critical need. Yet another important "funding" lesson learned was to include the contractor as a participant in the project funding. In the case of the XV-15 TRRA, this was accomplished contractually by an incentive fee arrangement tied to contractor cost performance. While the incentive fee did not prevent cost increases, it did provide for significant funding participation by the contractor through a negative fee arrangement.

Most important are the results of the TRRA flight test program. Within just over two years after the first full conversion of the XV-15 TRRA, sufficient data had been collected to determine that the primary proof-of-concept objectives were successfully completed. This included validation of rotor/pylon/wing dynamic stability, performance, and noise. The XV-15 met its predicted characteristics in all critical areas and was determined to be suitable for advanced flight research investigations, including evaluations of the tilt rotor aircraft's suitability of civil and military applications. These investigations and related advanced research have been conducted with the XV-15 for nearly twenty years after the completion of the proof-of-concept flight testing, demonstrating the tilt rotor aircraft's versatility and potential in many VTOL aircraft applications. Without question, the XV-15 TRRA has met or exceeded the goals as specified in the original Program Plan. Although the TRRA was built by the Bell Helicopter Company, it is significant to note this was the first time the Government (the Army and NASA) successfully wrote the specifications for and fostered the introduction of a new aircraft type into the aviation market.

---

[55] A discussion of the approach and key considerations of the TRRA and other flight research projects at Ames is contained in: David D. Few, "A Perspective on 15 Years of Proof-of-Concept Aircraft Development and Flight Research at Ames-Moffett by the Rotorcraft and Powered-Lift Flight Projects Division, 1970-1985," NASA Reference Publication 1187, August 1987.

Epilogue

The XV-15 continues to contribute to the advancement of aeronautical technology through its flight test activity at Bell, thereby further increasing the benefits derived from the TRRA project. It is appropriate, however, to note the costs incurred by the Government in the performance of this work. By September 1981, sufficient data had been acquired in the two research aircraft flight test program for the Government to declare that the primary proof-of-concept objectives had been successfully completed. At that time, the cost of the TRRA contract was $39.5M. An additional $5.0M was used during this period for supporting research and technology. Research and support work continued with the prime contractor (Bell) for several years under the same contract, and when it was terminated in August 1993, the final cost to the Government was $50.4M. Bell had contributed over $1.5M to the effort in accordance with the incentive fee arrangements of the contract. In recent years it has become apparent that the Government's investment in tilt rotor aircraft technology, through the new programs now under development, will likely provide thousands of new jobs and may even improve the U.S. balance of trade. The key events leading to the validation of tilt rotor technology by the XV-15, and the subsequent development of production tilt rotor aircraft (discussed later in this section) are listed in the chronology provided in Appendix C.

In addition, the contributions of many people associated with these projects over the years have been recognized by leading U.S. technical organizations and societies. A summary of the key awards and new speed and climb records set with the XV-15 are described in Appendix D. A collection of pictures showing the tilt rotor aircraft during the flight program is provided in the photo-gallery, Appendix E. Also, Appendix F contains a comprehensive bibliography of tilt rotor related publications.

The remarkable achievements, both technical and operational, of the XV-15 TRRA were directly responsible for the introduction of the world's first military and civil tilt rotor aircraft. Without the technology validation and the demonstrations provided by the TRRA, it would not have been possible for the leaders of industry and the Government to be confident enough to launch these new aircraft production programs. Thumbnail sketches of these programs, as well as brief summaries of the Government activities spawned by the TRRA project are provided here.

JVX/V-22 Osprey

Beginning in the late 1960s, and continuing for more than a decade, the Marines studied the options available for their future vertical assault role and transport needs. However, because of the relatively small number of vehicles required, coupled with the specialized missions, they could not establish the necessary level of support in the Department of Defense (DoD) and in the Congress to initiate acquisition of a new purpose-built aircraft. By the end of 1981, the DoD identified additional vertical lift missions for the Army and the Air Force which could make use of the same flight vehicle that would satisfy the Marine's requirements. If a common aircraft could be designed to fill the operational needs of these three services, the aircraft procurement might then be large enough to justify development and unit acquisition costs. Therefore, an assessment of the feasibility for identification of a single vehicle which could satisfactorily perform these diverse missions and the identification of the most suitable vehicle type for these applications was directed by the DOD. This study was conducted by a Joint Technology Assessment Group (JTAG) consisting of Government engineers and military specialists at the Ames Research Center, between February and May of 1982. Col. Jimmie Creech, USMC, was the study manager. The study was to include both current and advanced VTOL aircraft. Four vehicle types were selected for this investigation, with a team leader and a technical staff appointed to assess each type. The helicopter and compound helicopter teams were led by Dr. Michael Scully of the Army Advanced Systems Research Office (ASRO), the fan-in-wing team was headed by Sam Wilson of NASA Ames, and John Magee, also of NASA Ames, directed the tilt rotor study team. The latest design methodology and performance data were applied to develop a credible and practical design configured and sized to meet, to the best degree possible, the various and often conflicting mission requirements.

The results of the study made it clear that the tilt rotor aircraft was best suited to meet diverse missions. These included the Marine vertical assault, Navy rescue and logistics, Air Force long-range special operations, as well as the Army medical evacuation, long-range combat logistics support, and combat air assault support missions. With a single technical approach identified that could satisfy the requirements of the three military services, advocacy of the multiservice tilt rotor aircraft to the Congress and to the administration was initiated. The XV-15 proof-of-concept and flight research programs had established that performance, loads, and structural dynamics of the military tilt rotor transport could be predicted with high confidence. However, major changes occurred that affected the course of the JVX (Joint Vertical Experimental) program.

First, at the time of the advocacy of the new aircraft, the Army was engaged in the initiation of another major, high cost weapons system procurement, the LHX (Light Helicopter, Experimental). With a commitment to develop a world-class fighting machine that would use state-of-the-art structures, propulsion, avionics and weapon systems technology, it was not economically or politically feasible for the Army to simultaneously advocate and manage the development of a new technology transport rotorcraft. Since the primary user of the JVX aircraft would be the Marines, the task of managing this program was handed to the Navy, the weapon systems procurement agency for the Marine Corps.

Second, as the flight tests of the JVX aircraft, now called the V-22 Osprey, were about to get under way, a new administration came into office under President George Bush. With a focus on reducing DoD expenditures, Secretary of Defense Richard Cheney identified major procurements selected for cancellation. Since the JVX activity had recently begun and relatively little funding had been invested at this point, it became a target for elimination. The battle for the survival of the advanced rotorcraft transport aircraft would be waged for several years. Advocates included the potential military users, members of Congress, and elements of the rotorcraft industry. The opposition was the administration and the upper management of the DoD.

Other issues surfaced. In accordance with a longstanding DoD procurement policy, contractors for major new acquisitions were selected from competitive bids. In this case only two rotorcraft companies had sufficient technical expertise to bid. These were Bell and Boeing, and only Bell had extensive flight test experience with the tilt rotor aircraft. Furthermore, in the early 1980s, there was a DoD mandate for prime contractor teaming arrangements seen as a means of sharing Research and Development costs by the prime contractors, thus reducing the financial risk to any one company, as well as permitting the development of a broader technology base.

Figure 75.
The Bell-Boeing V-22 Osprey in cruise flight. (Ames Photograph AC89-0246-3)

To satisfy the teaming requirement, two companies that had been competitors, Bell and Boeing, joined forces. Although this would bring together the world's greatest resources of tilt rotor technology, it left no credible competitors in the U.S. rotorcraft industry. When the RFP for the V-22 was issued, only the Bell-Boeing team responded. While this presented a dilemma for advocates of competitive procurements, the qualifications of the team, coupled with strong political advocacy from the powerful Texas and Pennsylvania congressional representatives, provided the support needed to proceed.[56] The successful advocacy of this program is credited to strong congressional support, confirming the observation by political analyst Brenda Foreman that "if the politics don't fly, the hardware never will."

On March 19, 1989, the first flight of the Osprey was conducted at Bell's Flight Research Center at Arlington Texas, the site of the first XV-15 flight twelve years earlier. Bell test pilot Dorman Cannon (who was also onboard the XV-15 during its first test flight) and Boeing Helicopter test pilot Dick Balzer were at the controls. The first full conversion to airplane mode was flown on September 14, 1989. Figure 75 shows one of the V-22 EMD (Engineering Manufacturing

---

[56] An account by Brenda Forman of the factors leading to the approval of V-22 program funding is presented in "The Political Process in Systems Architecture Design," Program Manager, March-April 1993.

Figure 76.
The Bell tilt rotor eagle eye unmanned aerial vehicle. (Bell-Ames Photograph ACD99-0209-24)

Development) aircraft during early flight tests.

The flight test program of the V-22, however, was not without serious problems. Of the six Full Scale Development (FSD) aircraft planned for the flight test efforts (of which only five were completed), two crashed and were destroyed, with one crash taking the lives of all seven people on board. However, it was determined that these accidents were not due to the inherent characteristics of this vehicle type and the program survived.

As of late 1999, the V-22 Osprey is undergoing operational testing by the U.S. Navy and initial operational capability (IOC) is planned for the year 2001. On September 8, 1999, the first production V-22 delivered to the U.S. Marine Corps landed at the Pentagon for a tilt rotor demonstration hosted by Secretary of Defense William S. Cohen. A CH-46 (the helicopter that will be replaced by the V-22) and XV-15 proof-of-concept aircraft, in Coast Guard colors, landed along side the Osprey. After several members of Congress flew in the new V-22 tilt rotor transport, Secretary Cohen described it as a "revolution in military affairs." Based on the technology demonstrated by the XV-15 TRRA, the V-22 will bring capabilities to the U.S. armed services that are not available in any other vehicle.

UAV

Tilt rotor aircraft technology also offers performance and operational capabilities that are highly desirable for unmanned aircraft being developed for military applications. The ability to takeoff and land from a very small area, such as a landing pad onboard a ship, coupled with a large radius of action, high altitude performance, and a high cruise speed to get to the target area quickly provides a combination of attributes that meet the needs of the military users.

To demonstrate the readiness of tilt rotor technology for this application, Bell Helicopter Textron developed the Eagle Eye Unmanned Aerial Vehicle (UAV), (figure 76). This aircraft performed flight evaluations at the Naval Air Test Center, Patuxent River, Maryland, in 1995 and at the Proving Grounds in Yuma, Arizona, in 1998. The later activity demonstrated the ability to takeoff from and land within a 24-foot landing spot (and consistently touch down within a 10-foot square area), hover with the required fuel and payload, fly at over 200 knots, and cruise at 14,600-foot altitude with the 200-pound payload. The Eagle Eye uses a highly automated, command based flight control system, that includes two inertial navigation systems and a GPS (Global Positioning System).

As of this writing, Bell continues to explore missions and applications for the tilt rotor UAV.

Model 609

In November 1996, Bell and Boeing announced that they had agreed to jointly design and build the world's first production civil tilt rotor aircraft, the Bell Boeing 609 (BB 609). This major and multiyear commitment of company resources represented the culmination of the early research and technology efforts begun with flight tests of the XV-3 in the mid-1950s and completed with the technology validation provided by the XV-15 proof-of-concept tilt rotor research aircraft in the 1980s and 1990s.

Figure 77.
Mockup of the BA-Model 609 civil tilt rotor aircraft with Bell-Boeing markings. (Bell-Ames Photograph ACD97-0133-3)

In addition to the fundamental engineering and design capabilities provided by the joint Government and industry research programs, the model 609 will incorporate many features developed for the V-22 Osprey. This technology transfer will include state-of-the-art fly-by-wire flight controls and avionics, advanced composites in the rotors and structure, and Health and Usage Monitoring (HUM) systems. The 609 aircraft will have a crew of two and carry six to nine passengers. It is designed to cruise at 275 knots (316 miles per hour) and have a range of 750 nautical miles (863 statute miles), which is nearly twice the speed and range capability of current helicopters of the same payload class. Takeoff gross weight will be about 16,000 pounds with an approximate useful load of 5,500 pounds, which means that it can carry a full complement of passengers and plenty of cargo and/or baggage, an important consideration for civil aircraft. The fuselage will be pressurized to 5.5-psi pressure differential providing a passenger cabin altitude of 8,000 feet at a 25,000-foot ceiling. Although the BB 609 has VTOL capability, it is anticipated to be utilized as a fixed wing, turboprop airplane using rolling takeoffs during more than 90 percent of its operations. This will give it the ability to increase payload and/or range when VTOL operations are not required, thus lowering operating costs. Efforts are underway with the Federal Aviation Administration (FAA) and the European Joint Aviation Authorities (JAA) to establish certification for this aircraft type, anticipated by early 2001, followed by first deliveries of the aircraft later that year.

A full-scale mockup of the aircraft (figure 77) was displayed at the June 1997 Paris Air Show where the V-22 Osprey with the XV-15 TRRA flew daily flight demonstrations. The interest generated by the mockup and flight demonstrations was such that Bell received 36 advanced orders at that time for the new aircraft. Bell President Webb Joiner, speaking of the early customers for the Model 609, said that "These are not just customers, these are visionaries," noting their commitment to a new aircraft type two years before design freeze and four years in advance of first delivery. Bell further anticipates a market of up to 1000 Model 609's over the next 20 years, serving needs such as executive transport, offshore oil operations, search and rescue, emergency medical service, drug enforcement and border patrol.

In March of 1998, shortly after the Boeing Company purchased McDonnell Douglas Helicopters, and subsequently made the decision to focus on military helicopters only, Boeing removed itself as a major contributing partner in the BB 609 program. However, at the Farnborough Air Show in September of 1998, Bell announced a joint venture with the Agusta Helicopter Company of Italy wherein Agusta will participate in the development, manufacture, and final assembly of 609s delivered in Europe and other parts of the world. The 609 was now renamed the BA 609 (for Bell Agusta 609).

Agusta has had a long history of joint programs with Bell and also worked with other European aerospace companies on the development of tilt rotor technology under a program called EUROFAR (European Future Advanced Rotorcraft). Following the Bell-Agusta teaming announcement, Eurocopter, a French-German company, stated that it too was seeking funding for a civil tilt rotor project.

As a commuter aircraft operating in a growing worldwide short-haul commuter market, the BA 609 can operate to/from vertiports or conventional airports and will go a long way toward relieving congestion and delays at many of the world's major airport hubs. The BA 609 will be breaking new ground (or should we say "new air") in aviation.

CTRDAC

The development of the V-22 Osprey and the initiation of flight testing provided the encouragement needed by tilt rotor advocates to press for a civil application of this new aircraft type. Earlier FAA- and NASA-funded studies,[57] managed by Dr. John Zuk of NASA Ames, showed that the tilt rotor aircraft had potential worldwide market application and could be economically beneficial to the manufacturers as well as the operators. In late 1992, results were brought to the attention of members of Congress who directed Secretary of Transportation Samuel (Sam) Skinner to establish a Civil Tiltrotor Development Advisory Committee (CTRDAC) to examine the costs, technical feasibility, and economic viability of developing civil tilt rotor aircraft

---

[57] Anon., "Civil Tiltrotor Missions and Applications, Phase II: The Commercial Passenger Market," NASA CR 177576, February 1991.

(CTR).[58] The CTRDAC was to also consider issues associated with the integration of CTR aircraft into the national transportation system and assess the resulting national economic benefits. Furthermore, the Committee was charged with determining the required additional research and development, the needed regulatory changes to integrate the CTR into the transportation system, and how the CTR aircraft and related infrastructure development costs should be allocated between Government and industry.

The members appointed to the CTRDAC represented a broad spectrum of private and public sector agencies, companies, and associations, as well as the Department of Transportation (DOT), the National Aeronautics and Space Administration, and the Department of Defense. The chair of the CTRDAC was Frank E. Kruesi, Assistant Secretary for Transportation Policy (DOT). Among the 31 committee members were Dr. Hans Mark of the University of Texas (UT) (previously Director of the NASA Ames Research Center and later Chancellor of the UT), and Webb Joiner, president of Bell Helicopter Textron, Inc.

The findings of the Committee issued in December 1995[59] stated that the CTR is technically feasible and can be developed by the U.S. industry. However, additional research and development and infrastructure planning are needed before industry can make a CTR production decision. Furthermore, under the assumptions made during the study, it was concluded that a CTR system could be economically viable and could operate profitably without Government subsidies in heavily traveled corridors. The CTR, the Committee found, could reduce airport congestion, create jobs, and have a positive impact on the balance of trade.

The Committee recommended the creation of a public/private partnership to address CTR infrastructure issues and the initiation of associated planning. Work should begin, they stated, on regulatory and certification issues and on changes to the air traffic control system to safely and effectively use the capabilities of the CTR. In addition, the CTRDAC recommended that an integrated CTR aircraft and infrastructure research, development, and demonstration program should be conducted and the costs for this should be shared by the Government and industry.

In response, elements of work suggested by the CTRDAC have been included in the NASA rotorcraft program that are consistent with the NASA aeronautics technical thrusts.[60]

---

[58] The CTRDAC used a 40-passenger CTR as a baseline for its analysis. Earlier studies (see footnote 57) indicated that this size CTR has the greatest initial potential to provide societal benefits and achieve commercial success.

[59] Anon., "Civil Tiltrotor Development Advisory Committee Report to Congress in Accordance with PL102-581," December 1995.

[60] Anon., Aeronautics and Space Transportation Technology: Three Pillars for Success, National Aeronautics and Space Administration, Office of Aeronautics and Space Transportation Technology Brochure, March 1997.

Future Tilt Rotor Aircraft

By the early 1990s, an extensive tilt rotor data base had been developed from the Bell and Government XV-15 flight test activities. The larger military V-22 tilt rotor aircraft, which was designed using methodology validated with the XV-15 data, was well under way and was showing promise of meeting important performance goals. Also at that time, NASA's investigation of technical solutions to the growing air transport system congestion problems led to the identification of the tilt rotor aircraft as a part of the solution. However, significant advancements in several technology areas would be required before the tilt rotor aircraft could be accepted as a civil transport. To address these "barrier issues," researchers at the Ames, Langley, and Lewis Research Centers, led by Bill Snyder of Ames, developed a comprehensive effort called the Advanced Tiltrotor Transport Technology (ATTT) Program to develop the new technologies.

The research, started in 1994, was to be conducted as an element of NASA's Advanced Subsonic Technology Program. Due to funding limitations, the initial research activity, the Short-Haul Civil Tiltrotor (SHCT) Program (a subset of the ATTT Program), was restricted to issues of primary concern, noise and safety. The noise investigations focused on the reduction of the sound levels generated by transport-size tilt rotor aircraft while operating to and from downtown vertiports of major metropolitan areas. Community and regulatory acceptance requires much lower noise levels for this environment than is generated using V-22 technology. The research activity included the development of refined acoustics analyses, the acquisition of wind tunnel small- and large-scale proprotor noise data to validate the new analytical methods, analytical and wind tunnel investigations of innovative proprotor and blade configurations designed to reduce the most disturbing content of the noise signature, and flight tests to determine the effect of different approach profiles on terminal area and surrounding community noise. The Boeing and Bell Helicopter Companies, McDonnell Douglas Helicopter Systems, and the Sikorsky Aircraft Company, participated in the noise investigations. Mike Marcolini was the lead researcher at Langley Research Center for many of these efforts.

The safety effort was related to the projected need to execute approaches to and departures from confined vertiports. For these conditions the capability to operate safely with one engine inoperative (OEI) would be required and a safe/low pilot workload (referred to as Level 1 handling qualities by the FAA) must be maintained under adverse weather conditions. This area was addressed by conducting engine design studies seeking the ability to produce high levels of emergency power in the event of an OEI condition without adversely impacting weight, reliability, maintenance, or normal operation fuel economy. These studies were conducted by Allison, Allied Signal and General Electric under the technical guidance of Joe Eisenberg of Lewis Research Center (LeRC). Further safety investigations involved piloted simulations at the Ames Vertical Motion Simulator (VMS) to assess crew station issues, control law variations, advanced configurations such as the variable diameter tilt rotors, and terminal area approach path profiles including nacelle position variations. Bill Decker of Ames was the principal investigator for the simulation efforts.

As the SHCT Program nears the scheduled 2001 completion date, a new follow-on research effort is being developed by NASA to apply and evaluate relevant technologies that emerged during the SHCT activity. One key area of interest is the feasibility evaluation of Simultaneous Non-Interfering (SNI) terminal area operations. SNI operations are expected to increase the capacity of existing airports by allowing VTOL tilt rotor transport aircraft to takeoff and land using terminal area flight paths separate from that used by the fixed-wing transports. Furthermore, if short-haul aircraft utilize the SNI operations and are thereby removed from the runway queue, the larger capacity long-range aircraft would occupy the limited slots, thereby increasing the number of passengers that can be transported on existing airport runways. The planned research would identify the technologies and procedures needed for the aircraft and Air Traffic Management (ATM) system to obtain maximum aviation system benefits. The evaluations would involve the use of piloted simulations and flight tests, employing helicopters to represent the tilt rotor aircraft in near-terminal area operations. A separate program element includes ATM systems integration work and addresses adverse weather operations (such as icing conditions). This effort also deals with the automated cockpit and will examine methods of maintaining safe control during emergencies.

A new element of this follow-on activity is focused on Variable Diameter Tilt Rotor (VDTR) technology. This tilt rotor variant, being developed by Sikorsky, employs a proprotor system that provides a larger diameter and lower disc loading for higher efficiency in hover and low speed helicopter mode flight and, by the use of a blade retraction mechanism, a smaller diameter "prop" for airplane mode flight. The lower disc loading also contributes to safety by improving OEI performance and, if lower tip speeds were employed, would reduce the noise level. The planned five-year VDTR effort would address full-scale system design, system integration and reliability and would be conducted with shared funding by the Government and the contractor.

Additional investigations planned for this initiative address the application of conformable proprotor blade technology or other advanced proprotor designs to improve performance and reduce noise. The selected system would be wind tunnel and flight tested to validate predictions. The last major element deals with economic viability and passenger comfort issues. These issues include the improvement of high speed performance by reducing wing thickness while maintaining the required stability margins, the reduction of proprotor/airframe interaction losses, and the development of methods to control interior noise and reduce cabin vibrations.

In a more aggressive effort developed in response to the CTRDAC recommendations, NASA planners have proposed the advanced technology demonstrator tiltrotor aircraft program. This program carries some of the vehicle technology proposed in the SHCT follow-on program to flight demonstration with a highly modified V-22 Osprey. To accomplish this high cost program, it is expected that Government and industry would participate and cost share in order to make it affordable. While support for funding major new programs is usually difficult to obtain, Army planners have cited possible applications for the large tilt rotor aircraft technologies being considered here in their joint transport rotorcraft (JTR) program (for a CH-47 helicopter replacement) and in the recent "Army After Next" study of future Army tactics and related technology.

The rest of the tilt rotor aircraft story begins now. The dream has become a reality.

Appendix A—Aircraft Descriptions

Transcendental Model 1-G

The Transcendental Aircraft Corporation Model 1-G[61] (figure A-1), was a single-seat convertible rotorcraft with two counter-rotating three-bladed rotors located at the tips of its fixed wing. The high-wing Model 1-G incorporated a conventional empennage and a fixed tricycle landing gear. When the rotors were placed in the horizontal plane, they acted as normal helicopter rotors. The rotors could also be tilted forward 82 degrees to perform as traction propellers of a conventional fixed-wing aircraft. In this configuration lift was provided by the wing.

The four-cylinder Lycoming O-290-A, located in the fuselage behind the cockpit, powered the rotors through a two-speed reduction main gear box, spanwise drive shafts, and outboard gearboxes. In the helicopter mode, at the engine's maximum output of 3000 RPM, the rotors rotated at 633 RPM.

The rotor blade-angle control system employed two concentric tubes around the rotor shaft emanating from the outboard gearboxes. One of these tubes controlled cyclic blade pitch and the other the collective pitch. The change of the rotor position from the helicopter to the aircraft configuration was accomplished in approximately three minutes.

Figure A-1.
Transcendental Model 1-G hovering in ground effect.
(Ames AD98-0209-14)

---

[61] Model 1-G information from Janes, *All the World's Aircraft,* 1953-1954.

Model 1-G Characteristics

Powerplant
  Lycoming O-290-A
  Brake horsepower . . . . 160 HP @ 3000 RPM
Length . . . . 26 ft
Wing
  Span . . . . 21 ft
  Area . . . . 63 sq ft
  Chord . . . . 3 ft
  Loading. . . . . 27.7 lb/sq ft
  Airfoil section . . . . NACA 23015
  Width . . . . 38 ft (to outer tip of rotor disc)
  Height. . . . . 7 ft
Rotor
  No. of rotors . . . . 2, interconnected
  Type . . . . articulated
  Blades/proprotor 3
  Diameter . . . . 17 ft
  Chord . . . . 4 in
  Disc loading . . . . 3.6 lb/sq ft

Rotational speed
  Helicopter mode . . . . 633 rpm
Weight
  Empty . . . . 1450 lb
  Gross. . . . . 1750 lb
No. of seats. 1

Transcendental Model 2

The Transcendental Model 2 Convertiplane[62] (figures A-2 and A-3) was a high-wing monoplane with a helicopter-type rotor mounted at each wing tip. It was configured with a conventional airplane empennage and a fixed-position tricycle landing gear. In addition to vertical takeoff capability, the Model 2 Convertiplane was designed to perform rolling takeoffs combining the lift from the rotors and the wing at gross weights above the maximum vertical takeoff weight.

In hovering and slow flight, control was achieved by the use of conventional helicopter rotor cyclic and collective blade angle controls. At higher airspeeds the conventional fixed-wing airplane tail control surfaces and ailerons provided the means for flight path control.

A Lycoming O-435-23 opposed six-cylinder reciprocating engine was mounted vertically in the fuselage behind the crew area. Power was transmitted through a main transmission located above the engine to drive shafts which provide input to the outboard gearboxes. The spanwise shafts incorporated flexible couplings to accommodate the angular misalignments of the drive system. The outboard gearboxes and the shafts that drove the rotors could be tilted by the pilot through the use of electrical actuators. This permitted the rotors to be moved from a horizontal plane (for the hover and low speed flight mode) to a vertical plane (for higher speed forward flight) when sufficient airspeed was attained for the wings to support the aircraft.

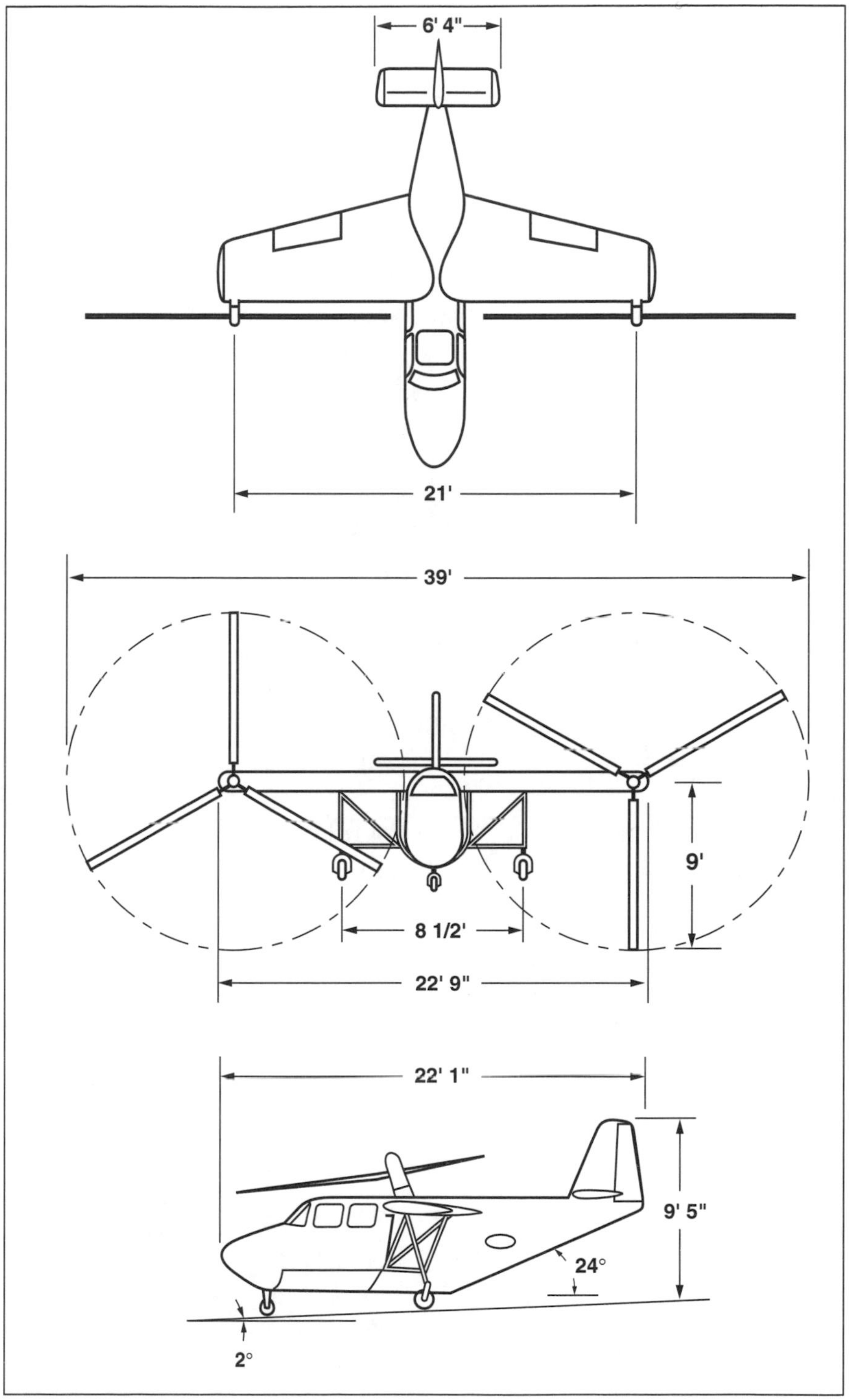

Figure A-2. Transcendental Model 2 tree-view drawing.

---

[62] Transcendental Model 2 information from Janes, *All the World's Aircraft,* 1955-1956.

Model 2 Characteristics

Powerplant

     One Lycoming O-435-23

     Brake horsepower . . . . 250 HP @ 3200 RPM

Length . . . . 22 ft 1 in

Wing

     Span . . . . 22 ft 9 in

     Area . . . . 100 sq ft

     Airfoil section . . . . NACA 23015

     Width . . . . 39 ft (to outer tip of rotor disc)

     Height . . . . 9 ft 5 in

Rotor

     No. of rotors . . . . 2, interconnected

     Type . . . . articulated

     Blades/proprotor 3

     Diameter . . . . 18 ft

     Chord (constant) . . . . 0.356 ft

     Disc loading . . . . 4.4 lb/sq ft

Weight

     Empty . . . . 1579 lb

     Gross. . . . . 2249 lb

     Useful load . . . . 670 lb

No. of seats. 2

Figure A-3.
Transcendental Model 2 cutaway drawing.

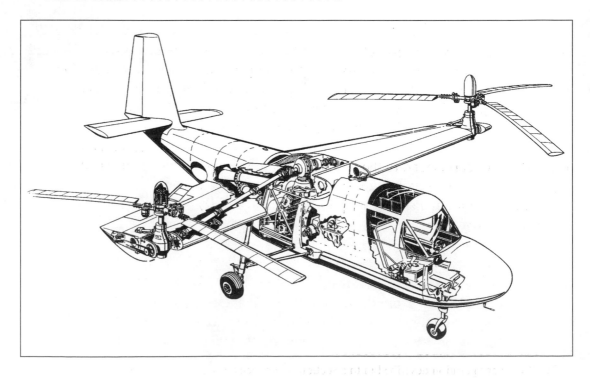

Bell XV-3

The XV-3[63] (figures A-4 and A-5) is a fixed mid-wing VTOL research aircraft developed to explore the flight characteristics of the tilt rotor aircraft. A two-bladed proprotor is mounted on a shaft assembly at each wing tip. The propro-tors can be rotated over a range of 90 degrees to permit hover and helicopter-, conversion-, and airplane-modes of flight. The aircraft has a conventional empen-nage plus a ventral fin below the vertical fin and rudder and uses a skid type landing gear. Small wheels can be attached for rolling takeoff and landing tests. The wing incorporates half-span 20 percent wing chord flaps and 22.5 percent wing chord ailerons. Fuselage-to-wing tip struts are incorporated to increase the stiffness of the wing.

A supercharged Pratt and Whitney R-985-AN-1 reciprocating radial engine is mounted in the fuselage aft of the wing center section. The standard rating for this engine is 450 BHP at 2300 rpm but, to increase performance for test purpos-es, the manufacturer authorized operation at 2400 rpm for takeoff, hovering and STOL flight conditions. Power is transferred from the engine to the proprotors through a short flexible-coupled drive shaft to the main (center) transmission located between the wing center section spars. From the main gear box, flexible-coupled shafts extend spanwise to the outboard wing tip (outboard) transmis-sions. The proprotor shafts extend from the outboard transmissions normal to the input drive shaft. The outboard transmissions are mounted on yokes which enable the proprotor shafts to be pivoted from the vertical to the horizontal.

The cockpit contains helicopter-type controls: a cyclic control stick, a collective pitch stick with a twist grip throttle, and rudder pedals. The longitudinal cyclic proprotor controls are mechanically reduced as the airplane mode configuration is approached. In the airplane mode no longitudinal cyclic response is provided. The differential collective controls (lateral stick inputs) are also reduced but one-third of the helicopter mode control is retained in airplane flight to increase maneuverability. The collective pitch is also automatically increased in the air-plane mode to correspond to the required operating range. The longitudinal, lat-eral, and collective controls are hydraulically boosted. There is no stability or control augmentation installed in the XV-3 and it does not have lateral cyclic proprotor controls.

The conversion system is powered by an electromechanical linear actuator con-nected to each outboard transmission yoke and is controlled by a "beep" switch on the cyclic stick. An interconnect-shaft links the right and left conver-sion systems to ensure synchronization and to permit the conversion cycle to be

---

[63] The XV-3 configuration described in this section (from Deckert and Ferry, footnote 7) reflects the characteristics of aircraft number 2 (tail number 4148) as flown during evaluations at the NASA Dryden Flight Research Center and the NASA Ames Research Center (from 1959 through 1962).

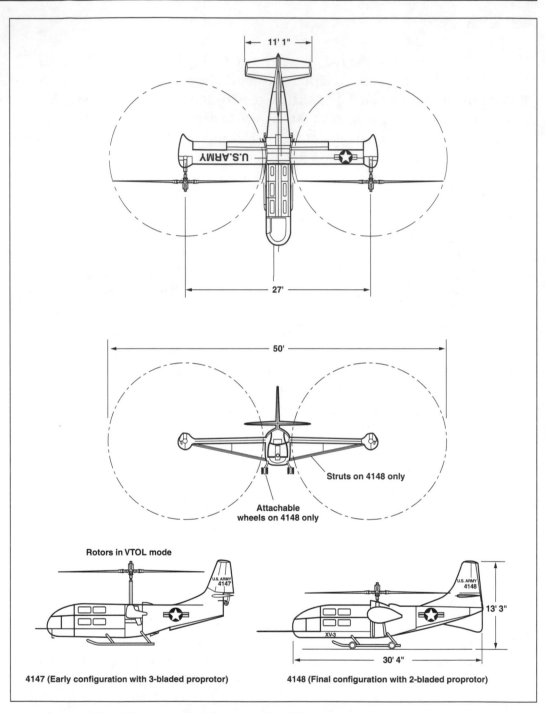

Figure A-4.
XV-3 three-view drawing.

completed with either actuator inoperative. The proprotors can be returned to the helicopter position by means of a hydraulic emergency reconversion clutch in the event of a complete electrical failure.

To accommodate the requirement for a high proprotor RPM for the high-thrust helicopter flight, and a lower RPM for airplane flight, the XV-3 incorporates a two-speed gear reduction capability in the center transmission. The gear shift, performed while flying in the airplane mode, is accomplished by means of an electrically controlled hydraulic clutch actuated by a switch in the cockpit.

Powerplant

    One Pratt and Whitney R-985-AN-1 reciprocating radial engine

    Brake horsepower . . . . 450 @ 2300 RPM

Length 30 ft 4 in

Wing

    Span . . . . 31 ft 2 in

    Area . . . . 116.0 sq ft

    Chord (constant) . . . . 3.75 ft

    Airfoil section . . . . NACA 23021

    Sweep/dihedral . . . . 0 degrees

    Aspect ratio 8.4

    Width . . . . 50 ft (to outer tip of proprotor disc)

    Height . . . . 13 ft 3 in

    Width . . . . 39 ft (to outer tip of rotor disc)

Horizontal tail

    Span . . . . 11ft 1 in

    Area . . . . 32.6 sq ft

    Chord . . . . 3 ft 10 in

Airfoil section

    root . . . . NACA 0015

    tip . . . . NACA 0012

    Aspect ratio 3.8

    Leading edge sweep . . . . 9.5 degrees

Vertical tail

    Area . . . . 32.8 sq ft

    Airfoil section . . . . NACA 0012

    Aspcct ratio 1.33

    Leading edge sweep . . . . 20 degrees

Proprotor

    No. of proprotors . . . . 2, interconnected

    Blades/proprotor 2

    Diameter . . . . 23 ft

    Chord (constant) . . . . 11.0 in

    Solidity 0.051

    Disc loading . . . . 5.66 lb/sq ft

    Airfoil section . . . . NACA 0015

    Twist (linear) . . . . 1 degree, 36 sec/ft

    Delta 3 angle . . . . 20 degrees

Rotational speed

    Helicopter mode . . . . 532 rpm

    Airplane mode . . . . 324 rpm

Weight

    Design . . . . 4700 lb

    Empty (actual) . . . . 4205 lb

Actual gross (at engine start) . . . . . . 4890 lb
Standard fuel . . . . 280 lb (600 lb capacity)
Instrumentation . . . . 160 lb
No. of seats. 1

Figure A-5.
XV-3 inboard drawing, side view.

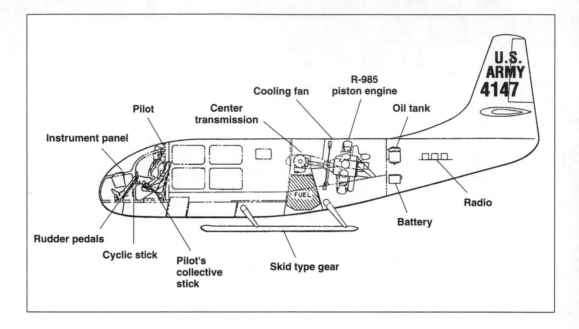

XV-15 Tilt Rotor Research Aircraft

XV-15 tilt rotor research aircraft was designed to be representative of the class of VTOL aircraft that employs large diameter, low disc loading, wingtip mounted proprotors that provide the thrust for vertical lift and forward flight. The XV-15 was sized to meet two requirements. First, it had to be large enough to properly demonstrate the performance, flight- and structural-dynamics, acoustics, and handling qualities of this vehicle class. Second, it had to be small enough to be accommodated in the test section of NASA Ames 40- by 80-foot wind tunnel for aerodynamics, loads, and systems performance evaluations.

The XV-15, shown in figure A-6, has 25-foot diameter proprotors and a design gross weight of 13,000 pounds. The proprotor axes rotate from 5 degrees aft of vertical for rearward flight or autorotation, to 90 degrees (vertical), the normal position for hover and helicopter flight, and to 0 degrees (horizontal) for airplane mode flight. The TRRA can also operate over a broad range of airspeeds at proprotor (or "nacelle") positions in between the helicopter and airplane modes. This flight region is referred to as the conversion mode and is depicted on the conversion envelope shown as figure A-7.

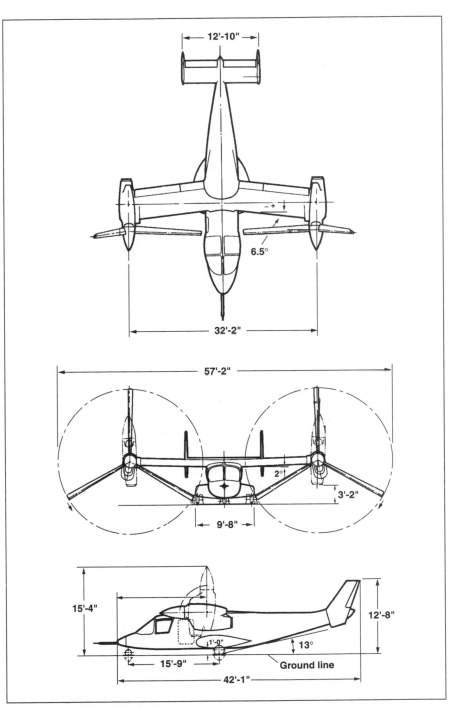

Figure A-6.
Three-view drawing of the XV-15 tilt rotor research aircraft.

Two Lycoming T-53-L-13B engines, modified for vertical starting and running (designated the LTC1K-4K) are installed in the wingtip nacelles. These engines are rated at 1,550 shp (shaft horsepower) for takeoff, with a normal (continuous operation) rating of 1,250 shp. The engines drive the proprotors through main transmissions also located in each nacelle. The two proprotors are also linked by a cross shaft system that allows both rotors to continue to be powered after the shut down of one engine. Upon the loss of a single engine during flight, it is disengaged from the drive system by an automatic clutch. Because of continuous

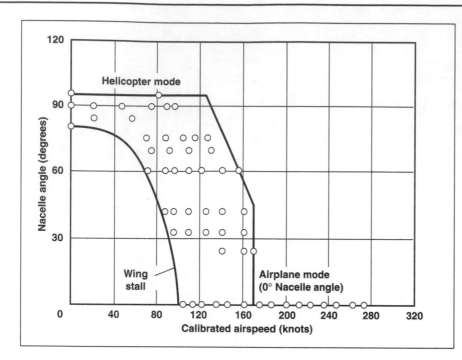

Figure A-7.
Conversion corridor of the XV-15 tilt rotor research aircraft.

torque transmission limitations, the engines on the XV-15 do not operate above 1,160 shp in the helicopter mode. A cross-shaft center gear box located below the wing in the fuselage accommodates the 6.5-degree forward wing sweep which is required to obtain proprotor-to-wing clearance in airplane mode flight. The free turbine engines permit the proprotor speed to be reduced during airplane mode flight to improve performance and reduce cruise noise.

The flight controls in the hover and helicopter modes resemble those of a lateral-tandem rotor helicopter. While the fixed-wing control surfaces remain active at all times, the primary low speed control forces and moments are provided by proprotor collective- and cyclic-blade angle (pitch) changes. Differential collective pitch produces aircraft roll and differential cyclic pitch results in yaw motions. The proprotor rpm is regulated by automatic control of the collective pitch. To reduce the hover performance loss resulting from the proprotor's wake impinging on the surface of the wing, the inboard flaps can be lowered to preset deflection positions. The outboard wing control surfaces are also deflected down when the flaps are deployed, but to a displacement less than two thirds of the flap position. The outboard wing control surfaces serve as ailerons in high speed flight and are referred to as "flaperons."

During conversion from helicopter flight to airplane mode flight, the helicopter-type control inputs to the proprotor are mechanically phased out and the conventional airplane control surfaces provide all flightpath-control forces and moments. By the time the nacelles are in the airplane position, the collective lever inputs to the proprotor are nulled and the total control of the collective pitch is transferred to the automatic rpm governor.

A stability and control augmentation system (SCAS) is provided with a three-axis (pitch, roll, and yaw) rate system that includes a pitch and roll attitude retention feature. SCAS characteristics are continuously varied from the helicopter to the airplane modes as a function of conversion angle to provide appropriate rate damping and control augmentation. The pitch and roll axes have dual channels and the yaw axis has a single channel system. SCAS-off flight has been routinely evaluated and demonstrated and, although damping and control are degraded, the XV-15 is still quite safe to fly, albeit with a higher pilot workload. A force feel system (FFS) provides stick and pedal forces proportional to control displacements while isolating the pilot's controls from SCAS feedback forces.

Force gradients are increased and trim rates are decreased with airspeed through an airspeed sensor. With the FFS off, pitch trim is available at a reduced rate and control forces are high but manageable.

The XV-15 aircraft has three independent transmission-driven 3000-psi hydraulic systems. The pump for each system is geared to the rotor side of the transmission clutch so that full hydraulic power can be provided with both engines shut down, as long as the rotors are turning within the normal speed range. Automatic shuttle valves are provided on some critical flight control actuators which switch the utility hydraulic system onto the critical actuator in the event of the loss of one of the primary hydraulic systems. The tricycle landing gear, operated by the utility hydraulic system, is automatically switched to a 3,000-psi pneumatic backup system for a one-time deployment when the normal hydraulics source becomes dedicated to the flight controls.

The electrical system includes two engine-mounted 300-ampere starter-generators. Each generator provides sufficient power to accommodate the aircraft's peak electrical load requirements. The XV-15's electrical system consists of two 28-volt dc busses and two 600 VA solid state inverters for ac power. Automatic dc bus interconnection is provided with pilot-controlled override switches in the cockpit. A 13-ampere-hour battery is connected to each dc bus during normal operation to prevent the bus voltage from dropping excessively during bus switching operations. The batteries also provide a self-contained engine-start capability.

The nacelles are tilted by ball-screw-jack actuators with hydraulic motors and electrically-powered servo valves. A triply redundant hydraulic power supply is provided for the conversion system because the XV-15 cannot be landed in the airplane mode without destroying the proprotor system. In the event of total electrical failure, the pilot still has mechanical access to hydraulic power to convert to the helicopter mode. The conversion system interconnect shaft provides a means to maintain both nacelles at the same angle and to provide power to drive the nacelle conversion in the event of a total power failure on one side. For flight operations, the pilot can select the normal 7.5-degree/per second rate continuous conversion (which completes the conversion in 12.5 seconds) or a slower rate of 1.5-degree/per second. The conversion can be stopped and steady flight performed at any point in the conversion envelope.

Fuel is supplied to each engine by separate fuel systems contained in each wing. Each system has two lightweight crash-resistant fuel cells which are interconnected to form a single tank. An electrically driven submerged boost pump is located at the lowest point of each tank. Interconnect valves and lines permit fuel transfer between tanks or supplying fuel to both engines from the same tank. With a complete loss of electrical power to both boost pumps, adequate fuel flow would be maintained by the engine-driven pumps up to an altitude of 10,000 feet. The 1,475 pounds of fuel carried in the wing allows a flight of one hour.

For ferry operations, Bell developed a removable internal tank that extends the duration of flight to more than two hours.

An environmental control system provides ventilation and temperature control. An air-cycle environmental control unit mounted in the aft fuselage is powered by bleed-air from the right engine. During hot day operation of the XV-15, the cooling capacity was found to be inadequate. To reduce crew station heating, the overhead windows were covered with an opaque coating during the late 1990s. Each crew seat is equipped with an oxygen system supplied from a 1,800-psi oxygen cylinder. Adequate oxygen for a one hour flight with a 20 percent reserve is carried onboard.

The design of the XV-15 TRRA incorporates many features and system redundancies intended to enhance the safety of this vehicle. Some of these are not expected to be included in civil aircraft of its weight class and, therefore, must be considered when evaluating the XV-15's weight and payload capacity. Among the additional items are the Rockwell International Model LW-3B ejection seats, capable of removing the crew members in flight or from a zero airspeed, ground-level (zero-zero) normal attitude condition. The ejection seats can be triggered independently or simultaneously by pilot command. In addition, the overhead and side windows can be removed by a mild detonator cord placed around the window frames. The window removal can be initiated from within the cockpit or from an external lever located under a door on the nose cone.

Figure A-8.
General layout and major components of the XV-15 tilt rotor research aircraft.

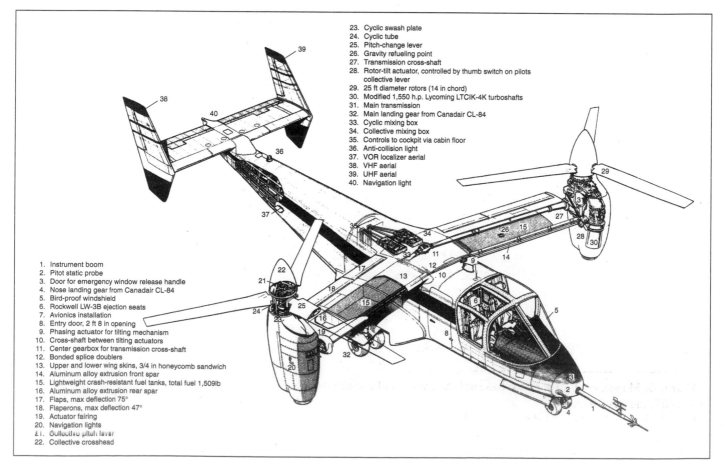

23. Cyclic swash plate
24. Cyclic tube
25. Pitch-change lever
26. Gravity refueling point
27. Transmission cross-shaft
28. Rotor-tilt actuator, controlled by thumb switch on pilots collective lever
29. 25 ft diameter rotors (14 in chord)
30. Modified 1,550 h.p. Lycoming LTCIK-4K turboshafts
31. Main transmission
32. Main landing gear from Canadair CL-84
33. Cyclic mixing box
34. Collective mixing box
35. Controls to cockpit via cabin floor
36. Anti-collision light
37. VOR localizer aerial
38. VHF aerial
39. UHF aerial
40. Navigation light

1. Instrument boom
2. Pitot static probe
3. Door for emergency window release handle
4. Nose landing gear from Canadair CL-84
5. Bird-proof windshield
6. Rockwell LW-3B ejection seats
7. Avionics installation
8. Entry door, 2 ft 8 in opening
9. Phasing actuator for tilting mechanism
10. Cross-shaft between tilting actuators
11. Center gearbox for transmission cross-shaft
12. Bonded splice doublers
13. Upper and lower wing skins, 3/4 in honeycomb sandwich
14. Aluminum alloy extrusion front spar
15. Lightweight crash-resistant fuel tanks, total fuel 1,509lb
16. Aluminum alloy extrusion rear spar
17. Flaps, max deflection 75°
18. Flaperons, max deflection 47°
19. Actuator fairing
20. Navigation lights
21. Collective pitch lever
22. Collective crosshead

A cutaway drawing showing the key components of the XV-15 is shown in figure A-8. Inboard profile drawings are provided in figures A-9 and A-10.[64]

As an example of the overall performance capabilities of the XV-15, the height-velocity flight envelope is shown in figure A-11. The variation of power with airspeed indicating the ability of the tilt rotor aircraft to operate over a broad range of airspeeds at power levels well below that required for hover is shown in figure A-12.[65]

Although only two XV-15 aircraft were built, the Government Project Office took the unusual step of directing the Bell Helicopter Company, under the TRRA Contract, to develop a complete flight manual. These manuals[66] became a valuable source of systems information for the flight and ground crews during the flight program and served as a training and familiarization tool for the many guest pilots.

---

[64] Martin D. Maisel, et al, "Tilt Rotor Research Aircraft Familiarization Document," NASA TM X-62.407, January 1975.

[65] W.L. Arrington, "Flight Test Report," Vol. I-V, NASA CR 177406 and USAACSCOM TR-86-A-1, June 1985.

[66] Anon., "XV-15 Flight Manual," Bell Helicopter Textron Report TP-78-XV-15-1, August 15, 1980.

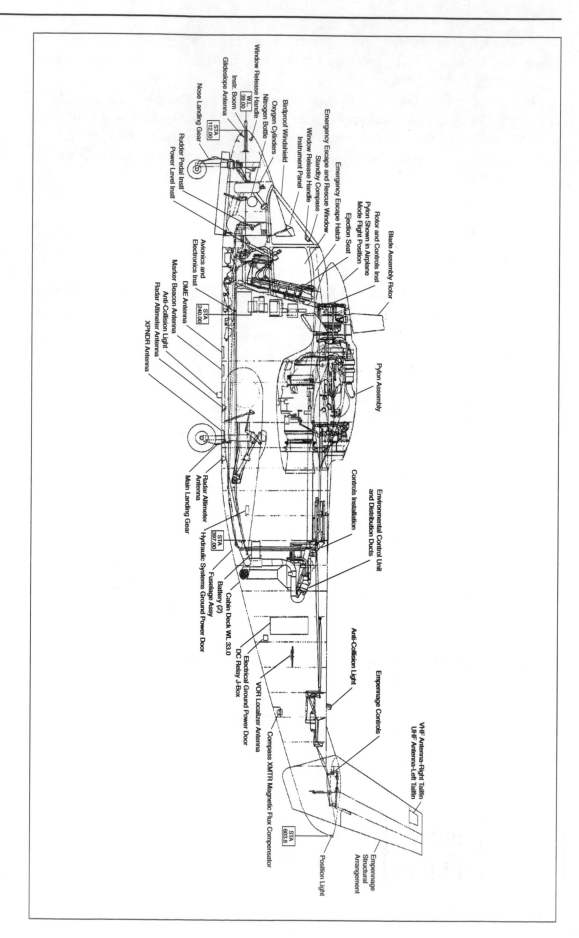

Figure A-9.
Side view inboard profile of the XV-15.

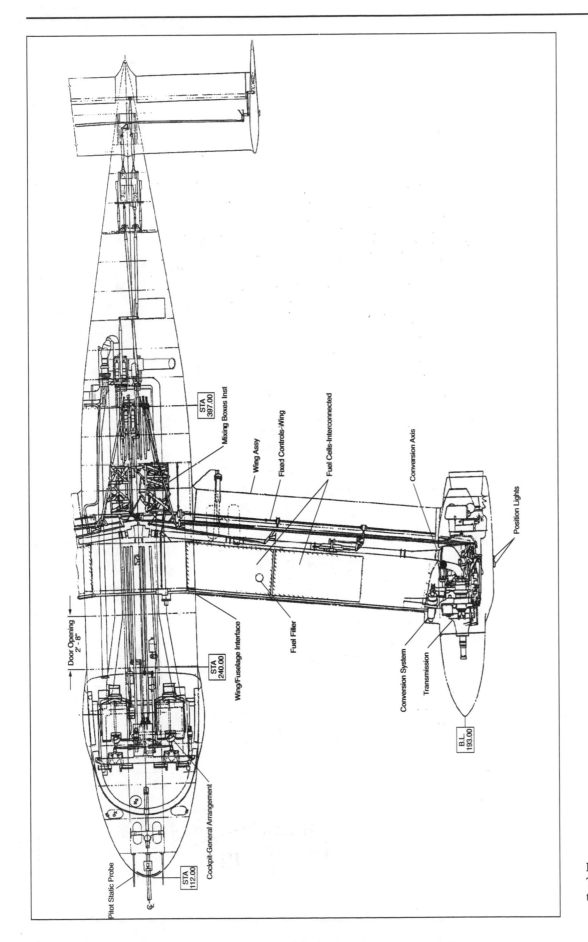

Figure A-10.
Top view inboard profile of the XV-15.

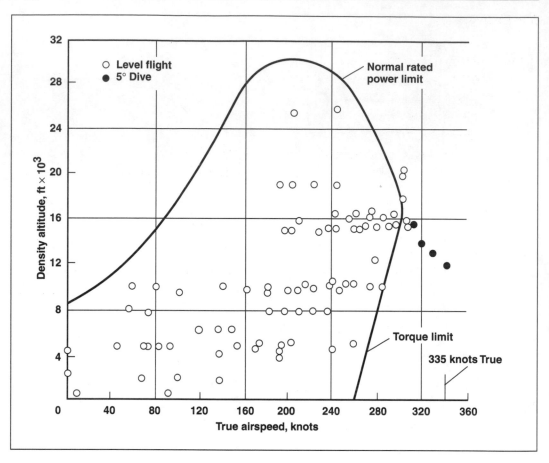

Figure A-11.
XV-15 height-velocity
envelope.

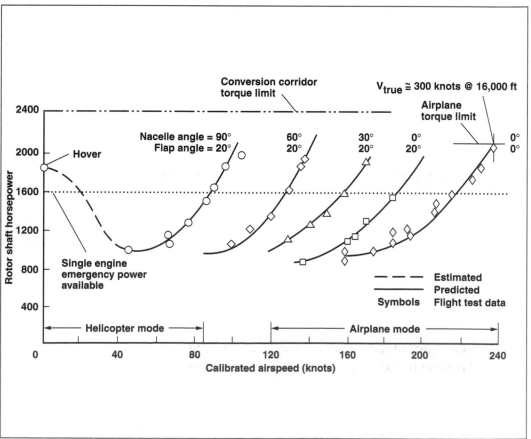

Figure A-12.
XV-15 variation of power
with airspeed.

Powerplant

    Two Lycoming LTC1K-41K turboshaft engines (modified T53L13B)

    Horsepower ratings

    Contingency (2 minutes) . . . . 1802 SHP

    Takeoff (10 minutes) . . . . 1550 SHP

    Normal (max. continuous) . . . . 1250 SHP

Length . . . . 42 ft 1 in (not including nose boom)

Wing

    Span . . . . 32 ft 2 in

    Area . . . . 169.0 sq ft

    Chord (constant) . . . . 5.25 ft

    Airfoil section . . . . NACA 64A223

    Sweep . . . . -6.5 degrees

    Dihedral . . . . 2.0 degrees

    Aspect ratio 6.12

Width . . . . 57 ft 2 in (to outer tip of
                                                proprotor disc)

Height . . . . 12 ft 8 in

Horizontal tail

    Span . . . . 12ft 10 in

    Area . . . . 50.25 sq ft

    Chord . . . . 3 ft 11 in

    Airfoil section . . . . NACA 64A015

    Aspect ratio 3.27

Vertical tail

    Area . . . . 50.5 sq ft

    Airfoil section . . . . NACA 0009

    Mean Aerodynamic Chord . . . . 3.72 ft

    Aspect Ratio 2.33

Proprotor

    No. of proprotors . . . . 2, interconnected

    Blades/proprotor 3

    Diameter . . . . 25 ft

    Chord (constant) . . . . 14.0 in

    Solidity 0.089

    Disc loading . . . . 13.2 lb/sq ft

    Twist, geometric (spinner to tip) . . . 36 degrees

    Delta 3 angle . . . . -15.0 degrees

Rotational speed

    Helicopter mode . . . . 589 rpm

    Airplane mode . . . . 517 rpm

Weight

        Design . . . . 13,000 lb

        Empty (actual). . . . . 10,083 lb

        Actual gross (at engine start) . . . . . . 13,248 lb

        Fuel . . . . 1,436 lb

        Research instrumentation. . . . . 1,148 lb

No. of seats. 2

Appendix B—Key Personnel

Key Tilt Rotor Research Aircraft Project Personnel[67]

WBS LEVEL: I II III IV	Bell	Army/NASA
V/STOL Tilt Rotor Research Aircraft Project		
Air Vehicle	Ken Wernicke	Kip Edenborough
	George Carter	Robby Robinson
Fuselage, Landing Gear, Empennage	George Carter	Robby Robinson
Fuselage	Ed Broman/Jerry Pickard	Robby Robinson
Landing Gear	George Carter	Robby Robinson
Empennage	George Carter	Robby Robinson
Wing, Nacelle	Pete Smith	Kip Edenborough
Wing	Pete Smith	Kip Edenborough
Nacelle	Ed Covington	Kip Edenborough
Rotors	Ernie Schellhase	Kip Edenborough
Blade Assembly	Ernie Schellhase	Kip Edenborough
Hub Assembly and Controls	Charlie Bradocks	Jim Weiberg
Transmission, Cross Shafting	J. D. Mooney	Jim Weiberg
Left/Right Transmission	J. D. Mooney	Jim Weiberg
Engine Coupling Gear box	J. D. Mooney	Jim Weiberg
Interconnect System	Norm Busbee	Jim Weiberg
Power Plant	Norm Busbee	Jim Weiberg
Engine	Norm Busbee	Jim Weiberg
Power Plant Installation	Norm Busbee	Marty Maisel
Fuel System	Jose Caero	Marty Maisel
Hydraulic System	Marvin Willis/Jim Sain	Marty Maisel
Electrical System	Ed Broman/	Marty Maisel
Environmental Control System	Claude Leibensberger	Shorty Schroers
Flight Control	Rod Wernicke/	Gary Churchill
Primary Flight Controls	Ray Conrad	Gary Churchill
Secondary Flight Controls	Ken Wernicke	Gary Churchill
Thrust/Power Management System	Paul Keefer	Gary Churchill
Automatic Flight Control	Paul Keefer	Gary Churchill
Crew Station	Paul Keefer	Shorty Schroers
Communication, Nav. Flight	Marvin Willis	Shorty Schroers
Instrument'n	Ken Wernicke	Al Gaehler/
	Dave Glass/	Mike Bondi
Research Instrumentation	Doug Winniford	John Hemiup
	Mike Kimbell/	John Hemiup
Support Equipment and Systems	Jerry Pickard	Dean Borgman/
Aircraft No. 1 Final Assembly	George Carter/	Marty Maisel
Analytical Integration	Pete Smith	John Hemiup
	Troy Gaffey/	Shorty Schroers
Aircraft No. 2 Final Assembly	Roger Marr	
Mock-up	Pete Smith	
	Pete Smith	

---

[67] Tilt rotor research aircraft project assignments, both at Bell and in the Government Project Office, changed during the activity. This list reflects the staff assignments during the project's first four years (1973-1977) when a large portion of the design, fabrication, and component testing was accomplished. The inclusion of a second name indicates where WBSE reassignments were made.

WBS LEVEL: I II III IV	Bell	Army/NASA
V/STOL Tilt Rotor Research Aircraft Project		
Test and Evaluation	Rod Wernicke	Kip Edenboroug
Component Acceptance Test	Mike Kimbell	Jim Lane
Component Development Tests	Rod Wernicke	Kip Edenborough
Systems Test	Mike Kimbell	John Hemiup
Structural Tests	Mike Kimbell	Kip Edenborough
Propulsion Tests	Mike Kimbell	Jim Welberg
Egress System Tests	Rod Wernicke/	
	Ray Conrad	Shorty Schroers
Integrated Systems Tests	Claude Liebensberger	
Ground Tiedown Aircraft Tests	Bill Martin	Al Gaehler
Wind Tunnel Aircraft Tests	Roger Marr	Jim Weiberg
Post Test Aircraft Refurbishment	Pete Smith	John Hemiup
Contractor Flight Tests	Roger Marr/	
Government Flight Tests	Shep Blackman	Shorty Schroers
Simulations	Roger Marr	Gary Churchill
Data and Documentation	Tommy Thomason	Dean Borgman
Test Plans, Procedures, and Test Reports	Mike Kimbell	John Hemiup
Design Reports and Specifications	Tommy Thomason	Dean Borgman
Inspection and maintenance Manual	Jerry Pickard	John Hemiup
Flight Operations Manual	Mike Kimbell	Shorty Schroers
Instrumentation and Data Acquisition Manual	Aaron Whitner/	Al Gaehler/
	Dave Glass	
System Safety and R&QA Plan		Mike Bondi
Spares	Tommy Thomason	Mike Carness
	Mike Kimbell/	
	Jerry Pickard	John Hemiup
Systems Project Management Plan	Lovette Coulter	Jim Diehl
Training	Jerry Pickard	Jim Diehl

Key Industry and Government Tilt Rotor Technology Personnel

Boeing Vertol (late 1960s to early 1970s)

V/STOL Technology Manager	Kenneth (Pip) Gilmore
Chief of Preliminary Design	David Richardson

Tilt Rotor Research Engineers

Aerodynamics Methodology	Allen Schoen
Preliminary Design and Performance	Harold (Hal) Rosenstein
Aeroelastics and Structural Dynamics	Harold (Alex) Alexander
Rotor Performance Methodology	John Magee
VTOL Propeller Design and Test	Marty Maisel
Aerodynamics	M. A. (Tony) McVeigh
Aerodynamics	Ross Clark
Aerodynamics	S. Jon Davis
VTOL Aircraft Design Unit Chief	Paul Dancik
Preliminary Design	Bernard (Bernie) Fry
Flight Controls	Gary Churchill

Bell Helicopter Company (late 1960s to early 1970s)

Director of Advanced Engineering, XV-3 Chief Engineer	Robert (Bob) Lichten
Chief of Advanced Design	Stanley (Stan) Martin
Manager, Applications Engineering	Richard (Dick) Spivey
IR&D Manager	Richard (Dick) Stansbury
Tilt Rotor Lead Design Engineer	Kenneth (Ken) Wernicke
Tilt Rotor Proposal Manager	Henry (Hank) Smyth

Tilt Rotor Research Engineers

Dynamics	Troy Gaffey
Dynamics	Jim Bilger
Dynamics	Kip Edenborough
Preliminary Design	Jack DeTore
Preliminary Design	Ken Sambell
Stress	Bob Gunderson
Design	Pete Smith
Fatigue Analysis	D. J. Reddy/Will Broekhuizen
Rotor Design	Ernie Schellhase/Ed Covington

US Army Air Mobility Research and Development Laboratory (late 1960s to early 1970s)

Director   Paul Yaggy
Deputy, Technical   Andrew (Andy) Morse
Test Pilot   Daniel (Dan) Dugan
Tilt Rotor Research Engineers
    Preliminary Design Methodology   Michael Scully
    Dynamics   Dave Sharpe
    Project Management   Dean Borgman

Aerodynamics, Performance   Marty Maisel (from 1970)
    Flight Controls   Gary Churchill (from 1971)
    Flight Test   Shorty Schroers (from 1972)
    Dynamics   Kip Edenborough (from 1972)

NASA Ames Research Center (late 1960s to early 1970s)

Director   Hans Mark
Director, Aeronautics and Flight Mechanics   Leonard Roberts
Deputy Director, Aeronautics and Flight Mechanics   John Boyd
Chief, V/STOL Projects Office   Woodrow L. (Woody) Cook
Manager, Advanced VTOL Projects Office   Wallace H. (Wally) Deckert
Chief, Full-Scale and Systems Research Division   Brad Wick
Research Engineers
    Dynamics   Wayne Johnson
    Rotor Dynamics Test   Jim Biggers
    V/STOL Wind Tunnel Test   Demo Giulianetti
    V/STOL Wind Tunnel Test   David Koenig
    V/STOL Wind Tunnel Test   William (Bill) Tolhurst
    Flight Data Acquisition   Herb Finger
    Instrumentation   Don Reynolds
    Test Pilot   Ronald (Ron) Gerdes

Tilt Rotor Research Aircraft Project Office

Bell

Program Manager	(1973-1975)	Henry (Hank) Smyth
	(1975-1981)	Tommy Thomason
	(1981-1984)	Lovette Coulter
	(1984-1990)	Ron Reber
Tilt Rotor IR&D Manager	(1990-1993)	William (Bill) McKinney
	(1993-1994)	Don Ferguson
XV-15 Project Manager	(1994-)	Colby Nicks
Deputy Program Manager	(1973-1975)	Tommy Thomason
	(1975-1981)	Lovette Coulter
	(1987-1989)	Jerry Pickard
Chief Project Engineer	(1973-1987)	Ken Wernicke
Chief Design Engineer	(1973-1978)	George Carter
Chief Technical Engineer	(1973-1975)	Troy Gaffey
Engineering Administrator	(1981-1990)	Mike Kimbell
Technology Manager		Roger Marr
Project Dynamicist		Jim Bilger
Test Pilots		Ron Erhart
		Dorman Cannon
		Roy Hopkins
		Tom Warren
		John Ball

Army/NASA

Project Manager	(1972-1977)	David Few
	(1977-1979)	Jim Brown
	(1979)	David Few (Acting)
	(1980-1984)	John Magee
	(1985-1994)	Bill Snyder
Deputy Project Manager	(1972-1974)	Dean Borgman
	(1975-1977)	Jim Brown
	(1977-1981)	Mike Carness
Deputy Project Manager, (Technical)	(1974-1979)	Kip Edenborough
	(1979-1980)	John Magee
Deputy Project Manager, (Army Liaison)	(1978-1981)	Clifford McKiethan
Resident Manager	(1973-1984)	Jim Lane

Army/NASA (continued)

Staff	(1972-1981)	Jerry Barrack
		Mike Bondi
		Dave Chappell
		Gary Churchill
		Kip Edenborough
		Al Gaehler
		John Hemiup
		Violet Lamica
		Jim MacDonnell
		John Magee
		Marty Maisel
		Robbie Robinson
		Shorty Schroers
		Victor (Tory) Stevens
		John Weyers
Test Pilots		Dan Dugan
		Ron Gerdes
		Grady Wilson
		George Tucker
		Rickey Simmons

XV-15 Principal Investigators

Discipline	Bell	Army/NASA
Flight Test Director	Shep Blackman	Shorty Schroers
	Bill Martin	Marty Maisel
	Colby Nicks	Brent Wellman
Flight Controls and Dynamics	Roger Marr	Gary Churchill
	Marvin Willis	Shorty Schroers
		Jim Weiberg
Structural Loads	Bob Gunderson	Dave Chappell
	D. J. Reddy	Shorty Schroers
	Jim Weiberg	
Aeroelastic Stability	M. J. Joglekar	Wally Acree
	Jim Bilger	Mark Tischler
Performance	Roger Marr	Marty Maisel
		Jim Weiberg
		Jerry Barrack
Acoustics	John Breiger	Marty Maisel
	Bryan Edwards	Dave Conner
	Suzanna Shank	Mike Marcolini
		Arnold Mueller
		Gloria Yamauchi
		Megan McCluer

XV-15 Ground Crew

Assignment	Bell	Army/NASA
Aircraft Manager/Engineer	Bill Martin	John Weyers
	Ted Turner	Jim McDonnell
	Jerry Pickard	Paul Espinosa
Crew Chief		Jerry Bree
		Dick Denman
Assistant Crew Chief		Dick Denman
		Kit Boyce
		Jim Lesko
Inspector		John Brown
		Jerry Bree
Instrumentation Engineer	Dave Glass	Tony Ogden
	Doug Winniford	John Lewis
Instrumentation Technician		Al Morningstar
		Duane Allen
		Alex Macalma
		John Wilson

Appendix C—Chronology

1452-1519	Leonardo da Vinci credited with the design of the first helicopter, basically a helical airscrew.
1924	Henry Berliner flies fixed-wing biplane with large diameter fixed-pitch propeller mounted on a tiltable vertical shaft near the tip of each wing.
September 1930	"Flying Machine" patent, issued to George Lehberger, employs use of a relatively low disc loading thruster (propeller) that can tilt its axis from the vertical (for vertical lift) to the horizontal (for propulsive thrust).
Late 1930s	Baynes Heliplane patent issued in England.
1937	Focke-Wulf Fw-61 (Germany) lateral-twin rotor helicopter flown.
1942	Focke-Achgelis FA-269 trail-rotor convertiplane project initiated.
Early 1940s	Platt-LePage Aircraft Company conduct preliminary design work on tilt rotor aircraft.
January 1947	Mario Guerrieri and Robert Lichten establish Transcendental Aircraft Company to develop convertiplane (tilt rotor aircraft).
August 1950	U. S. Army and U. S. Air Force announce competition to design a Convertiplane. Bell Helicopter and Transcendental Aircraft submit bids.
May 1951	USAF Air Research and Development Command awards contract to Bell to build mockup and begin detailed design of a flight tilt rotor aircraft.
October 1953	Award of U.S. Air Force contract for development, prototype construction, and testing of two XH-33 (later designated XV-3) full-scale "tilting-thrust-vector convertiplanes" to Bell Helicopter Company.
15 June 1954	First flight of Transcendental Aircraft Corporation Model 1-G tilt rotor aircraft.
15 February 1955	Platt patent of tilt rotor aircraft, No. 2,702,168 granted.
February 1955	First XV-3 rolled out.

20 July 1955	Transcendental Model 1-G crashes. Had previously flown from helicopter configuration to within 10 degrees of airplane configuration.
11 August 1955	First hover flight of XV-3. Piloted by Bell Chief Helicopter Test Pilot Floyd Carlson.
25 October 1956	XV-3 (tail number 4147) crashes due to a severe rotor instability injuring Bell test pilot Dick Stansbury.
1957	Transcendental Model 2 program terminated as Government funding shifts to Bell XV-3.
18 December 1958	XV-3 achieves first full in-flight conversion from helicopter to airplane mode and from airplane to helicopter mode. World's record event. Piloted by Bell XV-3 project test pilot Bill Quinlan.
6 February 1959	USAF Captain Robert G. Ferry first military pilot to execute full conversion of XV-3.
1 May 1959	XV-3 shipped to Edwards Air Force Base for Phase II Flight Test Program. Flight testing begins 15 May 1959.
12 August 1959	First hovering, altitude, and full conversion flight of XV-3 by a NASA test pilot Fred Drinkwater.
8 August 1961	U.S. Army test pilot Major E. E. Kluever conducts first flight evaluation of the XV-3 by an Army pilot.
June/July 1962	XV-3 (tail number 4148) with new rotor system tested in ARC 40- by 80-foot wind tunnel.
April 1966	Analysis explaining the tilt rotor aircraft rotor/pylon/wing aeroelastic instability issued by Dr. Earl Hall of Bell.
14 June 1966	NASA Ames Research Center announces completion of XV-3 testing. Total of 250 flights accomplished, 125 flight hours, 110 full conversions.
May 1968	Aeroelastic stability obtained for a gimbaled proprotor using positive pitch-flap coupling documented by Troy Gaffey of Bell.
October/November 1968	Ames wind tunnel test of modified XV-3 validated predicted rotor/pylon/wing aeroelastic stability.

1968	Boeing Vertol awarded contract NAS2-5025 from Ames to investigate the effect of blade twist on the performance of model-scale proprotors. Several performance tests were conducted between 1969 and 1973 in the Army 7- by 10-foot wind tunnel at Ames, the Ames 40-by 80-foot wind tunnel, and the ONERA (Office National d'Etudes et de Recherches Aerospatiales) 8-meter (26-foot) diameter S-1 wind tunnel in Modane-Avrieux, France.
1969	Contract NAS2-5386 awarded to Bell for the Ames 40-by 80-foot wind tunnel aeroelastic stability tests of 25-foot diameter gimbaled proprotor.
November 1970	Performance tests conducted with Bell 25-foot diameter proprotor in the Ames 40- by 80-foot wind tunnel as part of contract NAS2-5386.
1971	Woodrow L. Cook appoints manager of the V/STOL Projects Office (for the development and flight investigation of powered lift V/STOL aircraft) by Dr. Leonard Roberts, Director of the NASA Ames Aeronautics and Flight Mechanics Directorate. Cook's deputy and manager of the Advanced VTOL Projects Office was Wally Deckert.
August 1971	Contracts awarded to Boeing Vertol (NAS2-6598) and Bell (NAS2-6599) to conduct preliminary tilt rotor aircraft design studies.
18 September 1971	Robert Lichten, Bell's director of advanced engineering and chief engineer for the XV-3 project, dies following an automobile accident.
12 October 1971	NASA Ames Research Center awarded Bell contract for engineering study and a report to define future military and commercial applications of tilt rotor vehicles.
1 November 1971	"An Agreement Between the National Aeronautics and Space Administration and the Department of the Army for the Joint Development and Operation of Tilt Rotor Proof-of-Concept Research Vehicles at the Ames Research Center" signed.
January 1972	Boeing contract NAS2-6598 was extended to include a preliminary design of an advanced composite wing and to define a gust and blade load alleviation feedback control system for tilt rotor aircraft.

February 1972	Bell's tilt-fold-stowed tilt rotor tested in the Ames 40- by 80-foot wind tunnel under contract NAS2-5461.
August 1972	Boeing conducts dynamics tests of its 26-foot diameter hingeless, soft-in-plane proprotor in the Ames 40- by 80-foot wind tunnel under Army-funded contract NAS2-6505.
September, October, December 1972	Hover tests of 1/5 scale powered aeroelastic model of the Bell Model 300 tilt rotor aircraft conducted under Ames contract NAS2-6599 to examine performance and dynamic characteristics for near-ground operations.
20 October 1972	Two fixed-price contracts of $0.5M each awarded by Ames to Boeing-Vertol (contract NAS2-7259) and Bell (contract NAS2-7260) for preliminary aircraft design studies and the development of a program plan for a minimum-size tilt rotor research aircraft that could meet proof-of-concept objectives.
December 1972	Performance tests of Boeing 26-foot diameter hingeless, soft-in-plane proprotor conducted the Ames 40- by 80-foot wind tunnel.
22 January 1973	Proposals received at Ames from Boeing Vertol and Bell for the design, fabrication, and testing of two Tilt Rotor research aircraft.
January-March 1973	Low speed wind tunnel tests conducted by Bell to document the performance and static stability of a 1/5 scale powered aeroelastic tilt rotor model.
March 1973	Ames contracted with Bell (NAS2-7308) and made arrangements with the Air Force Aero Propulsion Laboratory (AFAPL) at Wright-Patterson Air Force Base for the hover performance test of the Bell 25-foot diameter proprotor.
13 April 1973	Bell Helicopter Company, Fort Worth, Texas, selected for negotiations leading to a contract for the design, fabrication, and testing of two tilt rotor aircraft.
31 July 1973	Phase II-A 60-day planning limited level of effort activity for the development of the tilt rotor research aircraft awarded to Bell.
30 September 1973	"Go-ahead" given to Bell for the design, fabrication, and test of two V/STOL tilt rotor research aircraft (Contract NAS2-7800).

November, December 1973	Initial piloted simulations conducted in the Ames Flight Simulator for Advanced Aircraft (FSAA) employing simulation math models developed by Boeing Vertol and Bell. The math model created by P. B. Harendra and M. J. Joglekar of Bell became the basis for the generic tilt rotor math model used for Ames piloted simulations into the late 1990s.
May 1974	Initial publication of aeroelastic stability analysis developed by Dr. Wayne Johnson was issued.
September 1974	Dr. Irving Statler becomes director, U.S. Army Air Mobility Research and Development Laboratory following retirement of Paul Yaggy.
July 1975	Demonstration of simultaneous XV-15 ejection seat operation.
14 October 1975	XV-15 tilt rotor research aircraft entered final assembly stage.
22 October 1976	Official roll-out ceremony for XV-15, N703NA at Bell.
1 May 1977	XV-15 N702NA completes ground tiedown development tests at Bell.
3 May 1977	First hover and low speed flight with XV-15 N702NA piloted by Bell Experimental Test Pilots Ron Erhart and Dorman Cannon.
23 March 1978	XV-15 N702NA transported to Ames Research Center, Moffett Field, California, onboard an Air Force C-5A.
4 May thru 23 June 1978	Ames 40- by 80-foot wind tunnel test of XV-15 N702NA.
July 1978	Army/NASA/Navy Memorandum of Agreement established providing Navy funding and for shipboard evaluation of TRRA.
27 August 1978	XV-15 N703NA begins ground run tests at Bell.
23 April 1979	First flight of XV-15 N703NA performed at the Bell Flight Test Center, Arlington Municipal Airport, Texas.
24 July 1979	First full in-flight conversion from helicopter-to-airplane mode accomplished by Bell with XV-15, aircraft N703NA.

5 December 1979	Uneventful landing of XV-15 N702NA following sudden in-flight engine failure.
5 June 1980	Major William S. "Bill" Lawrence, USMC becomes first military pilot to fly the XV-15.
9 June 1980	Major Ron Carpenter becomes the first U.S. Army evaluation pilot to fly the XV-15.
17 June 1980	XV-15 N703NA flown in the airplane mode, level flight at a record true airspeed of 301 knots (346 mph).
13 August 1980	XV-15 N703NA airlifted to DFRC from Bell.
30 October 1980	Formal Government acceptance ceremony of XV-15 N703NA held on at Dryden Flight Research Center.
28 April 1981	XV-15 N702NA transported to Farnborough, England, onboard a MAC C-5A and a C-141 aircraft.
4-14 June 1981	XV-15 performs daily flight exhibitions at the Paris Air Show, Le Bourget, France. First tilt rotor aircraft public demonstration.
September 1981	Army/NASA TRRA Project Office declares that the primary proof-of-concept project objectives have been successfully completed.
28 September 1981	Army/NASA TRRA team at Ames provides first guest pilot demonstration for General Story Stevens, Commander, U.S. Army Aviation and Troop Command.
26 October 1981	XV-15 N702NA ferried back to the Bell Flight Test Center at Arlington, Texas, from California to allow Bell to continue flight research and to conduct military applications evaluations. Longest cross-country flight to date covered 1700 statute miles with an average ground speed of 334 mph.
30 October 1981	U.S. Senator Goldwater becomes the first non-test pilot to fly in Tilt Rotor aircraft in Bell's guest pilot program. At end of flight he said, "The tilt rotor is the biggest advance in aviation in a quarter of a century."
December 1981	Deputy Secretary of Defense establishes Joint Services Advanced Vertical Lift Aircraft (JVX) Program.

24 March 1982	XV-15 demonstrated at NASA Langley, Virginia.
26 March 1982	Secretary of the Navy John Lehman flies XV-15 at Quantico USMC Air Station, Virginia.
29-30 March 1982	XV-15 demonstrated at Davison Army Air Field, Fort Belvoir, Virginia.
31 March 1982	XV-15 displayed at Pentagon.
7 June 1982	Bell Helicopter and Boeing Vertol announces teaming agreement to propose a tilt rotor aircraft for the Joint Services Advanced Vertical Lift Aircraft (JVX) Program competition.
8 July 1982	XV-15 low level nap-of-the-earth and evasive maneuver flight evaluations at Ft. Huachuca, Arizona.
July 1982	XV-15 flight demonstration at Yuma, Arizona.
2, 4, 5 August 1982	XV-15 demonstrates tilt rotor shipboard operations onboard *USS Tripoli* (LPH 10) in waters off the coast of southern California... . Fifty-four takeoffs and landings completed.
14 December 1982	Ten service-specific missions established for the proposed joint services aircraft in a Joint Services Operational Requirement (JSOR) document. This led to the establishment of the joint services tilt rotor, or JVX program. The JVX program marked the first time that an aircraft had been assigned a multimission role to serve all four services.
17 February 1983	Bell-Boeing Vertol proposes a tilt rotor aircraft to the U.S. Navy for the JVX Program.
19-24 May 1983	LCDR John C. Ball, USN, evaluates the potential of the tilt rotor aircraft to perform combat SAR and external lift applications. Demonstrated over-water rescue and cargo hookup capabilities at Dallas Naval Air Station, Texas.
10 October 1983	Completion of XV-15 military mission evaluation tests at Marine Corps Air Station, Yuma, Arizona.
8 June 1984	Naval Air Systems Command awarded Bell and Boeing contract for second stage of JVX tilt rotor preliminary design.

15 July 1984	Bell-Boeing submitted a joint Full-Scale Development JVX proposal to Naval Air Systems Command.
10-13 September 1984	XV-15 flown over the nap-of-the-earth course at Fort Rucker, Alabama.
18-26 September 1984	XV-15 demonstrates air-to-air evasive maneuvers, slope landings and aerial refueling capabilities at Patuxent River Naval Air Station, Maryland.
28 September- 2 October 1984	XV-15 demonstrated at USMC Air Station, Quantico, Virginia.
2 October 1984	XV-15 demonstrated flight from downtown New York City to downtown Washington, D.C., in 45 minutes.
5 October 1984	Bell completed a 3500-mile demonstration tour with XV-15... 54 flights in 20 flying days, 21 evaluation flights, five military pilots, and 16 guest pilots.
15 January 1985	Navy Secretary John Lehman announced that the official name for the JVX aircraft is "Osprey."
July 1985	Flight evaluation of a three-axis sidestick controller performed in XV-15 N703NA by Ames.
2 May 1986	U.S. Naval Air Systems Command awards Bell-Boeing Vertol contract for seven-year Full Scale Development Program for V-22.
21 May 1986	As part of the Bell "guest pilot" program Colonel Harry M. Blot, USNAVAIRSYSCOM V-22 program manager, flew the XV-15 for his first official tilt rotor flight.
June 1986	A new contract is awarded to the Bell-Boeing V-22 team by NAVAIR following a year of program reassessment and negotiations. The new contract called for a fixed-price development for the first three production lots, totaling 228 aircraft. Six prototype aircraft were to be built under the full-scale development contract.
18 December 1986	Department of Defense approved the full scale development program for the V-22 Osprey.

30 July 1987	FAA/NASA/DOD Tilt Rotor Applications Forum announces results of U.S. Government study on civil use of tilt rotor aircraft titled "Civil TiltRotor Missions and Applications: A Research Study."
30 July 1987	Port Authority of New York and New Jersey released results of their civil tilt rotor study that assesses the feasibility of tilt rotors in commercial air transportation infrastructure.
30 July 1987	U.S. Department of Transportation, Transportation Systems Center, released "Civil TiltRotor Industrial Base Impact Study."
31 August 1987	FAA Administrator T. Allan McArtor flew XV-15 and made TiltRotor certification a top priority of his agency.
22 October 1987	Cracks in the skins of two left proprotor blades grounded XV-15 N702NA.
13 November 1987	First hover flight of composite proprotor blades on XV-15 N703NA.
18 November 1987	Congressional hearing on "Civil Application of Tilt Rotor" sponsored by Subcommittee on Transportation, Aviation & Materials of the House Committee on Science, Space, and Technology.
18 November 1987	U.S. Army announces withdrawal from V-22 program.
16 May 1988	XV-15 N702NA returns to flight status with metal blades from N703NA.
23 May 1988	V-22 roll-out takes place in ceremonies at Bell's Flight Research Center.
20 July 1988	Bell-Boeing V-22 Joint Program Office formally applies to FAA for commercial certification of the V-22.
12 August 1988	Memorandum of Understanding signed between FAA and DoD allowing FAA participation in DoD's V-22 flight test program.
19 March 1989	First flight of V-22 aircraft no. 1.
14 September 1989	V-22 aircraft no. 1 achieved first full conversion to airplane mode.

9 November 1989	FAA published "National Civil TiltRotor Initiative Implementation Plan" which initiated civil tilt rotor activity in the Department of Transportation and other Government agencies.
1 December 1989	Deputy Secretary of Defense instructed Navy Secretary to terminate all contracts funded with FY89 advanced procurement funds which effectively would end the V-22 program.
February 1990	Department of Defense budget submission for FY91 contained no funds for V-22.
4 February 1990	XV-15 flew in opening ceremony of Helicopter Association International (Heli-Expo '90) in Dallas, Texas.
7 March 1990	General Accounting Offices charged Department of Defense acted improperly in terminating V-22 contracts funded with FY89 advanced procurement funds.
15 March 1990	XV-15 set five new world records: 1. Attained 3000 meters altitude in four minutes, 24.5 seconds. 2. Attained 600 meters altitude in eight minutes, 29 seconds. 3. Attained altitude of 22,600 feet. 4. Cruised in horizontal flight at 22,600 feet. 5. Flight altitude with payload (1,000 kg) record reached.
15 April 1990	XV-15 sets Federation Aeronautique Internationale time-to-climb records and maximum altitude records.
19 April 1989	Revised DoD budget for FY90 deleted—all V-22 funding.
25 April 1990	XV-15 N702NA landed on the east lawn of the Capitol during the time that the House Aviation Subcommittee held hearings on civil applications of tilt rotor technology.
1 May 1991	XV-15 N702NA wing was damaged by an in-flight collision with a bird. Aircraft was repaired and returned to flight 8 October 1991.
May 1990	First formal evaluation of V-22 by Government pilots completed. The V-22 demonstrated excellent potential for its intended missions.

6 May 1990	V-22 aircraft no. 2 conducts first cross-country flight from Arlington, Texas, to Wilmington, Delaware (1,210 nm, 1,392 miles) in 5.2 hours with a refueling stop in Atlanta, Georgia.
21 August 1990	V-22 reached 340 knots (391 mph) in level flight and 349 knots (402 mph) true air speed in a 1,200 feet per minute dive.
29 October 1990	Secretary of Transportation, Samuel Skinner, flew XV-15 and proclaimed the tilt rotor a commercial aircraft of the future.
November 1990	FAA publishes "Rotorcraft Master Plan" that includes the civil tilt rotor as a major Agency initiative.
4-7 December 1990	V-22 sea trials aboard *USS Wasp*.
4 February 1991	FY92 and FY93 Department of Defense budget submission contains no funding for the V-22.
19 February 1991	NASA publishes "Civil Tilt Rotor Missions and Applications Phase II: The Commercial Passenger Market." Press conference held in Washington.
11 June 1991	First flight of V-22 aircraft no. 5 terminated in a crash at Wilmington, Delaware, which result in a suspension of the V-22 flight test program.
6 September 1991	Failure of composite blade cuff retention causes emergency landing of XV-15 N703NA.
10 September 1991	V-22 full scale development flight tests resumed with flight of aircraft no. 3 at BHTI Flight Research Center.
9 October 1991	A bill is introduced in the House of Representatives that would establish a Civil TiltRotor Development Advisory Committee. A similar bill was introduced in the Senate on 26 November.
22 November 1991	Congress submitted National Authorization and Appropriation Bills for FY92 to the President that provided the V-22 program with $790 million which included $165 million from prior year funds for the development, manufacture, and operational test of three production representative aircraft and an additional $15 million for a special operations variant of the V-22.

26 November 1991	President signs Appropriations Act. Authorization Act signed 5 December 1991.
February 1992	The FY93 Department of Defense budget submission contained no funding for the V-22.
20 July 1992	V-22 aircraft no. 4 crashes in the Potomac River during ferry flight from Eglin Air Force Base to Quantico Marine Corps Air Station. All V-22 flight tests suspended. Later investigations found the cause of the crash was a correctable mechanical problem. No basic flaws were found in tilt rotor design or concept.
4 August 1992	Department of Defense awards a contract to Bell for the construction and flight demonstration of two short-range unmanned aerial vehicles (Bell Eagle Eye UAV).
20 August 1992	XV-15 (N702NA) crashes at Arlington, Texas, airport on completion of a demonstration flight as the result of a bolt that worked loose in a flight control connecting rod.
2 October 1992	U.S. Navy Mishap Board releases findings that a fire in the right-hand nacelle, coupled with a fire-induced failure of the interconnect drive shaft connecting the proprotor gearbox and the tilt-axis gearbox caused the crash of aircraft no. 4 on 20 July 1992.
23 October 1992	A new Engineering and Manufacturing Development letter contract was awarded to the Bell-Boeing Team for the V-22 Osprey program. The letter contract provided initial funding of $550 million on a contract that would total more than $2 billion.
31 October 1992	The President signs the Aviation Reauthorization Act that established a Civil TiltRotor Development Advisory Committee under the Department of Transportation to evaluate the technical feasibility of developing civil tilt rotor aircraft and a national system of infrastructure to support the incorporation of tilt rotor aircraft technology into the national transportation system.
18 May 1993	The U.S. Navy Air Systems Command cleared the V-22 to continue flight tests following the U.S. Navy Mishap Board findings of 2 October 1992.

14 June 1993	The Department of Transportation issues an order establishing the Civil TiltRotor Development Advisory Committee.
10 July 1993	The Bell eagle eye tilt rotor unmanned aerial vehicle successfully completed its first flight.
September 1993	President Bush reinstates production V-22 program.
21 April 1994	New Memorandum of Agreement signed between Army/NASA and Bell for bailment of XV-15 N703NA to Bell.
9 December 1994	Secretary of Defense, William Perry, announces that the V-22 will be produced for the United States Marine Corps and Special Operations Forces. Low rate initial production was announced for 1996 through 2001.
December 1994	Bell begins Model D-600 commercial tilt rotor program. (Later designated BB-609 and then BA-609)
Early 1995	NASA Administrator Daniel Goldin announced termination of flight operations at NASA ARC.
3 March 1995	XV-17 N703NA returns to flight at the Bell Flight Test Center, Arlington, Texas.
21 April 1995	XV-15 becomes first tilt rotor to land at the world's first operational vertiport, the Dallas Convention Center Heliport/Vertiport.
June 1995	XV-17 (N703NA) joins the Bell-Boeing V-22 Osprey at the 41st Paris Air Show.
10 July 1995	XV-15 puts on first tilt rotor flight demonstration in Canada at Bell Helicopter Mirabel facility near Montreal, Quebec.
11 July 1995	XV-15 is first tilt rotor to land at the Indianapolis Heliport.
December 1995	Findings of CTRDAC state that the civil tilt rotor transport is technically feasible and can be developed by the U.S. industry. However, additional research and development and infrastructure planning are needed.

August 1996	Boeing becomes partner with Bell in BB609 program.
February 1997	V-22 production contract awarded to Bell-Boeing team.
February 1997	First flight of first V-22 EMD (Engineering Manufacturing Development) aircraft (Ship Number 7).
June 1997	First public showing of full-scale BB-609 mockup at Paris Air Show.
March 1998	Boeing withdraws from BB-609 program.
September 1998	Bell announces a joint venture with the Agusta Helicopter Company of Italy in the now renamed BA-609 commercial tilt rotor aircraft program.
14 May 1999	Delivery of first production V-22 Osprey rotor aircraft to the U.S. Marine Corps.

Appendix D—Awards and Records

Over the years the engineers, designers, and test pilots of the tilt rotor aircraft have been recognized by leading American aviation technical organizations and societies for having made important contributions to the state of the art. These awards, including the most prestigious symbols of aeronautical achievement in the United States, indicated the high level of technical competence, perseverance, and commitment that the award recipients, and the entire tilt rotor "supporting cast" demonstrated to accomplish the project's goals. Looking back, it seems that the tilt rotor's technical problems were solved not by engineering alone, but by the magical effects of the positive spirit exhibited by the industry and Government tilt rotor team.

XV-3

8 May 1959
Dr. Alexander Klemin Award (American Helicopter Society) presented to Robert L. Lichten, Bell chief experimental project engineer, for development of the tilt rotor type convertiplane.

10 October 1959
Iven C. Kincheloe Award (Society of Experimental Test Pilots) presented to XV-3 test pilot USAF Major Robert G. Ferry, designating him as test pilot of the year.

XV-15

13 December 1976
Laurels (Aviation Week and Space Technology) to Tommy Thomason, Textron Bell Helicopter Div., and David Few, NASA/Army program director for driving the XV-15 tilt-rotor research program through budgetary knotholes to the prospects for technical success that open a promising line for rotary-wing vehicle future applications.

15 May 1978
Paul E. Haueter Memorial Award (American Helicopter Society) presented to Ken Wernicke, Bell Helicopter technical manager of tilt rotor programs.

16 November 1979
NASA Group Achievement Award awarded to the Bell and Army/NASA XV-15 tilt rotor research aircraft team.

16 November 1979
NASA Exceptional Service Medal awarded to David Few for leadership of the augmentor wing jet STOL research aircraft project and the tilt rotor research aircraft project.

13 May 1980
Frederick L. Feinberg Award (American Helicopter Society) presented to Bell Helicopter pilots Ron Erhart and Dorman Cannon for the most outstanding helicopter piloting achievement during 1979 testing of the XV-15.

1 October 1980	Iven C. Kincheloe Award (Society of Experimental Test Pilots) presented to Bell XV-15 test pilots Ron Erhart and Dorman Cannon, designating them test pilots of the year.
20 May 1981	Grover P. Bell Award (American Helicopter Society) presented to the NASA/Army/Bell XV-15 Project Team for "outstanding achievement in successfully demonstrating the feasibility and potential of TiltRotor technology."
10 September 1981	Kelly Johnson Award (Society of Flight Test Engineers) presented to the XV-15 flight test team.
18 October 1983	Aircraft Design Award (American Institute of Aeronautics and Astronautics) presented to Ken Wernicke, Bell Helicopter technical manager of tilt rotor programs.
29 May 1986	Harmon Trophy presented by President Ronald Reagan to XV-15 pilot Dorman Cannon for the most outstanding achievement in the art of flying in 1983.

V-22

7 May 1990	Paul E. Haueter Memorial Award (American Helicopter Society) presented to the Bell-Boeing and NAVAIR V-22 team for "significant contributions to development of VTOL aircraft other than helicopters."
17 May 1991	1990 Collier Trophy (National Aeronautics Association) presented to the V-22 tilt rotor team for the greatest achievement in aeronautics demonstrated by actual use during 1990.

Model 609

9 February 1998	Laurels (Aviation Week and Space Technology) to Webb Joiner and John P. Magee of Bell and Anthony M. Parasida of Boeing Aircraft and Missiles Systems for the "development of the 609 and the foresight to launch a unique mode of civil transportation using tilt rotor technology."

Records

The XV-15 TRRA provided an opportunity for setting new performance records for rotorcraft and Bell stepped up to the challenge. On June 17, 1980, XV-15 N703NA was flown in the airplane mode at a true airspeed of 301 knots (346 mph), exceeding the speed of any prior low disc loading rotorcraft not having a separate cruise-mode propulsion device, and establishing an unofficial world's speed record. In addition, the following six new FAI (Federation Aeronautique Internationale) official records were set with the XV-15, aircraft N702NA. On April 15, 1990, in the "without payload" category, the XV-15 achieved a time-to-climb record of 4 minutes and 24 seconds to reach an altitude of 3000 meters (9842 feet) and 8 minutes and 28 seconds to reach an altitude of 6000 meters (19684 feet). A record maximum altitude of 6,907 meters (22,660 feet) was reached and a record sustained horizontal flight altitude of 6,876 meters (22,560 feet) was recorded (also without payload). On the second flight of that day, a record altitude for this category with 1,000 kg (2,205 lb.) of payload was obtained (6,879 meters, 22,560 feet). The official record for speed of 247.56 knots (284.89 mph) over a recognized course was set on April 4, 1990, during a flight from Arlington Municipal Airport, Texas, to Baton Rouge, Louisiana, a distance of 611.5 kilometers (380 statute miles).

Figure D-1.
Jean Tinsley, first woman to fly the XV-15 tilt rotor aircraft.
(Ames Photograph A90-0218-1)

Another interesting first occurred on April 23, 1990, when Jean Tinsley, an accomplished aviatrix and member of the renowned "Whirly Girls" club, became the first woman to pilot a tilt rotor aircraft (figure D-1). This "first" added to several rotorcraft records already credited to her.

Appendix E—Photo Gallery

Figure E-1.
XV-3 at Bell ramp, 1953.
(Bell Photograph XV-3-35)

Figure E-2.
Bell XV-3 personnel in front of the XV-15 research aircraft.
(Bell Photograph 308597)

Figure E-3.
XV-15 flying by the
Statue of Liberty.
(Ames Photograph
AC86-0410-4)

Figure E-4.
XV-15 flying near the
Washington Monument.
(Ames Photograph
AC86-0410-2)

Figure E-5.
XV-15 flyby at the
Jefferson Memorial.
(Ames Photograph
AC86-0410-3)

Figure E-6.
XV-15 landing at the
Capitol Building.
(Bell Photograph 037868)

Figure E-7.
Bell test pilots Roy Hopkins
and Dorman Cannon.
(Bell Photograph 037868)

Figure E-8.
XV-15 in executive
transport markings.
(Bell Photograph 043100)

Figure E-9.
XV-15 in camouflage
markings.
(Bell Photograph 024741)

Figure E-10.
XV-15 in Navy gray
flying over the *USS Tripoli*,
August 1982.
(Ames Photograph
AC82-0612-25)

Figure E-11.
Ken Wernicke, Bell tilt rotor
design engineer, 1965.
(Bell Photograph 262938)

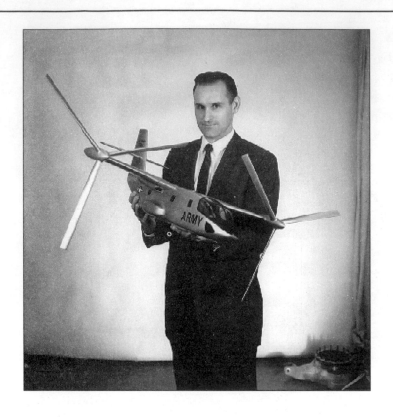

Figure E-12.
Ken Wernicke after
flying XV-15.
(Bell Photograph 05590)

Figure E-13.
XV-15 N702NA crew
station (1982).
(Ames Photograph
AC82-0493-6)

Figure E-14.
Composite photograph
showing V-22 Osprey in
hover, conversion, and
airplane mode flight.
(Bell Photograph 039956)

Appendix F—Bibliography

Tilt Rotor Related Publications

Acree, C. W.; Jr. Tischler, M. B. "Using Frequency-Domain Methods to Identify XV-15 Aeroelastic Modes." NASA TM-100033, November 1987.

Acree, C. W., Jr. "An Improved CAMRAD Model for Aeroelastic Stability Analysis of the XV-15 With Advanced Technology Blades." NASA TM-4448, 1993.

Acree, C. W., Jr.; Tischler, M. B. "Identification of XV-15 Aeroelastic Modes Using Frequency Sweeps." *Journal of Aircraft,* vol. 26 no. 7, July 1989, pp. 667-674.

Acree, C. W., Jr.; Tischler, Mark B. "Determining XV-15 Aeroelastic Modes from Flight Data with Frequency-Domain Methods." NASA TP-3330 and ATCOM Technical Report 93-A-004, 1993.

Acree, C. W., Jr.; Tischler, Mark B. "Frequency-Domain Identification of Aeroelastic Modes." NASA Tech Brief ARC-12407, 1991.

Acree, Cecil W., Jr.; Tischler, Mark B. "Identification of XV-15 Aeroelastic Modes Using Frequency-Domain Methods." NASA TM-101021, 1989.

Ahuja, K. K. "Tilt Rotor Aircraft Noise: A Summary of the Presentations and Discussions at the 1991 FAA/Georgia Tech Workshop." DOT/FAA/RD-91, 1992.

Alexander H. R.; Amos, A. K.; Tarzanin, F. J.; Taylor, R. B. "V/STOL Dynamics and Aeroelastic Rotor-Airframe Technology." AFFDL-TR-72-40, vol. 2, Boeing Vertol Co., September 1972.

Alexander, H. R.; et al: "Preliminary Design Study of Advanced Composite Blade and Hub and Nonmechanical Control System." NASA CR-152336, November 1979.

Alexander, H. R.; Hengen, L. M.; Weiberg, J. A. "Aeroelastic Stability Characteristics of a V/STOL Tilt Rotor Aircraft with Hingeless Blades: Correlation of Analysis and Test." AHS Preprint 835, Presented at AHS 30th National Forum, Washington, D.C., May 1974.

Alexander, H. R.; Kuntz, W. H.; Wasserman, L. S. "Dynamically Similar Model Tests of Rotary Wing and Propeller Types of VTOL Aircraft." U.S. Air Force V/STOL Technology and Planning Conference, Las Vegas, NV, September 1969.

Alexander, Harold R.; Maisel, Martin D.; Giulianetti, Demo J. "The Development of Advanced Technology Blades for Tilt-Rotor Aircraft." 11th European Rotorcraft Forum, London, England, September 10–13, 1985.

Amos, A. K., Alexander, H. R. "Simulation Study of Gust Alleviation in a Tilt Rotor Aircraft." Vols. I and II, NASA CR-152050/1, June 1977.

Anon. Bell's XV-3. *AEROPHILE,* vol. 2, no. 1, ISSN0147-7668, June. 1979.

Anon. "Civil TiltRotor Development Advisory Committee Report to Congress in Accordance With PL102-581." December 1995.

Anon. "Civil TiltRotor Missions and Applications, Phase II: The Commercial Passenger Market." NASA CR 177576, February 1991.

Anon. "Full-Scale Hover Tests 25-Foot Low Disk Loading Tilt Rotor." NASA CR-114626, May 1973.

Anon. "Large Scale Wind Tunnel Investigation of a Folding Tilt Rotor." NASA CR 114464, Bell Helicopter Co., May 1972.

Anon. The XV-15, Bell's Tilting Test Bed. *AEROPHILE,* vol. 2, no. 2, ISSN0147-7668, October 1979.

Anon. *V/STOL Tilt-Rotor Research Aircraft*, Vols. 1–4. Bell Helicopter Co., Reports 301-199-001 to 004, 1975.

Anon. "V/STOL Tilt-Rotor Aircraft Study, Vol. II—Preliminary Design of Research Aircraft." NASA CR-114438, Boeing-Vertol Co., March 1972.

Anon. "V/STOL Tilt-Rotor Study, Task II—Research Aircraft Design." NASA CR-114442, Bell Helicopter Co., March 1972.

Anon. "Wind Tunnel Results. Advancement of Proprotor Technology, Task II." NASA CR-114363, Bell Helicopter Co., September 1971.

Anon. "Wind Tunnel Test Results of 25-Foot Tilt Rotor during Autorotation." NASA CR-137824, February 1976.

Anon. "XV-15 Flight Manual." Bell Helicopter Textron Report TP-78-XV-15-1, August 15, 1980.

Arnold, James R.; Farrell, Michael K. "One Engine Inoperative Takeoff Climb Performance of the XV-15 Tilt Rotor." SAE, Aerospace Technology Conference and Exposition, Long Beach, California, October 5–8, 1987.

Arrington, W. L.; Kumpel, M.; Marr, R. L.; McEntire, K. G. "XV-15 Tilt Rotor Research Aircraft Flight Test Report." Vol. I-V, NASA CR 177406 and USAAVSCOM TR-86-A-1, June 1985.

Baird, Eugene F.; Bauer, Elmer M.; Kohn, Jerome S. "Model Tests and Analyses of Prop-Rotor Dynamics for Tilt-Rotor Aircraft." Mideast Region Symposium of the AHS, Philadelphia, Pennsylvania, October 1972.

Ball, J. C. "XV-15 Shipboard Evaluation." Presented at the AHS, 39th Annual Forum, St. Louis, Missouri, May 9–11, 1983.

Ball, J. C.; Bowes, R. H. "Second Interim Report-USN/USMC Assessment of the XV-15 Tilt Rotor Research Aircraft." NATC Report No. RW-29R-83, September 29, 1983.

Ball, J. C.; DuFresne, D. A. "Shipboard Evaluation of the XV-15 Tilt Rotor Research Aircraft." NATC Report No. RW-54R-82, April 18, 1983.

Ball, John C. "Tilt-Rotor Memories." Naval Helicopter Association Rotor Review, Number 19, November 1987.

Bartie, K.; Alexander, H.; McVeigh, M.; Lamon, S.; Bishop, H. "Hover Performance Tests of Baseline Metal and Advanced Technology Blade (ATB) Rotor Systems for the XV-15 Tilt Rotor Aircraft." NASA CR-177436, 1986.

Becker, C. L.; Bowes, R. H.; Kolwey, S.; Clark, W. J. "Evaluation of the XV-15 Tilt Rotor Aircraft Concept for JVX Missions." NATC Report No. RW-13R-85, May 12, 1986.

Beroul, Frederic; Bassez, Pascal; Gardarein, Patrick. "EUROFAR Rotor Aerodynamic Tests." Presented at the Eighteenth European Rotorcraft Forum, Avignon, France, September 15-18, 1992.

Beziac, G. "Composite Blade for a 5-m Diameter Tilt Rotor." Fourth European Rotorcraft and Powered Lift Aircraft Forum, Stresa, Italy, September 1978.

Bilger, J.M.; Zahedi, A. "Results of Structural Dynamics Testing of the XV-15 Tilt Rotor Research Aircraft." *Journal of the American Helicopter Society,* vol. 27, no. 2, April 1982.

Bilger, J. M.; Marr, R. L.; Zahedi, Ahmed. "In-Flight Structural Dynamic Characteristics of the XV-15 Tilt Rotor Research Aircraft." AIAA Paper 81-0612, 1981.

Bilger, J. M.; Marr, R. L.; Zahedi, Ahmed. "Results of Structural Dynamic Testing of the XV-15 Tilt Rotor Research Aircraft." Presented at the 37th Annual AHS Forum, New Orleans, Louisiana, May 1981.

Bilger, J.; et al. "Interim Flight Test Data Report for XV-15 Tilt Rotor Research Aircraft (Flights 1–27, April–August 1979)." Bell Helicopter Textron Report No. 301-989-010, November 1979.

Bondl, M. "Tilt Rotor—'Copter and Plane in One." *Mechanical Engineering,* vol. 108, 1986.

Boorla, Raghupati. "Damage Tolerance Analysis of Dynamic Components of Rotary Wing Aircraft." *Journal of the American Helicopter Society,* vol. 34, October 1989.

Brandt, D. E. "Aeroelastic Problems of Flexible V/STOL Rotors." AGARD CP No. 46, April 1969.

Brieger, John T.; Maisel, Martin D.; Gerdes, Ronald. "External Noise Evaluation of the XV-15 Tilt Rotor Aircraft." AHS National Specialists' Meeting on Aerodynamics and Aeroacoustics, Arlington, Texas, February 25–27, 1987.

Brigadier, William L. "Analysis of Control Actuator Authority Requirements for Attitude and Translational Rate Command Augmentation Systems for the XV-15 Tilt Rotor Research Aircraft." NASA TM-81,243 (AVRADCOM Technical Report TR-80-A-13), 1980.

Brown, J. H.; Edenborough, H. K.; "XV-15 Tilt Rotor Test Status." Presented at the 33rd Annual National Forum of the AHS, Washington, DC, AHS Paper No. 77.33-64, May 1977.

Brown, J. H.; Edenborough, H. K.; Few, D. D. "XV-15 Tilt Rotor Progress Report." Presented at the Aerospace Meeting of the SAE, Los Angeles, California, SAE Paper No. 770953, November 14-17, 1977.

Brown, J. H.; Edenborough, H. K.; Wernicke, K. G. "Evaluation of the Tilt Rotor Concept—The XV-15's Role." Presented at the Flight Mechanics Panel Symposium on Rotorcraft Design of the AGARD, Moffett Field, California, AGARD Paper No. 16, May 1977.

Calise, A. J.; Rysdyk, R. "Research in Nonlinear Flight Control for Tilt Rotor Aircraft Operating in the Terminal Area." NASA CR-203112, 1996.

Carpenter, R. B.; Ball, J. C.; Becker, C. "XV-15 Experience—Joint Service Operational Testing of an Experimental Aircraft." SETP, Report to the Aerospace Profession; Proceedings of the 27th Symposium, Beverly Hills, California, September 28–October 1, 1983.

Carpenter, Ronald B.; Churchill, Gary B. "The XV-15 Experience from Wind Tunnel and Simulations to Joint Services V/STOL Aircraft." Presented at the Army Operations Research Symposium, Ft. Eustis, Virginia, October 4–5, 1983.

Cerbe, T. M.; Reichert, G.; Schrage, D. P. "Short Takeoff Optimization for the XV-15 Tilt Rotor Aircraft." European Rotorcraft Forum, Berlin, Germany, September 24–26, 1991.

Churchill, G. B.; Dugan, D. C. "Simulation of the XV-15 Tilt Rotor Research Aircraft." NASA TM-84222, AVRADCOM TR-82-A-4, March 1982.

Churchill, G. B.; Gerdes, R. M. "Advanced AFCS Developments on the XV-15 Tilt Rotor Research Aircraft; Automatic Flight Control System." AHS, 40th Annual Forum, Arlington, Virginia, May 16–18, 1984.

Coffen, Charles D.; Albert R. "Prediction of XV-15 Tilt Rotor Discrete Frequency Aeroacoustic Noise with WOPWOP." NASA CR-187684, 1990.

Coffen, Charles D.; George, Albert R. "Analysis and Prediction of Tilt Rotor Hover Noise." AHS 46th Annual Forum and Technology Display, Washington, D.C., May 21–23, 1990.

Coffen, Charles D.; George, Albert R.; Hardinge, Hal; Stevenson, Ryan. "Flow Visualization and Flow Field Measurements of a 1/12 Scale Tilt Rotor Aircraft in Hover." AHS and Royal Aeronautical Society, Technical Specialists' Meeting on Rotorcraft Acoustics/Fluid Dynamics, Philadelphia, Pennsylvania, October 15–17, 1991.

Coffen, Charles David. "Tilt Rotor Hover Aeroacoustics." NASA CR-177598, 1992.

Conner, David A.; Wellman, J. Brent. "Hover Acoustic Characteristics of the XV-15 With Advanced Technology Blades." NASA TM-111578, 1993.

Cook, W. L.; Poisson-Quinton, P. "A Summary of Wind Tunnel Research on Tilt Rotors from Hover to Cruise Flight." Presented at Fluid Dynamics Specialist Meeting—AGARD, Marseilles, France, September 13-15, 1972.

Curtiss, H. G., Jr.; Komatsuzaki, T.; Traybar, T. "The Influence of Feedback on One Aeroelastic Behavior of Tilt Proprotor Aircraft including the Effects of Fuselage Motion." Princeton University, TR No. 1441, July 1979.

Dadone, Leo; Liu, John; Wilkerson, Joseph; Acree, C. W. "Proprotor Design Issues for High Speed Tilt Rotors." Presented at the 50th Annual Forum of the AHS, Washington, D.C., May 11-13, 1994.

Davis, C. E. "Practice V/STOL—The XV-3 Story." *AHS Newsletter.* Vol. 6, no. 6, June 1960.

Davis, C. E.; Lichten, R. L. "Flight Test Experience With the XV-3 Low-Disc-Loading V/STOL Aircraft." Presented at the IAS 29th Annual Meeting, New York, New York, January 1961.

Decker, William A. "Piloted Simulator Investigations of a Civil Tilt-Rotor Aircraft." AHS 48th Annual Forum, Washington, D.C., June 3-5, 1992.

Decker, William A.; Bray, Richard S.; Simmons, Rickey C.; Tucker, George E. "Evaluation of Two Cockpit Display Concepts for Civil Tilt Rotor Instrument Operations on Steep Approaches." AHS Conference on Flying Qualities and Human Factors, San Francisco, California, January 1993.

Deckert, W. H.; Ferry, R. G. "Limited Flight Evaluation on the XV-3 Aircraft." TR-60-4 ARDC XV3, May 1960.

Deckert, Wallace H.; McCloud, John L., III. "Considerations of the Stopped Rotor V/STOL Concept." *Journal of the American Helicopter Society,* vol. 13, no.1, pp. 27-43, 1968.

DeLarm, Leon N. "Whirl Flutter and Divergence Aspects of Tilt-Wing and Tilt Rotor Aircraft." U.S. Air Force V/STOL Technology and Planning Conference, Las Vegas, Nevada, September 1969.

DeTore, J. A.; Gaffey, T. M. "The Stopped-Rotor Variant of the Proprotor VTOL Aircraft." *Journal of the American Helicopter Society,* vol. 15, no. 3, July 1970, pp. 45–56.

DeTore, J. A.; Gaffey, T. M. "The Stopped-Rotor Variant of the Proprotor VTOL Aircraft." Presented at the AIAA/AHS VTOL Research, Design and Operations Meeting, Atlanta, Georgia, February 17-19, 1969.

DeTore, J. A.; Sambell, K. W. "Conceptual Design Study of 1985 Commercial Tilt Rotor Transports." Vol. 1, VTOL Design Summary, Bell Helicopter Co., Report No. D312-099-002, November 15, 1974.

DeTore, John. "Tilt Rotor—An Effective V/STOL Concept." Presented at the 38th Annual Conference of the SAWE, New York, New York, Paper No. 1273, May 7-9, 1979.

Dugan, D. C. "The XV-15 Tilt-Rotor Flight-Test Program." NASA TM 86846, 1985.

Dugan, D. C.; Erhart, R. G.; Schroers, L. G. "The XV-15 Tilt Rotor Research Aircraft." NASA TM-81244 (AVRADCOM Technical Report 80-A-15), 1980.

Dugan, D. C.; Erhart, R. G.; Schroers, L. G. "The XV-15 Tilt Rotor Research Aircraft." Presented at the SETP Annual Meeting, September 1980.

Dugan, D.C. "Designing The V-22 Tilt Rotor: A Flight Test Pilot's Perspective." *Vertiflite,* Summer 1998.

Dugan, D.C. "Don't Look Now!—Tilt Rotors Are Coming." Presented at the SETP Annual Meeting, September 1997.

Edenborough, H. K. "Investigation of Tilt-Rotor VTOL Aircraft Rotor-Pylon Stability." Presented at AIAA 5th Aerospace Sciences Meeting, New York, New York, AIAA Paper 67-17, January 1967.

Edenborough, H. K.; Gaffey, T. M.; Weiberg, J. A. "Analysis and Tests Confirm Design of Proprotor Aircraft." Presented at AIAA 4th Aircraft Design, Flight Test, and Operations Meeting, Los Angeles, California, Paper 72-803, August 1972.

Edenborough, H. Kipling. "Investigation of Tilt-Rotor VTOL Aircraft Rotor-Pylon Stability." Journal of Aircraft, vol. 5, no. 2, March–April 1968, pp. 97–105.

Edmunds, R. S.; Vangaasbeek, J. "Pilot Modeling and Control Augmentation for the XV-15 in In-Ground-Effect Hover." AIAA Paper 84-1892, 1984.

Edwards, Bryan D. "XV-15 Tilt Rotor Aircraft Noise Characteristics." AHS 46th Annual Forum and Technology Display, Washington, D.C., May 21-23, 1990.

Espinosa, Paul S.; Groepler, David R. "TiltRotor Research Aircraft Composite Blade Repairs: Lessons Learned." NASA TM-103875, 1991.

Farrell, Michael K. "Aerodynamic Design of the V-22 Osprey Proprotor." Presented at the 45th Annual Forum and Tech. Display of the AHS, Boston, Massachusetts, May 22-24, 1989.

Felker, F. F.; Maisel, M. D.; Betzina, M. D. "Full-Scale Tilt-Rotor Hover Performance." AHS, 41st Annual Forum, Fort Worth, Texas, May 15–17, 1985.

Ferguson, S. W.; Hanson, G. D.; Churchill, G. B. "Simulation Validation of the XV-15 Tilt Rotor Research Aircraft." AHS, 40th Annual Forum, Arlington, Virginia, May 16–18, 1984.

Ferguson, Samuel W.; Kocurek, J. David. "Rotorwash Flow Fields: Flight Test Measurement, Prediction Methodologies, and Operational Issues." Presented at the AHS Vertical Lift Design Conference, San Francisco, California, January 17-19, 1991.

Few, D. D.; Edenborough, H. K. "Tilt-Proprotor Perspective." Aeronautics and Astronautics, December 1977.

Fradenburgh, Evan. "Improving Tilt Rotor Aircraft Performance With Variable Diameter Rotors." Presented at the Fourteenth European Rotorcraft Forum, Milan, Italy, September 20-23, 1988.

Frick, J. K.; Johnson, W. "Optimal Control Theory Investigation of Prop Rotor/Wing Response to Vertical Gust." NASA TM X-62384, September 1974.

Gaffey, T. M.; Yen, J. G.; Kvaternik, R. G. "Analysis and Model Tests of the Proprotor Dynamics of a Tilt-Proprotor VTOL Aircraft." U.S. Air Force V/STOL Technology and Planning Conference, Las Vegas, Nevada, September 1969.

Gaffey, Troy M. "The Effect of Positive Pitch-Flap Coupling (Negative d3) on Rotor Blade Motion Stability and Flapping." Paper No. 227, Presented at the 24th Annual Forum of the AHS, Washington, DC, May 8–10, 1968.

Gaffey, Troy M.; Maisel, Martin D. "Measurement of Tilt Rotor VTOL Rotor Wake-Airframe-Ground Aerodynamic Interference for Application to Real-Time Flight Simulation." Presented at AGARD Conference on V/STOL Aerodynamics, CPP-143, Delft, Netherlands, April 1974.

George, A. R.; Coffen, C. D.; Ringler, T. D. "Advances in Tilt Rotor Noise Prediction." Proceedings of the DGLR/AIAA Aeroacoustics Conference, Aachen, Germany, May 11–14, 1992.

George, Albert R.; Smith, Charles A.; Maisel, Martin D.; Breiger, John T. "Tilt Rotor Aeroacoustics." Presented at the 45th Annual Forum and Tech. Display of the AHS, Boston, Massachusetts, May 22-24, 1989.

Gibs, J.; Stepniewski, W.; Spencer, R.; Kohler, G. "Noise Reduction of a Tilt Rotor Aircraft Including Effects on Weight and Performance" (NASA Contract NAS2-6784). NASA CR-114638, Boeing Report D222-10062-1, June 1973.

Gillmore, K. B. "Survey of Tilt Rotor Technology Development." AGARD Flight Mechanics Panel Meeting, Langley Research Center, September 20-23, 1971.

Golub, Robert A.; Conner, David A.; Becker, Lawrence E.; Rutledge, C. Kendall; Smith, Rita A. "Some Far-Field Acoustics Characteristics of the XV-15 Tilt Rotor Aircraft." AIAA Paper 90-3971, 1990.

Haffner, R. "The Case for the Convertible Rotor. Tenth Cierva Memorial Lecture." *Journal of the Royal Aeronautical Society,* vol. 75, August 1975.

Hall, W. E. "Preliminary Flight Test Planning for XV-15 Tilt Rotor Aircraft." NASA CR-152392, 1979.

Hall, W. Earl, Jr. "Prop-Rotor Stability at High Advance Ratios." *Journal of the American Helicopter Society,* vol. 11, no. 2, April 1966, pp. 11–26.

Ham, N. D.; et al. "A Study of Gust and Control Response of Model Rotor-Propellers in a Wind Tunnel Airstream." NASA CR-137756, August 1975.

Ham, N.D.; Whitaker, H. P. "A Wind Tunnel Investigation of the Tilt-Rotor Gust Alleviation Systems." NASA CR-152264, January 1978.

Harendra, P. B.; Joglekar, M. J.; Gaffey, T. M.; Marr, R. L. "A Mathematical Model for Real-Time Flight Simulation of the Bell Model 301 Tilt Rotor Research Aircraft." NASA CR-114614, April 1973.

Harris, D. J.; Simpson, R. D. "Technical Evaluation of the Rotor Downwash Flow Field of the XV-15 Tilt Rotor Research Aircraft." NATC Report No. SY-14R-83, July 28, 1983.

Hoad, Danny R.; Conner, David A.; Rutledge, Charles K. "Acoustic Flight Test Experience with the XV-15 Tilt Rotor Aircraft with the Advanced Technology Blades (ATB)." Proceedings of the DGLR/AIAA Aeroacoustics Conference, 14th, Aachen, Germany, May 11–14, 1992.

Hofmann, L. G.; Hoh, R. H.; Jewell, W. F.; Teper, G. L. "Development of Automatic and Manual Flight Director Landing Systems for the XV-15 Tilt Rotor Aircraft in Helicopter Mode." NASA CR-152140, 1978.

Hotz, E. R.; Holsapple, D. E. "Test Report on 25-Foot Diameter Prop/Rotor." Air Force Flight Dynamics Laboratory Report AFFDL/FYT-73-2, May 1973.

Houbolt, J. C.; Reed, W. H., III. "Propeller-Nacelle Whirl Flutter." *Journal of the Aeronautical Sciences,* vol. 29, no. 3, March 1962, pp. 333-346.

Huston, Robert J.; Golub Robert A.; Yu, James C. "Noise Considerations for Tilt Rotor." Presented at the AIAA/ASME/SAE/ASEE 25th Joint Propulsion Conference, Monterey, California, July 10-12, 1989.

Johnson, W. "An Assessment of the Capability to Calculate Tilting Prop-Rotor Aircraft Performance, Loads and Stability." NASA TP-2291, 1984.

Johnson, W. "Comparison of Calculated and Measured Blade Loads on a Full-Scale Tilting Proprotor in a Wind Tunnel." NASA TM-81228, September 1980.

Johnson, W. "Dynamics of Tilting Prop/Rotor Aircraft in Cruise Flight." NASA TN D-7677, May 1974.

Johnson, W. "The Influence of Pitch-Lag Coupling on the Predicted Aeroelastic Stability of the XV-15 Tilting Proprotor Aircraft." NASA TM-X-73213, 1977.

Johnson, Wayne. "Analytical Model for Tilting Proprotors Aircraft Dynamics, Including Blade Torsion and Coupled Bending Modes, and Conversion Mode Operation." NASA TM X-62369, August 1974.

Johnson, Wayne. "Analytical Modeling Requirements for Tilting Proprotor Aircraft Dynamics." NASA TN D-8013, July 1975.

Johnson, Wayne. "Optimal Control Alleviation of Tilting Proprotor Gust Response." NASA TM X-62494, October 1975.

Johnson, Wayne. "Predicted Dynamic Characteristics of the XV-15 Tilting Prop-Rotor Aircraft in Flight and in the 40- by 80-Ft. Wind Tunnel." NASA TM X-73158, June 1976.

Johnston, Robert A. "Parametric Studies of Instabilities Associated with Large Flexible Rotor Propellers." Preprint No. 615, 28th Annual Forum of the AHS, Washington, D.C., May 1972.

Jordan, D. E.; Patterson, W.; Sandlin, D. R. "An Experimental and Analytical Method for Approximate Determination of the Tilt Rotor Research Aircraft Rotor/Wing Download." NASA CR-176790, 1985.

Jumper, Stephen J.; Prichard, Devon; Golub, Robert A. "Tilt Rotor Ground Noise Reduction from Rotor Parametric Changes as Predicted by ROTONET." AHS and Royal Aeronautical Society, Technical Specialists' Meeting on Rotorcraft Acoustics/Fluid Dynamics, Philadelphia, Pennsylvania, October 15–17, 1991.

Kingston, L.; DeTore, J. "Tilt Rotor V/STOL Aircraft Technology." Presented at the Second European Rotorcraft and Powered Lift Aircraft Forum, Buckeburg, Germany, Paper No. 36, September 1976.

"Blade-Vortex Interaction Noise." Presented at the 53rd Annual Forum of the AHS, Washington, D.C., April 29-May 1, 1977.

Kleuver, Emil E. "Pilot Evaluation of the Bell Model XV-3 Vertical Takeoff and Landing Aircraft." U.S. Army Aviation Test Office, Edwards AFB, California, Report ATO-TR-62, February 1962.

Koenig, D. G.; Grief, R. K.; Kelly, M. W. "Full-Scale Wind Tunnel Investigation of the Longitudinal Characteristics of a Tilting Rotor Convertiplane." NASA TN D-35, December 1959.

Kottapalli, Sesi; Meza, Victor. "Analytical Aeroelastic Stability Considerations and Conversion Loads for an XV-15 Tilt-Rotor in a Wind Tunnel Simulation." AIAA 92-2258, 1992.

Kvaternik, R. G.; Kohn, J. S. "An Experimental and Analytical Investigation of Proprotor Whirl Flutter." NASA TP 1047, 1977.

Kvaternik, Raymond G. "A Historic Overview of Tiltrotor Aeroelastic Research at Langley Research Center." NASA TM 107578, April 1992.

Kvaternik, Raymond G. "Studies in Tilt Rotor VTOL Aircraft Aeroelasticity." Vol. 1, NASA TM-X-69497, June 1, 1973, and Vol. 2, NASA TM-X-69496, June 1, 1973.

Lacy, Clay. "Tiltrotor Technology." *Professional Pilot,* September 1998.

Lambert, M. "Bell Tilt-Rotor—The Next V/STOL." *Flight International,* vol. 117, 1980.

Lambert, Mark. "Flying the XV-15 and V-22 Tilt Rotors." *Interavia,* vol. 43, 1988.

Lawrence, W. S.; Allison, W. A.; DuFresne, D. "Final Report, Advanced Helicopter Rotor Systems, First Navy Evaluation of the XV-15 Tilt Rotor Research Aircraft." NATC, Patuxent River, Maryland, NATC Technical Report No. RW-44R-80, December 1980.

Lawrence, W. S.; DuFresne, D. A. "The XV-15—An Initial Navy Look." Presented at the AIAA 19th Aerospace Sciences Meeting, January 12–15, 1981, St. Louis, Missouri, AIAA Paper 81-0155, January 1981.

Lebacqz, J. V.; Scott, B. C. "Ground-Simulation Investigation of VTOL Airworthiness Criteria for Terminal Area Operations." Atmospheric Flight Mechanics Conference, Seattle, Washington, August 21–23, 1984.

Lebacqz, J. V.; Scott, B. C. "Ground-Simulation Investigation of VTOL Instrument Flight Rules Airworthiness Criteria." AIAA 84-2105, 1984.

Lee, A.; Mosher, M. "An Acoustical Study of the XV-15 Tilt Rotor Research Aircraft." AIAA Paper 79-0612, 1979.

Lee, Albert; Mosher, Marianne. "An Acoustical Study of the XV-15 Tilt Rotor Aircraft." AIAA Paper 74-0612, 1974.

Lichten, R. L. "Some Aspects of Convertible Aircraft Design." *Journal of the Aeronautical Sciences,* October 1949.

Lichten, R. L. "Some Performance and Operating Characteristics of Convertiplanes." SAE National Aeronautical Meeting, Los Angeles, California, October 1957.

Lichten, R. L.; et al. "A Survey of Low-Disc-Loading VTOL Aircraft Designs." AIAA Paper No. 65-756, Aircraft Design and Technology Meeting, November 1965.

Lichten, R. L.; Mertens, J. R. "Development of the XV-3 Convertiplane." Presented at the Twelfth Annual National Forum of the AHS, May 1956.

Liebensberger, Claude E. "Some Conclusions on Flight Characteristics and Future Developments Based on XV-3 Convertiplane Tests." Presented at the Semi-Annual Meeting of the ASME, St. Louis, Missouri, June 1959.

Liu, J.; McVeigh, Michael A. "Design of Swept Blade Rotors for High-Speed Tiltrotor Application." Presented at the AIAA Aircraft Design Systems and Operations Meeting, Baltimore Maryland, September 23-25, 1991.

Liu, John; McVeigh, Michael A. Mayer, Robert.; Snider, Royce W. "Model and Full-Scale Tiltrotor Download Tests." Presented at the 55th Annual Forum of the AHS, Montreal, Quebec, Canada, May 25–27, 1999.

Lyle, Karen H. "XV-15 Structural-Acoustic Data." NASA TM-112855, 1997.

Lynn, R. R. "The Rebirth of the Tilt Rotor–The 1992 Alexander A. Nikolsky Lecture." *Journal of the American Helicopter Society,* vol. 38, no. 1, January 1993.

Magee, J. P. "The Tilt Rotor Research Aircraft (XV-15) Program." American Planning Association Proceedings of the Monterey Conference on Planning for Rotorcraft and Commuter Air Transportation, 1983.

Magee, J. P.; Alexander, H. R. "A Hingeless Rotor XV-15 Design Integration Feasibility Study." NASA CR-152310, March 1978.

Magee, J. P.; Alexander, H. R. "A Hover Test of a 1/4.62 Froude Scale Rotor Designed for a Tilt Rotor Aircraft." NASA Contract NAS2-8048. NASA CR-137945, July 1976.

Magee, J. P.; Alexander, H.R. "V/STOL Tilt Rotor Aircraft Study Wind Tunnel Tests of a Full-Scale Hingeless Prop/Rotor Designed for the Boeing Model 222 Tilt Rotor Aircraft." NASA Contract NAS2-6505. NASA CR-114664, October 1973.

Magee, J. P.; Clark, R. D.; Giulianetti, D. "Rotary-Wing Aircraft Systems for the Short Haul Market." Presented at the 11th Annual Meeting of the AIAA, Washington, D.C., AIAA Paper 75-275, February 1975.

Magee, J. P.; Clark, R. D.; Widdison, C.A. "Conceptual Engineering Design Studies of 1985 Era Commercial VTOL and STOL Transports that Utilize Rotors." NASA CR-2545, May 1975.

Magee, J. P.; Clark, R.; Alexander, H. R. "Conceptual Design Studies of 1985 Commercial VTOL Transports That Utilize Rotors." NASA Contract NAS2-8048. Vol. I: NASA CR-137600, Vol. II: NASA CR-137599, November 1974.

Magee, J. P.; et al. "Wind Tunnel Test of a Powered Tilt Rotor Performance Model." AFFDL-TR-71-62, vol. V, October 1971.

Magee, J. P.; Pruyn, R. "Prediction of the Stability Derivatives of Large Flexible Prop/Rotors by a Simple Analysis." Paper 443, 26th Annual Forum Proceedings of the AHS, 1970.

Magee, J. P.; Taylor, R. B. "Wind Tunnel Tests of a Conversion Process of a Folding Tilt Rotor Aircraft Using a Semispan Unpowered Model." AFFDL-TR-71-62, vol. IV, parts I and II, August 1971.

Magee, J. P.; Wernicke, K. "XV-15 Tilt Rotor Research Aircraft Program Report." AIAA Paper 79-54, Atlantic Aeronautical Conference, Williamsburg, Virginia, March 1979.

Magee, John P. "Tilt Rotor Technology Thrusts." Presented at the Aerospace Congress and Exposition, Long Beach, California, October 3–6, 1983.

Magee, John P.; Maisel, Martin D.; Davenport, Frank J. "The Design and Performance Prediction of Propeller/Rotors for VTOL Applications." Paper No. 325, 25th Annual Forum of the AHS, Washington, D.C., May 14–16, 1969.

Maisel, M. D., et al. "Tilt Rotor Research Aircraft Familiarization Document." NASA TM X-62,407, January 1975.

Maisel, M; Harris, D. "Hover Tests of the XV-15 Tilt Rotor Research Aircraft." Presented at the 1st Flight Testing Conference, Las Vegas, Nevada, AIAA Paper 81-2501, November 11-13, 1981.

Maisel, Martin D.; McKiethan, Clifford M. "The Tilt Rotor—Expanding Rotorcraft Horizons." *Vertiflite,* May-June 1980.

Maisel, Martin D.; McKiethan, Clifford M. "Tilt Rotor Aircraft." Army RD&A, May-June 1980.

Maisel, Martin D.; Weiberg, James A.; Brown, James H., Jr. "A Review of the Design and Acoustics Considerations for the Tilt Rotor Aircraft." Presented at the NASA Quiet, Powered-Lift Propulsion Conference, Lewis Research Center, November 1978.

Maisel, Martin; Laub, Georgene. "Aerodynamic Characteristics of Two-Dimensional Wing Configurations at Angles of Attack Near –90∞." NASA TM 88373, December 1986.

Marcolini, Michael A.; Burley, Casey L.; Conner, David A.; Acree, C. W., Jr. "Overview of Noise Reduction Technology in the NASA Short Haul (Civil Tilt Rotor) Program," SAE International Powered Lift Conference, Jupiter, Florida, November 18 20, 1996.

Mark, Hans; Lynn, Robert R. "Aircraft Without Airports–Changing the Way Men Fly." *Vertiflite,* May/June 1988.

Mark, Hans. "Straight Up into the Blue," *Scientific American,* October 1997.

Marr, R. L. "XV-15 Flight Simulator Period No. 1 (FSAA Simulator, December 1973)." Prepared under Contract No. NAS2-7800 by Bell Helicopter Textron, February 13, 1974.

Marr, R. L. "XV-15 Flight Simulator Period No. 2 (FSAA Simulator, July 1974)." Prepared under Contract No. NAS2-7800 by Bell Helicopter Textron, August 30, 1974.

Marr, R. L. "XV-15 Flight Simulator Period No. 3 (FSAA Simulator, September 1975)." Prepared under Contract No. NAS2-7800 by Bell Helicopter Textron, January 13, 1976.

Marr, R. L.; Blackman, S.; Weiberg, J. A.; Schroers, L. G. "Wind Tunnel and Flight Test of the XV-15 Tilt Rotor Research Aircraft." Presented at the 35th Annual National Forum of the AHS, Washington, D.C., Paper No. 79-54, May 1979.

Marr, R. L.; Neal, G. T. "Assessment of Model Testing of a Tilt Prop-Rotor VTOL Aircraft." Presented at AHS Symposium on Status of Testing and Modeling Techniques for V/STOL Aircraft, October 1972.

Marr, R. L.; Sambell, K. W.; Neal, G. T. "Hover, Low Speed and Conversion Tests of a Tilt Rotor Aeroelastic Model." *V/STOL Tilt Rotor Study,* vol. VI, Bell Helicopter Co., NASA CR-114615, May 1973.

Marr, R. L.; Willis, T. M.; Churchill, G. B. "Flight Control System Development for the XV-15 Tilt Rotor Aircraft." Presented at the 32nd Annual National V/STOL Forum of the AHS, Washington, D.C., May 1976.

Marr, Roger L.; Churchill, Gary B. "Piloted Simulation in the development of the XV-15 Tilt Rotor Research Aircraft." AGARD, Flight Simulation, 1986.

Marr, Roger L.; Neal, Gordon T. "Assessment of Model Testing of a Tilt-Proprotor VTOL Aircraft, Status of Testing and Modeling Techniques for V/STOL Aircraft." Proceedings of the Mideast Region Symposium, AHS, Essington, Pennsylvania, October 26-28, 1972.

Marr, Roger L.; Roderick, W. E. B. "Handling Qualities Evaluation of the XV-15 Tilt Rotor Aircraft." Presented at the 30th Annual National Forum of the AHS, Washington, D.C., May 1974.

Martin, Stanley, Jr.; Erb, Lee H.; Sambell, Kenneth W. "STOL Performance of the Tilt Rotor." Presented at the Sixth European Rotorcraft and Powered Lift Forum, Bristol, England, September 16-19, 1980.

Martin, Stanley, Jr.; Peck, William B. "JVX Design Update." AHS, 40th Annual Forum, Arlington, Virginia, May 16–18, 1984.

McCroskey, W. J.; Spalart, Ph.; Laub, G. H.; Maisel, M. D.; Maskew, B. "Airloads on Bluff Bodies, with Application to the Rotor-Induced Downloads on Tilt-Rotor Aircraft." Presented at the Ninth European Rotorcraft Forum, Stresa, Italy, September 13-15, 1983.

McVeigh, M. A. "Pilot Evaluation of an Advanced Hingeless Rotor XV-15 Simulation." NASA CR-152034, 1977.

McVeigh, M. A. "Preliminary Simulation of an Advanced Hingeless Rotor XV-15 Tilt Rotor Aircraft." NASA CR-151950, December 1976.

McVeigh, M. A. "Synthesis of Rotor Test Data for Real-Time Simulation." NASA CR-152311, 1979.

McVeigh, M. A.; Rosenstein, H. J.; McHugh, F.J. "Aerodynamic Design of the XV-15 Advanced Composite Tilt Rotor Blade." AHS, 39th Annual Forum, St. Louis, Missouri, May 9-11, 1983.

McVeigh, Michael A.; Rosenstein, Harold J.; McHugh, Francis J. "Aerodynamics Design of the XV-15 Advanced Composite Tilt Rotor Blade." Presented at the AHS, 39th Annual Forum, St. Louis, Missouri, May 9–11, 1983.

McVeigh, Michael A. "The V-22 Tilt-Rotor Large-Scale Rotor Performance/ Wing Download Test and Comparison with Theory." Presented at the 11th European Rotorcraft Forum, London, England, September 10–13, 1985.

McVeigh, Michael A.; Grauer, William K.; Paisley, David J. "Rotor/Airframe Interactions on Tiltrotor Aircraft." Presented at the 44th Annual Forum of the AHS, Washington, DC, June 1988.

Menger, Ross P.; Hogg, Charles B. "Recent Investigations in Tilt Rotor Flight Technology Through XV-15 Flight Testing." Presented at the AHS, 43rd Annual Forum, St. Louis, Missouri, May 18–20, 1987.

Narramore, J. C. "Advanced Technology Airfoil Development for the XV-15 Tilt Rotor Vehicle." AIAA Paper No. 81-2623, 1981.

Paisley, David J. "Rotor Aerodynamic Optimization for High Speed Tilt Rotors." Presented at the AHS, 43rd Annual Forum, St. Louis, Missouri, May 18-20, 1987.

Peck, W. B.; Schoen, A. H. "The Value of Various Technology Advances for Several V/STOL Configurations." Presented at the Fourth European Rotorcraft and Powered Lift Forum, Stresa, Italy, September 13–15, 1978, *Journal of the American Helicopter Society,* vol. 24, no. 4, July 1979, pp. 4–10.

Polak, David R.; George, Albert R. "Experimental Aerodynamic and Aeroacoustic Investigation of a Scaled Tilt Rotor in Hover." Presented at the 50th Annual Forum of the AHS, Washington, D.C., May 11-13, 1994.

Quigley, H. C.; Koenig, D. C. "A Flight Study of the Dynamic Stability of a Tilting-Rotor Convertiplane." NASA TN D-778, 1961.

Reed, W. H., III. "Propeller-Rotor Whirl Flutter, A State of the Art Review." Presented at the Symposium of the Noise and Loading Actions on Helicopter V/STOL Aircraft and Ground Effect Machines, Southampton, England, August 30-September 3, 1965.

Reed, W. H., III; Bland, S. R. "An Analytical Treatment of Aircraft Propeller Precession Instability." NASA TN D-659, 1961.

Reed, Wilmer H., III. "Propeller-Rotor Whirl Flutter: A State of the Art Review." *Journal of Sound and Vibration,* vol. 4, no. 3, November 1966, pp. 526–544.

Reed, Wilmer H., III. "Review of Propeller-Rotor Whirl Flutter." NASA TR R264, 1967.

Reeder, John P.; Drinkwater, Fred J. III. "Limited Flight Experience With Several Types of VTOL Aircraft." Proceedings of a NASA Briefing on VTOL/STOL Aircraft Research, given at the U.S. Army Transportation Command, Ft. Eustis, Virginia, December 15, 1959.

Richardson, David A. "The Application of Hingeless Rotors to Tilting Prop/Rotor Aircraft." AHS Paper No. 403, AHS National Forum, Washington, D.C., 1970.

Richardson, J. R.; Naylor, H. F. W. "Whirl Flutter of Propellers with Hinged Blades." Report No. 24, Engineering Research Associates, Toronto, Canada, March 1962.

Ringland, Robert F.; Craig, Samuel J. "Simulated Limit Cycle Behavior in the Collective Control Linkage of the XV-15 Aircraft." Working Paper 10488-11, Systems Technology, Inc., Hawthorne, California, November 1975.

Ropelewski, R. R. "Flexibility is Offered by XV-15 Tilt-Rotor Concept." *Aviation Week and Space Technology,* vol. 116, 1982.

Rutledge, Charles K.; George, Albert R. "A Comparative Analysis of XV-15 Tiltrotor Hover Test Data and WOPWOP Predictions Incorporating the Fountain Effect." NASA CR-189455, 1991.

Saberi, H. A.; Maisel, M.D. "A Free Wake Rotor Analysis Including Ground Effect." Presented at the 43rd Annual Forum of the AHS, St. Louis, Missouri, May 18–20, 1987.

Sambell, K. W. "Application of the Low Disc-Loading Proprotor to a Series of Aircraft for the Short-Haul Market." AIAA 3rd Aircraft Design and Operations Meeting, Seattle, Washington, July 1971.

Sambell, Kenneth W. "Proprotor Short-Haul Aircraft—STOL and VTOL." *Journal of Aircraft,* vol. 9, no. 10, October 1972, pp. 744–750.

Sandford, R. W.; Magee, J. P.; et al. "Design Studies and Model Tests of the Stowed Tilt Rotor Concept." Summary of Design Criteria and Aerodynamic Prediction Techniques, AFFDL-TR-71-62, vol. VIII, October 1971.

Schillings, John J.; Roberts, Bradford J.; Wood, Tommie L.; Wernicke, Kenneth G. "Maneuver Performance Comparison Between the XV-15 and an Advanced Tiltrotor Design." *Journal of the American Helicopter Society,* vol. 35, April 1990.

Schillings, John J.; Roberts, Bradford J.; Wood, Tommie L.; Wernicke, Kenneth G. "Maneuver Performance of Tiltrotor Aircraft." Presented at the AHS, 43rd Annual Forum, St. Louis, Missouri, May 18–20, 1987.

Schmitz, F. H.; Stepniewski, W. Z.; Gibs, J.; Hinterkeuser, E. "A Comparison of Optimal and Noise-Abatement Trajectories of a Tilt-Rotor Aircraft." NASA CR-2034, January 1972.

Schmitz, F.; Stepniewski, W. Z. "The Reduction of VTOL Operational Noise through Flight Trajectory Management." AIAA Paper 71-991, 8th Annual Meeting and Technical Display, Washington, D.C., October 25–28, 1971.

Schroers, L. G. "Dynamic Structural Aeroelastic Testing of the XV-15 Tilt Rotor Research Aircraft." AGARD Paper No. 18, October 1981.

Schroers, L. G. "Initial Flight Test Results Compared to Design Predictions." Presented at the AIAA 18th Aerospace Sciences Meeting, Pasadena, California, January 14-16, 1980, AIAA Paper 80-0235, January 1980.

Schroers, L. G.; Dugan, D. C.; Marr, R. L.; Erhart, R. C. "Operating Flexibility Exhibited on Flight Test of the XV-15 Tilt Rotor Research Aircraft." Presented at the 36th Annual Forum of the AHS, Washington, DC, Paper No. 80-58, May 1980.

Schroers, L. "Dynamic Structural Aeroelastic Stability Testing of the XV-15 Tilt Rotor Research Aircraft." AGARD Paper No. 339; also NASA TM-84293, December 1982.

Shank, Suzanna S. "Tiltrotor Interior Noise Characteristics." Presented at the AHS and Royal Aeronautical Society, Technical Specialists' Meeting on Rotorcraft Acoustics/Fluid Dynamics, Philadelphia, Pennsylvania, October 15–17, 1991.

Simmons, Rickey C. "Selection of the Safest Cockpit Thrust Control Inceptor Design for the Civil Tiltrotor Transport Aircraft Based on Pilot Preference." Research Project. Embry-Riddle Aeronautical University, Extended Campus, Moffett Field, California, December 1997.

Smith, K. E.; Alexander, H. R.; Maisel, M. D. "Design Aspects of the XV-15 Advanced Technology Blade Program." AHS, 41st Annual Forum, Fort Worth, Texas, May 15–17, 1985.

Snyder, William J.; Zuk, John; Mark, Hans. "Tilt Rotor Technology Takes Off." *Aerospace America,* AIAA, April 1997.

Stepniewski, W. Z.; Schmitz, F. H. "Possibilities and Problems of Achieving Community Noise Acceptance of VTOL." *The Aeronautical Journal,* vol. 77, no. 750, Royal Aeronautical Society, June 1973.

Studebaker Fletcher, Karen; Decker, William A.; Matuska, David G.; et al. "VMS Simulation of a Variable Diameter Tiltrotor." Presented at the 53rd Annual Forum of the AHS, Washington, D.C., April 29-May 1, 1977.

Studebaker, Karen; Abrego, Anita. "Ground Vibration Test of the XV-15 Tiltrotor Research Aircraft and Pretest Predictions." Presented at the Gear-Up 2000: Women in Motion Technical Paper Contest for Women, 1994.

Thomason, T. H. "The Promise of Tilt Rotor." *Professional Pilot,* December 1977.

Thomason, T. "XV-15 Program Update." *Vertiflite,* vol. 28, 1982.

Tiller, F. E., Jr.; Nicholson, Robert. "Stability and Control Considerations for a Tilt-Fold-Proprotor Aircraft." *Journal of the American Helicopter Society,* vol. 16, no. 3, July 1971, pp. 23–33.

Tischler, M. B. "Frequency-Response Identification and Verification of XV-15 Tiltrotor Aircraft Dynamics." NASA TM-89428, May 1987.

Tischler, M. B.; Leung, J. G. M.; Dugan, D. C. "Frequency-Domain Identification of XV-15 Tilt-Rotor Aircraft Dynamics." AIAA 83-2695, 1983.

Tischler, M. B.; Leung, J. G. M.; Dugan, D. C. "Frequency-Domain Identification of XV-15 Tiltrotor Aircraft Dynamics in Hovering Flight." *Journal of the American Helicopter Society,* April 1985.

Tischler, M. B.; Leung, J. G. M.; Dugan, D. C. "Identification and Verification of Frequency-Domain Models for XV-15 Tilt-Rotor Aircraft Dynamics." NASA TM-86009, 1984.

Tischler, M. B.; Leung, J. G. M.; Dugan, D. C. "Identification and Verification of Frequency-Domain Models for XV-15 Tiltrotor Aircraft Dynamics in Cruising Flight." *Journal of Aircraft,* vol. 9, No. 4, July-August 1986.

Tischler, Mark B. "Advancements in Frequency-Domain Methods for Rotorcraft System Identification." *Vertica,* vol. 13, no. 3, 1989.

Tischler, Mark B.; Kaletka, Juergen. "Modeling XV-15 Tilt-Rotor Aircraft Dynamics by Frequency and Time-Domain Identification Techniques." AGARD, Rotorcraft Design for Operations, 1987.

Totah, Joseph J.; Madden, John F., III. "Rotor and Control System Loads Analysis of the XV-15 With the Advanced Technology Blades." Innovations in Rotorcraft Test Technology for the 90s. Proceedings of the AHS National Technical Specialists' Meeting, Scottsdale, Arizona, October 8–12, 1990.

Totah, Joseph J.; Madden, John F., III. "Rotor and Control System Loads Analysis of the XV-15 With the Advanced Technology Blades." NASA TM-102876, 1991.

Unger, G. "Tilt Rotor Aircraft and the U.S. Navy." Fourth European Rotorcraft and Powered Lift Aircraft Forum, Italy, September 1978.

VanWagensveld, D.; Magee, J. P.; et al. "Wind Tunnel Test of the Aerodynamics and Dynamics of Rotor Spin Up and Stopping and Folding a Semispan Folding Tilt Rotor Model." AFFDL-TR-71-62, vol. VIII, October 1971.

Weiberg, J. A.; Dugan, D. C.; Gerdes, R. "XV-15 N703 Takeoff Performance." NASA Ames Memo dated January 4, 1983.

Weiberg, J. A.; Dugan, D. C.; Gerdes, R.; Tucker, G. "Climb Performance of N703." NASA Ames Memo dated April 7, 1983.

Weiberg, J. A.; Maisel, M. D. "Wind-Tunnel Tests of the XV-15 Tilt Rotor Aircraft." NASA TM-81177 and AVRADCOM TR-80-A-3, April 1980.

Wellman, Brent. "Advanced Technology Blade Testing on the XV-15 Tilt Rotor Research Aircraft." AHS 48th Annual Forum, Washington, D.C., June 3-5, 1992.

Wernicke, K. G. "Performance and Safety Aspects of the XV-15 Tilt Rotor Research Aircraft." Presented at the 33rd Annual National Forum of the AHS, Washington, D.C., AHS Paper No. 77.33-14, May 1977.

Wernicke, K. G. "Tilt Proprotor Composite Aircraft, Design State of the Art." *Journal of the American Helicopter Society,* vol. 14, no. 2, April 1969, pp. 10–25.

Wernicke, K. G. "Tilt-Proprotor Composite Aircraft, Design State of the Art." Presented at the 24th Annual Forum of the AHS, Washington, D.C., May 8-10, 1968.

Wernicke, K. G.; Edenborough, H. K. "Full Scale Proprotor Development." Preprint No. 501, 27th Annual National V/STOL Forum of the AHS, Washington, D.C., May 1971.

Wernicke, K. G.; Magee, J. P. "XV-15 Flight Test Result Compared with Design Goals." Presented at AIAA Aircraft Systems and Technology Meeting, New York, New York, AIAA Paper 79-1839, August 1979.

Wernicke, Kenneth G. "Mission Potential of Derivatives of the XV-15 Tilt Rotor Research Aircraft." AGARD Paper No. 19, Paris, France, April 6-9, 1981.

Wernicke, Kenneth G.; Edenborough, H. Kipling. "Full-scale Proprotor Development." *Journal of the American Helicopter Society,* vol. 17, no. 1, January 1970, pp. 31–40.

Wernicke, R. K. "A Tilt Rotor Design That Provides Economical Extended Range VTOL Transportation to Off-Shore Oil Platforms." Presented at the AIAA Aircraft Systems and Technology Meeting, Anaheim, California, Paper No. 80-1822, August 1980.

Wernicke, R. K. "Prediction of Tilt Rotor Outwash." Presented at the AIAA 19th Aerospace Sciences Meeting, January 12-15, 1982, St. Louis, Missouri, AIAA Paper 81-0013, January 1981.

Wernicke, R. K. "XV-15 Tilt Rotor Aircraft and Preliminary Design of a Larger Aircraft for the U.S. Navy Subsonic V/STOL Mission." Presented at the Fourth European Rotorcraft and Powered Lift Aircraft Forum, Stresa, Italy, Paper No. 45, September 1978.

Wernicke, R. K.; Fischer, J. N. "An Evaluation of Advanced Rotorcraft Configurations for Emerging Military Applications." Presented at the 37th Annual AHS Forum, New Orleans, Louisiana, May 1981.

Wernicke, R. K.; Wernicke, K. G.; Borgman, D.C. "Mission Potential of Derivatives of the XV-15 Tilt Rotor Research Aircraft." Presented at the 36th Annual Forum of the AHS, Washington, D.C., Paper No.80-11, May 1980.

Whitaker, H. L.; Cheng, Yi. "Use of Active Control Systems to Improve Bending and Rotor Flapping Responses of a Tilt Rotor VTOL Airplane." NASA CR-137815, October 1975.

Widdison, C. A.; Magee, J. P.; Alexander, H. R. "Conceptual Design Study of a 1985 Commercial STOL Tilt Rotor Transport." NASA Contract NAS2-8048. NASA CR-137601, November 1974.

Wolkovitch, Julian; Wainfan, Barnaby; Ben-Harush, Ytzhak; Johnson, Wayne. "Application of the Joined Wing to Tiltrotor Aircraft." NASA CR-177543, 1989.

Yasue, M. "A Study of Gust Response for a Rotor-Propeller in Cruising Flight." NASA CR-137537, August 1974.

Yen, J. G.; Weber, Gottfried E.; Gaffey, Troy M. "A Study of Folding Proprotor VTOL Aircraft Dynamics." AFFDL-TR-71-7, vol. 1, September 1971.

Yen, Jing, G.; Weber, Gottfried E.; Gaffey, Troy M. "A Study of Folding Proprotor VTOL Dynamics." AFFDL-TR-71-7, February 1971.

Young, Maurice I.; Lytwyn, Roman T. "The Influence of Blade Flapping Restraint on the Dynamic Stability of Low Disk Loading Propeller-Rotors." *Journal of the American Helicopter Society,* vol.12, no. 4, October 1967, pp. 38–54; see also Wernicke, Kenneth G.; Gaffey, Troy M. "Review and Discussion." *Journal of the American Helicopter Society,* vol. 12, no. 4, October 1967, pp. 55–60.

About the Authors

Martin D. Maisel

After graduating in 1960 from the Polytechnic Institute of Brooklyn with a BS in aeronautical engineering, Martin Maisel worked on propeller and rotor aerodynamic design and technology development at the Hamilton Standard Division of United Technologies Corporation, Windsor Locks, Connecticut, and then at the Boeing Helicopter Company, Riddley Park, Pennsylvania, where he was involved in advanced VTOL aircraft design. While at Hamilton Standard, he did additional graduate work at the Rensselaer Polytechnic Institute, East Hartford, Connecticut, Graduate Center. In 1970, Mr. Maisel moved to the Army Air Mobility Research and Development Laboratory (now the Army Aeroflightdynamics Directorate) at the NASA Ames Research Center, Moffett Field, California, and became a member of the NASA/Army project team that developed the XV-15 tilt rotor research aircraft. His project responsibilities included aerodynamics integration, subsystem development, and systems, wind tunnel, and flight testing. After managing the XV-15 for the last two years of flight test activity at Ames, he continued to participate in the development of tilt rotor technology for civil transport application as part of the NASA Short-Haul Civil Tilt Rotor (SHCT) Project Office. Since early 1998, Mr. Maisel has been serving as the airworthiness officer for Army flight operations at Ames, in support of the joint Army/NASA rotorcraft technology activity. He has authored over 20 papers and technical reports on the design, performance, acoustics, and operations of the tilt rotor aircraft. With a lifelong interest in aviation, he is also a licensed private pilot.

Demo J. Giulianetti

Demo Giulianetti's 42-year career as a Government research engineer began in 1956 at the NACA Ames Aeronautical Laboratory (later, the NASA Ames Research Center), Moffett Field, California. For the first 15 years, his work focused on small- and large-scale wind tunnel investigations of conventional and advanced aircraft, including new V/STOL configurations. In 1975, he joined the Tilt Rotor Research Aircraft Project Office and participated in the development of two XV-15 aircraft. His technical efforts in this Office included analytical evaluations, aircraft systems and hardware development, and wind tunnel and flight test investigations. He also participated in the development and testing of the first all-composite rotor blades for this aircraft type. Prior to his retirement in 1998, he was a senior staff engineer in the Advanced Tiltrotor Transport Technology Office, responsible for the management of major rotorcraft task order contracts with four major U.S. rotorcraft companies which concentrated on supporting the short-haul civil tilt rotor program. He graduated from San Jose State University with a BS in general engineering followed by one year of graduate work. He has authored and co-authored numerous NASA technical reports. He is currently a consultant to the Eloret Institute in Sunnyvale, California.

Daniel C. Dugan

Daniel Dugan graduated from West Point in 1955 and began his Army aviation career with primary flight training at Gary AAF, San Marcos, Texas. Following various military aviation assignments, he attended Virginia Polytechnic Institute at Blacksburg, Virginia, earning a master's degree in aerospace engineering in 1963. After serving in Korea, he attended the U.S. Naval Test Pilot School at Patuxent River, Maryland, graduating in 1965. He was then assigned to the Army aviation test activity at Edwards AFB, California, as an experimental test pilot. There he was assigned as the project pilot on the YUH-1C gunship (XM-30), the ACH-47A armed and armored Chinook, and the YCH-47B. After a tour in Vietnam (1968-1969), he was assigned to the Army's aviation laboratory at Ames Research Center, after completing a year at the Command and General Staff College. At Ames, Mr. Dugan flew the XV-5B lift fan, YOV-10A rotating cylinder flap research aircraft, and was the project pilot for the UH-1 V/STOLAND research helicopter and the XV-15 tilt rotor research aircraft. He remained the NASA project pilot on the XV-15 for 14 years and accumulated 200 hours in this unique aircraft. From 1990 through 1995, Mr. Dugan was assigned to Patuxent River as the NASA member of the V-22 test team. He is currently on the staff of the rotorcraft division at Ames Research Center and is assigned to a civil tilt rotor team for the development of tilt rotor displays, symbology, and operational procedures. Dan has authored over 20 technical reports and papers, many of which are tilt rotor related. He holds airline transport pilot certificates for both airplanes and helicopters and has accumulated over 7,000 hours of flight time.

Index

Monographs in Aerospace History

Launius, Roger D., and Gillette, Aaron K. Compilers. *The Space Shuttle: An Annotated Bibliography.* (Monographs in Aerospace History, No. 1, 1992).

Launius, Roger D., and Hunley, J.D. Compilers. *An Annotated Bibliography of the Apollo Program.* (Monographs in Aerospace History, No. 2, 1994).

Launius, Roger D. *Apollo: A Retrospective Analysis.* (Monographs in Aerospace History, No. 3, 1994).

Hansen, James R. *Enchanted Rendezvous: John C. Houbolt and the Genesis of the Lunar-Orbit Rendezvous Concept.* (Monographs in Aerospace History, No. 4, 1995).

Gorn, Michael H. *Hugh L. Dryden's Career in Aviation and Space.* (Monographs in Aerospace History, No. 5, 1996).

Powers, Sheryll Goecke. *Women in Aeronautical Engineering at the Dryden Flight Research Center, 1946-1994.* (Monographs in Aerospace History, No. 6, 1997).

Portree, David S.F. and Trevino, Robert C. Compilers. *Walking to Olympus: A Chronology of Extravehicular Activity (EVA).* (Monographs in Aerospace History, No. 7, 1997).

Logsdon, John M. Moderator. *The Legislative Origins of the National Aeronautics and Space Act of 1958: Proceedings of an Oral History Workshop.* (Monographs in Aerospace History, No. 8, 1998).

Rumerman, Judy A. Compiler. *U.S. Human Spaceflight: A Record of Achievement, 1961-1998.* (Monographs in Aerospace History, No. 9, 1998).

Portree, David S.F. *NASA's Origins and the Dawn of the Space Age.* (Monographs in Aerospace History, No. 10, 1998).

Logsdon, John M. *Together in Orbit: The Origins of International Cooperation in the Space Station Program.* (Monographs in Aerospace History, No. 11, 1998).

Phillips, W. Hewitt. *Journey in Aeronautical Research: A Career at NASA Langley Research Center.* (Monographs in Aerospace History, No. 12, 1998).

Braslow, Albert L. *A History of Suction-Type Laminar-Flow Control with Emphasis on Flight Research.* (Monographs in Aerospace History, No. 13, 1999).

Logsdon, John M. Moderator. *Managing the Moon Program: Lessons Learned from Project Apollo.* (Monographs in Aerospace History, No. 14, 1999).

Perminov, V.G. *The Difficult Road to Mars: A Brief History of Mars Exploration in the Soviet Union.* (Monographs in Aerospace History, No. 15, 1999).

Tucker, Tom. *Touchdown: The Development of Propulsion Controlled Aircraft at NASA Dryden.* (Monographs in Aerospace History, No. 16, 1999).

Those monographs still in print are available free of charge from the NASA History Division, Code ZH, NASA Headquarters, Washington, D.C. 20546. Please enclose a self-addressed 9x12" envelope stamped for 15 ounces for these items.

ISBN 0-16-050276-4

90000

9 780160 502767